This book contains the most fundamental documents and arguments of the emerging Earth Federation, a federation dedicated to the creation of democratic world government under the *Constitution for the Federation of Earth*. The book includes the "Declaration of the Rights of People" to create a decent, democratic world order under enforceable world laws. It also includes the "Manifesto of the Earth Federation" that describes the many global crises that we face today and presents the compelling reasons why democratic world government under the *Constitution* is our only viable, common sense option.

Most importantly, this volume includes the well-known *Constitution for the Federation of Earth* that has already been translated into twenty-two languages and distributed worldwide. Finally, it includes the Pledge of Allegiance to the Earth Federation that was approved at the Seventh Session of the Provisional World Parliament. These documents are supplemented by an Introduction, extensive commentary, and several essays by the President and other officers of the World Constitution and Parliament Association. The entire volume investigates the numerous global crises faced by humanity in the twenty-first century and presents the many reasons why the only practical solution to *today's catastrophic world disorder* is ratification of the *Earth Constitution*.

Glen T. Martin is Professor of Philosophy and Religious Studies at Radford University in Virginia. He is Secretary-General of the World Constitution and Parliament Association (WCPA) (www. wcpa.biz), President of International Philosophers for Peace (IPPNO) (www.radford.edu/~peace/ippno/), and Vice-President of the Institute On World Problems (IOWP) (www.worldproblems.net).

Dr. Martin has lectured, published, and traveled in many countries of the world in the service of world peace and a transformed future for humankind. He is author of *From Nietzsche to Wittgenstein - The Problem of Truth and Nihilism in the Modern World* (1989), *Millennium Dawn - The Philosophy of Planetary Crisis and Human Liberation* (2005), and Co-editor of *Emerging World Law - Key Documents and Decisions of the Global Constituent Assemblies and the Provisional World Parliament* (2005). He is also author of dozens of articles on a variety of topics in political commentary, comparative philosophy, the spirituality of human liberation, economic democracy, democratic world government, and global social issues. His personal home page is found at www.radford.edu/~gmartin.

World Constitution and Parliament
Association (WCPA)

www.wcpa.biz
Organizing Agent for Sessions of the
Provisional World Parliament

Cooperating with the

Institute On World Problems (IOWP)

www.worldproblems.net
The IOWP is a non-profit 501-C3 educational
organization registered in the USA.
Donations to IOWP are tax deductible.

North America Offices:
313 Seventh Avenue, Radford, VA 24141 USA
gmartin@radford.edu,
govt_rules@yahoo.com,

Asia Offices:
41, Dias Place, Colombo 12, SRI LANKA
fax/phone: 94-11-2345483

Africa Offices:
B.P. 680, Kara, TOGO, West Africa
fax: 228-660-1812 and 228-660-1104

President: Dr. Terence P. Amerasinghe,   Sri Lanka
Honorary President for Life: Sir Dr. Reinhart Ruge, Mexico

Secretary - General: Dr. Glen T. Martin, USA
Deputy Secretary General: Ms. Eugenia Almand, USA

Coordinator for Africa: Dr. Dominique Balouki
World Peace Envoy: The Most Venerable Bhikkhu
Ariyawanso (former Dr. Suchart Kosolkitiwong), Thailand
Youth Coordinator: H.M. Sarwar Alam, Canada/Bangladesh

WORLD

REVOLUTION

THROUGH

WORLD

LAW

WORLD REVOLUTION THROUGH WORLD LAW

BASIC DOCUMENTS OF THE EMERGING EARTH FEDERATION

Edited with an introduction
and other writings by

Glen T. Martin

IED
Institute for Economic Democracy
Publisher
9936 West Camden Ave., Sun City, AZ, 85351 USA

In cooperation with the
Institute On World Problems
313 Seventh Ave., Radford, VA 24141, USA

The Institute for Economic Democracy is a Non-Profit Organization
dedicated to publishing quality books
for progressive social change.
www.ied.info

Publisher's Cataloging-in-Publication Data

World revolution through world law:
basic documents of the emerging earth federation /
edited with an introduction and other writings
by Glen T. Martin.
1st ed.
p. cm.
Includes bibliographical references and index.
ISBN 0-9753555-2-X (pbk.)
ISBN 0-9753555-3-8 (hc)

I. Martin, Glen T., 1944-
1. International organization. 2. International law
JZ5566.4.W67 2005   341.2'1   QBI05-200101
3. World federation 4. Global issues

Book cover design by Chris Carter, Bill Kovarik, and Linda Burton
First Edition 2005

This book is dedicated to

Dr. Terence Amerasinghe,
Professor Philip Isely,
and Dr. Reinhart Ruge,

three great visionaries and leaders
who have lived their lives
in the service of one world
and a decent future
for all humanity.

And in memory of

Niklan Jones-Lezema (1964-2004)
activist, freedom-fighter, and friend,
who suggested the title
"world revolution through world law"

and Dr. Rashmi Mayur (1932-2004)
who inspired a generation
of world citizens
with his vision,
eloquence,
and commitment.

Acknowledgments

The purpose of this book is to disseminate these ideas and documents as widely as possible. Permission is granted to copy any particular chapters or documents for study and dissemination as long as (a) no charge is made for these copied items and (b) proper credit is given to this book as the source.

This book includes the work of the several thousand people who worked on the *Constitution for the Federation of Earth*, the major document contained herein, most of whom must remain unnamed. The signatures of only a few of them appear on the signature pages at the end of the *Constitution*.

It is also the work of the several hundred people who were involved in the Seventh and Eighth Sessions of the Provisional World Parliament who studied and approved the Manifesto, the Declaration of the Rights of Peoples, and the Pledge. They also must remain unnamed, although their names may well appear in future history books.

For help with reading or preparing the manuscript, I am very thankful to Eugenia Almand, Dr. Terence Amerasinghe, Dr. Roger Kotila, Dr. William Kovarik, and Phyllis Turk. I am especially grateful to Chris Carter, organizer, web mistress, and creative specialist for the Institute On World Problems. I am responsible for whatever flaws remain.

TABLE OF CONTENTS

FOREWORD

Dr. Terence P. Amerasinghe
President, Graduate School of World Problems

Books describing the chaotic state of the world today are plenty. Most authors stop short concerning how we can end the rot and turn the corner to an ordered world. Our world violence, poverty, and chaos are not mere theoretical issues. Ordinary citizens the world over are fully aware of these evils because they are presently experiencing them. We must find real solutions to the world's multiple and interrelated crises or we may soon perish.

Alone among authors of this category of books, Dr. Glen T. Martin has had the courage and vision to unfold a road-map that is practical, simple, and common sense. He does it within the space of a short volume, as against the 1000 page U.N. reports or the ten-year studies like the Commission on Global Governance. These reports end, to the reader's annoyance, in a no-man's land of indecision, pious platitudes, and cowardly recommendations for incremental changes to the present corrupt world system.

In offering a genuine road-map, Dr. Martin takes us ahead of Mahatma Gandhi's "civil disobedience" that won independence for India. When British rule in India lost its legitimacy, the Mahatma urged the Indian masses to civil disobedience. However, he did not live to raise the world's masses to the higher level of "civil obedience."

Just as with colonial rule, today all national governments have become illegitimate due to their inability to promote the security, peace, freedom, and prosperity of their peoples. Our globalized world disorder makes it impossible for even the most powerful governments to protect their citizens from global warming, ozone depletion, global loss of agricultural lands, forests, and fisheries, or terrorist attack. Dr. Martin responds to this illegitimacy by calling for an act of obedience: *civil obedience* to a democratic federal world government.

The Mahatma often declared that he only wished to live in a truly federated world. Dr. Martin, in his short volume, proves to be the Mahatma's greatest disciple in that he extends Gandhi's philosophy to its logical and destined goal. Martin declares that people doing "civil disobedience" to illegitimate institutions today are no longer moving toward a state of anarchy disrespecting all laws (as the vested interests protecting the old order like to claim).

The *Constitution for the Federation of Earth* provides non-violent "lawbreakers" with a complementary act of civil obedience. We must switch our loyalties to what is truly the legal expression of the sovereignty of the people of Earth. We must act on our world citizenship, which is prior to all national citizenship.

This small volume will do for the world what the *Communist Manifesto failed to do*. The *Communist Manifesto* was flawed by the fact that it concentrated only on a segment of the world's people: the workers. It is a document that divides people from one another, whereas *World Revolution Through World Law* unites everyone under the principle of universal sovereignty of the people of Earth. This book is essential reading for all – precisely because we are all world citizens first and foremost. It presents for us, clearly and logically, the only truly practical and common sense road-map for human survival on Earth.

Chapter One: Introduction

Restoring the Legitimacy of Nations Through the Supreme Act of Civil Obedience

The future of our world at the dawn of the twenty-first century is obscured by a dark cloud of hopelessness and despair. Violence, militarism, and war destroy the lives and hopes of millions each day. Millions more each day, including thirty thousand children, die of starvation or starvation-related conditions. Crippling diseases and plagues tear through thousands of communities in Africa, Asia, and South America.

Global warming threatens to disrupt the entire ecosystem of our planet while oil production increases daily. Yet everyone knows that the burning of oil is one of the main causes of global warming. Agricultural lands, fresh water sources, and ocean fisheries continue collapsing worldwide. Weapons of mass destruction are built and deployed with the intent of world domination and conquest. A fleet of Trident Submarines slithers across the bottom of the oceans of Earth. Each submarine, upon receiving the order to fire, or as the consequence of some terrible accident, is capable of wiping out 123 cities worldwide.

For giant profit-making enterprises, gigantic war industries, media conglomerates, and corporate prostitutes of consumer whims, it is business as usual. They are in the business of protecting the status quo which is the source of their exorbitant profits. And for millions of first-world consumers wallowing in their self-indulgent and unsustainable lifestyles, it is also business as usual. While the majority of humankind writhes in a living hell, they flash their credit cards, indulge their mindless entertainment, and covet their corrupt luxuries.

All human beings share the same fundamental spirit, a spirit arising from the very heart of the sacred universe. In the light of this spirit, we understand that we are all brothers and sisters capable of living together in peace, harmony, mutual respect, even love, on this precious planet Earth, which is our home. But the dominant institutions of our world alienate us from our fundamental spirit. They have taken on a life of their own that is threatening to destroy not only humankind, but the sacred Earth that has been entrusted to us as our home.

It is ordinary people, and the ordinary person in each of us, who must act together now to save the Earth and our common future. This book is based on the gigantic truth that such action is not only necessary but very possible. Humanity is at the verge of a breakthrough to a new world order. We do not need to wait for some "miraculous" transformation of a corrupt human nature. We need only transform the humanly-made, flawed institutions that alienate and distort our common humanity. We can rapidly and easily build those practical and common-sense institutions that allow our common humanity to flower in peace and prosperity.

The rule of universal law, applying equally to all and enforced fairly in the service of all, is a fundamental mainstay of human civilization. And it is *democratically legislated* universal laws that are the foundation of a transformed world order of peace, justice, and prosperity. The world has never yet had full democracy, not because some good constitutions have not been written, but because an interdependent world requires universal democratically legislated laws in the service of everyone.

You cannot fracture the Earth into approximately 191 competing territories and expect peace, justice, and prosperity to be the result. Humanity has the technical ability, the intelligence, and the spiritual capacity, at the dawn of the twenty-first century, to easily create a transformed future for the Earth (Martin, 2005). Now is the time.

This book contains all the essentials for creating that new and decent world order for the Earth. It provides a blueprint for a nonviolent revolution that founds the world order on genuine political and economic justice for all nations, peoples, and persons on Earth. As such, this small book may be one of the most important you will ever read. It is truly history in the making. You hold in your hand the key to justice, freedom, sustainability, and peace upon the Earth. Treasure it; think about it, and act on it. The survival of humanity and a future for our children are what is at stake.

1. The History Behind the Documents in this Book

There has been a great demand among the worldwide membership of the World Constitution and Parliament Association and related movements to produce a small volume containing the basic documents of the coming "revolution through world law." This book is our response to this demand. It has been kept intentionally short so that it might be inexpensive and easily acquired by its readers. Some have given it a nickname: "The Blue Book."

Those who wish to study the amazing history and legal accomplishments of this fast-expanding movement in more detail (including provisional world laws enacted to date) should acquire *Emerging World Law – Key Documents and Decisions of the World Constituent Assemblies and Provisional World Parliament*, edited by Eugenia Almand and myself, with a Preface by Dr. Terence Amerasinghe. This larger volume includes the four documents from the present volume as well as extensive chapters of commentary, analysis, history, provisional world laws passed to date, development of the World District Courts, etc.

The four documents collected below are official documents of the World Constituent Assemblies and the Provisional World Parliament. The Constituent Assemblies and their representatives wrote, debated, and approved the *Constitution for the Federation of Earth* as described in this Introduction. The Provisional World Parliament approved both the *Manifesto of the Earth Federation* and the Pledge of Allegiance to the Constitution at its Seventh Session in Chennai, India, in December 2003 and passed the "Declaration of the Rights of the People of Earth to create and ratify a World Constitution and hold sessions of the Provisional World Parliament" at its Eighth Session in Lucknow, India, in August 2004. These four together are perhaps the most fundamental documents in our revolutionary movement to create a decent world order on planet Earth for the first time in history.

In 1958, an agreement to call a World Constitutional Convention was initiated by four persons and circulated worldwide for signatures, with a request that both national governments and people of each country send delegates. From this call began a movement of world citizens from many countries to create a constitution for the Earth and initiate democratic world government.

With this initiative, a World Committee for a World Constitutional Convention formed. Thousands signed the initial agreement, including many prominent leaders. The organizers of this action traveled around the world to enlist support. Between 1961 and 1962, a definitive call to the World Constitutional Convention was adopted. Many persons signed, including the heads of five national governments. During the next four years, two Preparatory Congresses were held, first in Denver, Colorado, USA, and then in Milan, Italy. An outline of democratic procedures for debate and the drafting of a world constitution was formulated.

In 1967, the decision was made at the Third Preparatory Congress to hold a World Constitutional Convention in 1968, even if there were no governmental delegates who had signed up. 300 people's delegates pledged. The first World Constitutional Convention was held accordingly at Interlaken, Switzerland, and Wolfach, Germany. It was attended by 200 people's delegates from 27 countries and five continents. At this Convention, work was begun on drafting the *Constitution for the Federation of Earth.*

During the next seven years, a strategy for "Reclaiming Earth for Humanity" was circulated and directions were developed and given to the drafting commission to write the *Constitution* according to the guidelines developed at the first World Constitutional Convention. This commission of four persons worked together consistently, nearly completing the first draft of the *Earth Constitution.* Between 1973 and 1975, the first draft was finished, printed in 1974, and circulated worldwide for comment, together with the call to the second session of the World Constitutional Convention (now defined as the "World Constituent Assembly") in 1977. Comments on the first draft were compiled and the drafting commission met once again to write the second draft. This was completed and circulated worldwide in 1976.

In June 1977, the Second Session of World Constituent Assembly was held in Innsbruck, Austria. The proposed *Earth Constitution* was debated paragraph by paragraph, amended, then adopted with 138 original signers from 25 countries and 6 continents. A worldwide call for ratification by the nations and peoples of Earth was issued. The *Constitution* was sent to U.N. General Assembly and to all national governments.

From 1978-1980, the *Earth Constitution* was again circulated worldwide for debate and ratification. The Third Session of World Constituent Assembly was held January 1979, in Colombo, Sri Lanka. The Assembly adopted the "Rationale For A World Constituent Assembly" and defined the right of people to convene the Assembly, draft the *Constitution*, and obtain ratification. (This "Rationale" was the predecessor of the "Declaration of Rights of People" included in this volume.) A worldwide appeal was issued for national parliaments to ratify. Under the authority of Article 19 of the *Constitution*, the people of Earth begin holding sessions of the Provisional World Parliament in 1982 in Brighton, England.

The process of the development and elaboration of provisional world law had begun, continuing at the Second Session of the Provisional World Parliament in New Delhi, India, in 1985 and the Third Session in Miami Beach, Florida, in 1987. A continuing discussion at these meetings of Parliament over details within the *Constitution* revealed the need to hold a Fourth Session of the World Constituent Assembly, which was held in Troia, Portugal, in 1991. Delegates adopted 59 amendments to the *Earth Constitution* (mostly small, precise changes in wording), and the document took on the final form that is now included in this volume. During the course of its 33-year development, literally thousands of world citizens worked at developing the *Earth Constitution* in the form that we have it today. It is the only world constitution in existence that has undergone such a rigorous process of democratic, participatory development.

Since 1991, the campaign for ratification of the *Constitution* has continued, with thousands of people and organizations becoming personal ratifiers of the document. (Official, final ratification must, of course, take place in accordance with the provisions set forth in Article 17 of the *Constitution.*) A network of organizations and people was formed called the Global Ratification and Elections Network, to promote ratification of the *Constitution.* This network is now being integrated into the newly emerging *Earth Federation Movement,* a movement which may soon have chapters in every country on Earth, devoted exclusively to getting the nations of the world to ratify the *Earth Constitution.*

The process of developing a body of provisional world law has also proceeded through the Fourth Session of the Provisional World Parliament in Barcelona, Spain, in 1996, the Fifth Session on the island of Malta in 2000, the Sixth Session in Bangkok, Thailand, in March 2003, the Seventh Session in Chennai, India, in December 2003, and the Eighth Session in Lucknow, India, in August 2004. The Ninth Session is currently being developed for Libya in Africa for the end of February 2006. When the World Parliament is finally activated (upon ratification of the *Constitution* under Article 17), the urgent work of the Earth Federation will already be partially in place, with a body of high-quality world law available for the World Parliament to accept, reject, or modify.

The *Manifesto of the Earth Federation* presents the reasons why we urgently need to build the Earth Federation and work to have the people and nations of Earth ratify the *Constitution.* The "Declaration of the Rights of the People of Earth to create and ratify a World Constitution and hold sessions of the Provisional World Parliament" presents, in a brief form, the official justification for our work of building the Earth Federation independently of the approval of the illegitimate collection of so-called "sovereign" nation-states.

The *Constitution* is the solution to the nightmare conditions on planet Earth: conditions, as the *Manifesto* points out, that are the direct result of the system of "sovereign" nation-states in cooperation with exploitative, monopoly capitalism. It is the only viable, practically available solution that we have before us today. It may not be a perfect document (no document could be perfect and non-controversial to all thinking persons). But it is an excellent and brilliantly conceived document, the official ratification of which would almost overnight create a decent world order for humanity.

The Pledge of Allegiance, adopted at the Seventh Session of the Provisional World Parliament, is an instrument by which the people of Earth can affirm their commitment to a new and decent world order independently of the corrupt system that now dominates the Earth and holds all governments hostage to its destructive power. Even prior to the adoption of the pledge, many thousands of people were becoming personal ratifiers of the *Constitution*, putting their names on file with the World Constitution and Parliament Association as recognizing the *Constitution for the Federation of Earth* as the supreme law of planet Earth. By doing this, they at least partially extricated themselves from participation in the corruption of the present world system and expressed their affirmation of a world system that includes and respects all human beings on the planet equally.

Today, the Pledge serves this function. People are signing the Pledge and sending a copy to the World Constitution and Parliament Association to keep on file for posterity and history. They are also posting it on the walls of their offices and their homes, on street corners and in public places. By doing so they transmit their support for a new and just world order and their rejection of the corruption and disintegration of our present world order. The Pledge is fast becoming a key document in the development of the new world within the dying husk of the old.

In every country people are also acting to build the *Earth Federation Movement*, a movement unlike any political party that has ever existed. The *Earth Federation Movement* is not attempting to take power in any country, nor to influence the ways any country is run according to a political platform. The Earth Federation Movement's goal is not to take power of any sort but to have all nations ratify the *Constitution for the Federation of Earth*. The goal is not power for some organization or interest group. The goal is for the people of Earth to take power under a *Constitution* that enshrines their rights, protects all of them equally, and recognizes their sovereignty over all parties, organizations, and nations.

2. World Revolution as a Paradigm Shift from Fragmentation to Unity-in-Diversity

Today, it is becoming apparent to millions of people that nonviolent world revolution is our only option and that world law is the only practical route to that option. It does not matter whether one focuses on environmental issues, human rights issues, health care issues, worker safety or exploitation issues, poverty issues, democracy issues, civil liberties and freedom issues, or any number of other issues facing our world – the conclusion is the same. There will be no positive solution to any of these issues without world revolution.

World revolution is defined as a new order established on principles that eliminate the present system of domination, exploitation, and destruction of people and nature on Earth and establishes the just rule of democratically legislated law for our planet. We need a new order premised on justice, sustainability, equity, freedom, and universal prosperity. We will see that this is not a "utopian dream" but very possible, even necessary.

The ongoing destruction of the global environment, the rapid diminishing of agricultural lands, fresh water, and ocean fisheries, the assumption of ever-greater wealth and power by the few at the expense of the many, the unspeakable poverty and misery that a large portion of humanity must endure for their entire lives, the destruction of human liberty and human rights everywhere on Earth, the continued development and manufacture of weapons, and the use of war as an instrument of foreign policy as well as U.N. policy – all of these facts about our world lead to the conclusion that world revolution through law is our only option.

A fuller account of these crises is included in the *Manifesto* that comprises Chapter Three below. The study of these issues that has appeared in book after book shows that all of them are deeply interrelated. (For a list of such books, see the bibliography to this volume.) We live in a world system that inevitably produces these horrors and has led to this gigantic world crisis that we face today.

These deeply interrelated crises are not accidents of history. The are products of the dominant institutions of our modern world that evolved five or six centuries ago and are singularly unsuited for planetary protection of human life and the environment in the twentieth and twenty-first centuries. Thousands of books have exposed the fatal flaws in these institutions, yet the dominant powers and dominant media use every resource at their command to prevent an understanding of these institutions from developing in the people of Earth. The dominant institutions of our world are global monopoly capitalism integrated with the system of "sovereign" nation-states.

The origins of these institutions with the birth of the modern world during the Renaissance, along with the rise of science and the scientific method, defines the character of "modernity." When these institutions were born much of our planet was still unknown. People living on one continent did not know about those living on other continents. Nature seemed to be an infinite and inexhaustible resource there for the taking and exploiting. Exploitative capitalism and the early "sovereign" nation-state seemed institutions that could produce wealth for many and glory and security for nations. It did not seem to matter that the world was divided into thousands of competitive corporate and national units, all operating out of self-interest without regard to nature or people.

The fragmentation of these early modern institutions was not questioned because the world itself was not understood as single unit. There was little conception of a single human race trying to become successfully interdependent on a tiny "spaceship Earth." There was little or no conception of a planetary environment integrated into a single ecosystem that could be fatally disrupted by human activity (Harris, 2000).

Today, despite the best efforts of the corporate-owned dominant media to prevent understanding, and despite the immense propaganda spewed forth by imperial governments, more and more people worldwide are realizing that the world has no future under these institutions. For the global crisis that we face is precisely the product of these institutions, forms of organization five centuries old that were never intended to regulate the whole of our tiny, planetary ecosystem or to integrate and harmonize the vast multiplicity of the Earth's people.

If we are to survive on this planet much longer, if we are to eliminate the nightmare conditions in which a large portion of the Earth's population are forced to live out their lives, if we are to preserve the collapsing planetary ecosystem, if we are to abolish militarism and war as instruments of nation-states, we need new institutions designed for the world as we face it today: a fragile, integrated, interdependent whole.

This means planetary revolution. It means founding human civilization and our relationship with the global environment on new, planetary institutions. The old systems of fragmentation have taught us much that is useful. In the political sphere, they have taught us about democracy, human rights, multicultural respect for one another, and the need for freedom, justice, and basic equality of all.

Modern science has taught us about the dynamic "field" nature of our universe, where parts are inseparable from wholes (from the macro to the micro levels) and particular things and events are incomprehensible apart from unifying systems within which they are integrated. Science has taught us about the balanced and delicate ecosystems that form an integrated series of ecosystems up to the planetary level. Across the board, every area of twentieth-century science has shown that the parts are inseparable from the whole (Harris, 2000).

All these understandings are built into the *Constitution for the Federation of Earth*. Planetary revolution means establishing planetary democratic government based on the goal of protecting our global environment and serving equally all the diverse people that live upon the Earth. It means replacing the fragmented and failed institutions of global exploitative capitalism and the system of "sovereign" nation-states with the unity-in-diversity of democratic world government. It does not mean abolishing diversity but truly protecting it for the first time.

Under the systems of fragmentation, those parts that are bigger, stronger, or more aggressive than other parts (whether cultures, religions, ethnic groups, corporations, or nation-states) dominate or assimilate those parts that are smaller, weaker, or less aggressive. Under systems of fragmentation there is no true diversity but only the chaos of a war of all against all, inevitably resulting in the imperial domination of the strongest corporation, religion, or nation-state.

Even when military wars are not proceeding, economic, cultural, and ideological wars continue unabated. Minorities, indigenous peoples, small religious groups, weaker ethnic groups, or weaker nations have always suffered persecution, domination, exploitation, or assimilation. Only the collective force of democratic world government under the *Constitution for the Federation of Earth* can give the Earth that unity-in-diversity that is at the heart of the universe, of our planetary ecosystem, and of human civilization on this planet (Martin, 2002).

The fragmented systems by which we have been operating for five centuries have led to the global crisis that we now face. These systems are clearly the underlying cause of this crisis. They cannot be reformed, because it is not some particular feature of these systems that is the problem but the set of assumptions themselves that make up these systems (Martin, 1999).

The new paradigm, affirmed by all the sciences of the twentieth and twenty-first centuries, is unity-in-diversity. This principle applied in the human realm means the integration of all the parts (cultures, ethnic groups, religions, corporations, nations) into a whole (democratic world government) without losing their unique character as parts. Indeed, as we have seen, it is only the collective force of the democratic whole that can protect and preserve this uniqueness and individuality. The *Constitution* is explicitly based on the principle of unity-in-diversity.

3. The Twisted Logic of the Nation-State System

In a world divided into nearly 200 territorial units, competing with one another politically, militarily and economically, there is a perpetual danger of total disaster. It is *the logic of the nation-state system* itself that lays the ground for disaster, not corruption of peoples or leaders. Rather, the system corrupts both peoples and leaders due to its implacable logic, inherently destructive of democracy, freedom, justice, and peace.

a. The most obvious danger inherent in the logic of nation-states is that of war. War and militarism destroy all four values identified here, even if the war, or the militarism, is promoted as a "defense of democracy." National sovereignty is by its very nature a root cause of war, because every national sovereign government regards security and defense against possible invasion or aggression as a first and most vital interest. Most sovereign states, therefore, seek to maintain as powerful an arsenal of weaponry as they can afford and spend inordinate amounts of their wealth on armaments, which other states view as a potential threat. The result is an ever-increasing arms race in the attempt to maintain a balance of power, which generates international tensions and crises that constantly tend to explode into war (Harris, 2000).

As Errol E. Harris points out in his essay "Are We Unteachable?" below, the United Nations cannot prevent this, because Article 2 of its Charter commits it to uphold the sovereign status of its members, and Chapter VII provides, as its means of "peace-keeping," only warlike measures "by land, sea, and air." Accordingly, as long as states remain sovereign and independent, world peace cannot be maintained and neither can the legitimacy of nation-states. The U.N. is premised on the same flawed logic of nation-states that belie the noble ideals enshrined in its Charter.

b. In a world where corporations operate with the goal of accumulating wealth regardless of the common good and outside of independent oversight of their activities, democracy, freedom, justice, and peace will again be the victims. An economics predicated on the secret machinations of self-interest will see any of these four values that interferes with its self-interest as negative values to be defeated. The most obvious example is militarism where giant corporations have a vested interest in the continuation of the war system and in promoting the war system with the governments of their respective nation-states.

Today, some multinational corporations operate autonomously, outside of any individual nation-state and hence beyond the possibility of effective regulation by any and all governments. They use the anarchic system of a multiplicity of governments to their own advantage, regardless of the good of peoples or the Earth itself. Some corporations have assets larger than the nation-states within which they operate.

Under this system, they strive for power and influence over governments. Governments are colonized into the service of private, profit-making institutions, unaccountable to the common good or the welfare of the community they are supposed to be governing. There is an anarchy of greed, exploitation, and cynical self-interest.

c. Third, the system of "sovereign" nation-states gives institutional support to the lowest aspects of our common "human nature": blind territoriality, the tendency to submerge our individuality into a collectivism of state worship, and a tendency to blind obedience to state authorities and their military mandarins. This means the possibility of fascism is always present. Fascism requires enemies to bind the nation into a unit submerged in the power of the state. It requires the complicity of corporations who see their link with state power as the source of undreamed-of profit and wealth. And it crushes diversity and individual rights and freedoms, submerging citizens in an obsessive "patriotism" that asks no questions and hates the diversity and uncertainty of democracy.

As long as the "territorial instinct" is exacerbated by dividing the world into nearly two hundred autonomous units, as if the Earth could be the "private property" of the people who happen to be born at a particular place, there will be the danger of obsessive nationalism and fascism. Any honest history course covering the modern period will reveal the havoc this territoriality has played with the values of democracy, freedom, justice, and peace. Only a united world, premised on the principle of unity-in-diversity can overcome this ever-present consequence of the logic of nation-states.

d. Under the logic of nation-states, mass media tend to operate in the service of the nation with which they identify. Mass media dedicated to the freedom of information and the creation of an educated and informed public are essential to the values of democracy, freedom, justice, and peace. Yet the mass media of each nation-state tend to reflect the dominant values of that state and its system of power. The "news" is disseminated to the population of each nation from the point of view of the national establishment with its dominant governmental and business elites (who often own or control the mass media). The result simply reflects the destructive logic of the system of nation-states, promoting international misunderstanding, war, fascist tendencies, imperialism, and injustice.

e. The logic of the modern nation-state system creates a near inevitability that powerful states will act to dominate and exploit weaker states. Inherent in the modern world system are the aspirations to empire and hegemony of the strong over the weak. The entire history of modernity bears this out. Imperialism, colonialism, economic exploitation, hegemony, spheres of influence, and secret pacts and intrigues not open to the public comprise the history of "sovereign" nation-states. It is not ambitious rulers and compliant populations that are primarily at fault. Rather the logic of the system itself recruits ambitious rulers and promotes blind "patriotism" in compliant populations.

These five flaws in the logic of the nation-state system make a world of democracy, freedom, justice, and peace nearly impossible. The ideals of democracy, freedom, justice, and peace have developed at the heart of the modern project, especially in terms of the "Enlightenment" project of the eighteenth century. They form the greatest legacy of modernity as well as the highest hope for our future on this planet. But the principles of democracy have their own inner logic that is in fundamental contradiction with the logic of the nation-state system as outlined here.

Democracy can only be world democracy. The twisted logic of the "sovereign" nation-state system gives us the world described above of militarism, corporate manipulation of governments, the ever-present threat of fascism, systematic media distortion of information, and imperialism. Under these conditions, authentic democracy within nations is nearly impossible. Decisions and conditions from outside the nation impact individual nations in ways beyond the control of citizens. Governments necessarily have to keep their foreign and military policies secret from their own citizens, defeating civilian oversight of government which is the essence of democracy. Economic and other decisions within the nation necessarily impact people in other countries. Citizen control of their lives (democracy) becomes an impossibility.

The only real freedom must be world freedom, guaranteed to every citizen of Earth. Freedom is impossible under this current world system. Governments routinely restrict freedom because of the uncertainties created by the chaos of nation-states. They maintain elaborate immigration protection systems, elaborate systems of visa restrictions, and elaborate security arrangements because of the threat of terrorism, subversion, or machinations of other nation-states. None of this would be necessary in a world where gross injustices have been eliminated and every nation and person has equal rights to participate in government. Only democratic world government can secure real freedom for the peoples of Earth.

Justice can only be world justice. As long as some nations have substantially more wealth, power, and influence than others, there will never be a just world order. The logic of nation-states, we have seen, ensures that there will never be economic, environmental, juridical, or democratic justice among the diverse peoples of Earth. Only world government under the *Earth Constitution,* with the clear mandate to treat all equally and to create a just world order, can succeed at this task.

Finally, peace can only come to humanity as world peace. All of the consequences of the logic of the nation-state system work to destroy the possibility of peace in the world. Militarism, unregulated corporate power, the tendency to fascism and blind patriotism, the distortion of news and the media, and imperialism all work to destroy the possibility of peace. War is a criminal activity. The production of weapons of war is a criminal activity. Only when these activities are recognized for what they are and abolished by enforceable world law will there be peace on the Earth. Only when substantial justice has been created for the peoples of Earth will there be peace. No force on Earth can create world peace except democratic world government.

Throughout the history of nation-states in the modern period of the past 500 years, one or more of these logical consequences of the nation-state system have coalesced to perpetually destroy democracy, freedom, justice, and peace in our world. This history is there for all to see. Today, with the technology of weapons of mass destruction brought nearly to perfection, this system portends the self-destruction of the Earth and our common human project. Today, all five of these negative consequences of the nation-state system have coalesced in the global empire of the United States.

4. Are We Inside the Belly of a Beast or the Box of Our Own Assumptions?

As a number of scholars have pointed out, the people living within the global imperial center today are the most propagandized, manipulated, and brainwashed population in the world (Chomsky, 1989). The people within the U.S. experience job loss, outrageous health-care and insurance costs, environmental degradation, decaying infrastructure in their cities, repression of civil liberties, privatizing of social security, growth of the prison industry, draconian laws targeting minorities and the poor, and growing social disintegration.

At the same time, when U.S. troops invade or bomb other countries, yellow ribbons appear on autos and in windows saying "support our troops." It does not matter if the troops invaded another country, if they are committing mass murder of civilians, if they are engaged in torture or repression. The mantra is "support our troops." The propaganda system (in the service of the ruling class) is just that effective. Exploited and marginalized people in the U.S. often support the very system that diminishes their lives.

The mass media focus on the atrocities of "official enemies." The people are told these others are "enemies" based upon secret evidence. Fictitious "evil" actions of these enemies are even published for public consumption according to misinformation created by the CIA or their own government. The public is told they must trust their government (that operates in secret) as it attempts to protect them from horrible enemies in a dangerous world. Democracy is a sham and voter apathy is notorious.

The mass media uncritically repeat the formulas, photos, selection of certain information, and ideological framework provided by government and the ruling powers within the imperial centers. Two to four million people are slaughtered in Vietnam and the American people mourn only 65,000 of these deaths. U.S. troops invade Iraq and slaughter its people, and the mass media speak of those courageous Iraqis who resist as "insurgents" or "rebels."

Military personnel in brutal dictatorships are trained by the imperial troops to repress their own people (or their neighboring countries), as happened in Indonesia, East Timor, Columbia, El Salvador, Guatemala, and elsewhere, and the media within the U.S. are silent about the connection, the massacres, and the implications of this "foreign policy." Perhaps 200,000 people are slaughtered in the first two years of the U.S. invasion of Iraq, and the American people only mourn 1,800 of these.

Are the American people so hopelessly corrupt that they would support such horrific acts on their part of their military and care only about their own forces? This is not the case. The problem, we have seen, is not "the American people" but the system of "sovereign nation-states" that institutionalizes a system of blind loyalty towards the country where one happens to be born. The people of Germany supported Nazi troops in the same way: *Deuschland über alles!* they chanted, and organized civic groups to "support our troops" in the field.

Imperial nation-states cultivate and promote "patriotism" in order to maintain popular, blind support for their systems of domination and exploitation. In the U.S. the slogan is "God bless America." The fact that this translates into the destruction and domination of other peoples worldwide is of no concern, since America, in the popular mind, is the chosen one of God. The problem is not the people of the United States. The problem is the world system of sovereign states where such blind loyalty is promoted everywhere, destroying, in turn, democracy, freedom, justice, and peace.

The military oppression of other peoples by the imperial centers functions in the service of economic exploitation. The wealthy imperial centers want control of oil, diamonds, gold, manganese, forests, coal. They want "financial stability" for their investments. The kinds of countries in the world system that can be counted on most to provide this "financial stability" are dictatorships and authoritarian regimes whose governments operate on behalf of the tiny wealthy elite in their countries who do business with the multinational corporations and the tiny wealthy elite of the imperial centers (Chomsky, 1993).

Democracy is considered an "unstable form of government" in the foreign policy of the U.S. and has been routinely subverted, overthrown, or suppressed in dozens of countries since the ascendancy of the U.S. to global dominance at the close of World War Two (Blum, 2000) That is because a fragmented world system cannot support the unity-in-diversity of democracy. Only the sovereignty of all the people who live on Earth institutionalized in the *Earth Constitution* can achieve the goals inherent in democracy: peace, equity, freedom, and prosperity.

Citizens of the imperial centers of capital are not so much trapped in the belly of a corrupt beast as within the box of their own limited assumptions. From inside the "box" of these institutions, the future is indeed hopeless. But there is no reason why human beings cannot think outside that box to a new order premised on the whole of our planet, the whole of its ecosystem, the whole of the human population, and the common good of all peoples. Without this gestalt switch, without this simple paradigm shift, the murderous evils of our current world system will continue unabated.

Real revolution is not violent revolution. Very often violent revolutions establish a new government on the same flawed assumptions as the old. Real revolution is thinking outside the box of outmoded institutions. Real revolution involves solving the crisis in civilization and governance by establishing a new, more adequate paradigm. The simple switch to the principle of unity-in-diversity for planet Earth, expressed in the *Constitution for the Federation of Earth*, will cut through our immense problems and create a decent life for all the diverse peoples of our planet. It is not violence, but leaving the constricting box of our old institutions, that constitutes real revolution.

From within the belly of the beast, the point is not to overthrow or destroy "the beast." For history is a series of "beasts" all preying upon their weaker neighbors, all eventually overthrown to be superseded by another "beast." Without changing the assumptions behind economics and the nation-state system, there will always be another beast, another imperial center, or another "world war" of competing imperial centers.

No country or its people is intrinsically evil. It is the flawed world system that impels countries to act in evil ways. A new world system under the rule of democratically-legislated world law will transform this "beast" nature of all powerful countries. It is the assumptions behind the system of "sovereign" nation-states that creates imperialism. The world must demilitarize and solve its problems through democratic processes. The only legitimate route to world revolution is through world law.

5. Global Monopoly Capitalism

The second dominant institution of the modern world, global capitalism, is inextricably linked to the first. The nation-state system and global capitalism are both destructive of freedom, prosperity for the majority, peace, justice, the environment, and a decent world order (Martin 2005, ch. 9). World revolution is necessary to achieve any and all of these goals. And the only way that world revolution can possibly succeed is for the world to ascend to the level of genuine, enforceable, democratically-legislated world law.

The consequences of not doing this, that is, the consequences of the present world system, are horrible and intolerable to all decent, informed people. These consequences can only be changed by a simple change in the premises by which we operate. Instead of the fragmentation of "sovereign nation-states" and global exploitative capitalism, we need a united world under a democratic federal world government with an economic policy designed to promote prosperity for all those who live on Earth.

As a worker on behalf of the *Earth Constitution* since 1995, and as Secretary-General of WCPA since 2003, I have traveled to many countries and seen for myself the inhuman, nightmarish conditions in which people are forced to live. They are literally "forced" to live like this, enforced by the global economic system, backed up by imperial military might, often by the repressive forces of their own governments trained and equipped from imperial centers, and trapped by an international visa system that prevents them from going elsewhere. It does not have to be this way.

I have also read many of the excellent books that have appeared concerning the savagery of empires past and present as well as books on the global economic system, the nation-state system, the global crises that the world currently faces, and the historical foundations of the current world disorder (see the bibliography). The *Manifesto of the Earth Federation* expresses not only extensive research into our current world system but a great deal of personal experience as well.

The global system of domination and exploitation has been maintained for five centuries through the military, economic, and political might of the imperial nation-states. The system has involved the interbreeding of the two dominant institutions of the modern world – the nation-state system and monopoly capitalism. The marriage of these two institutions has led to the horrific world we live in today – a world where one fifth of the Earth's population live in "absolute poverty," where wars proceed unhindered all over the globe, where the environment is being rapidly degraded, and where the future appears more and more without hope.

Global capitalism destroys democracy. Inevitably, uncontrolled concentrations of wealth interfere in politics and the law-making process on behalf of their own amoral pursuit of wealth and power. Inevitably, "freedom" is defined not as respecting the individual rights and dignity of individuals worldwide but as the license of corporations to rob and exploit and manipulate government and press as they please (Chomsky, 1996, pp. 86-91). Inevitably global capitalism results in a few winners with stupendous wealth and power with the majority of humankind as exploited and dominated losers. Finally, war, growth of a prison industry, violent conflicts, the counter-terrorism business, global "security" measures, and the consumption of weapons and ammunition are sources of immense profit for global capitalism. World peace is an impossibility under this system, which is inextricably linked, as we have seen, to the system of "sovereign" nation-states.

6. Economics: Inequality Structured into Law

In the Europe of feudal times, independent city-states realized that the resources necessary for production and wealth lay in the countryside. They would organize raids into the countryside to destroy the early industrial technology of the surrounding towns and villages and make these rural areas dependent on the city for processing their raw materials into the products necessary for life (Smith, 2005a). This process of domination was institutionalized in the laws passed by the governments of the cities and forced upon the weaker towns and villages. They understood, even then, that all wealth comes from a combination of nature's resources, human labor power, and industrial capital. They took steps to control this process in their own interest.

With the development of modern nations after the Renaissance in Europe, this same policy was implemented by the ruling powers of these nations. They understood that capital was not accumulated through "free trade," but through establishing monopoly control over the *wealth-producing-process*. This was done through both private property laws and by maintaining a low-tech periphery that supplied cheap raw materials to the industrial centers of capital to be manufactured into goods and sold back to the periphery or other consumers at great profit.

"Sovereign" nation-states began to compete with one another for colonies and for control of technology, resources, and markets. They understood that monopoly control of the wealth-producing process is the key to the capital accumulation of great wealth and power. The military forces of these European nations were deployed to ensure domination over the colonies, the enforcement of laws that prohibited the development of technology or machines of production in the colonies, and to defend the colonies against encroachment by rival European nations also bent on controlling the wealth-producing process in their own interests.

The British were the first to discover the great propaganda value of promoting an Adam Smith "free trade" doctrine to the world while they took careful steps to ensure control of the *wealth-producing-process* for England and its ruling elite. Nations acted to control technology, cheap resources, and markets in their own interest while preaching to the rest of the world the need for "free trade" (Smith, 2005a). The private property laws, the laws of trade and exchange, and international trade laws were promoted as "democratic" and as giving "equal opportunity" to all. In reality, they functioned to privilege the few at the expense of the many and to favor the imperial nation at the expense of the periphery (Korton, 2001).

However, all the European nations understood this same principle and engaged in tremendous rivalry to colonize the world and control the wealth-producing process in their own interest. This led to the two world wars. Nations made trade and military pacts with other nations in order to promote their own power and self-interest and increase their colonial spheres of hegemony in the interest of wealth accumulation for the motherland and her ruling elite. This rivalry led to gigantic world wars in which the imperial nations of the world exhausted their resources in the battle (Smith, 2005a, Introduction; Hudson, 2003).

From this carnage, the United States emerged as a leading world power after the First World War. The allies whom it had aided were now deeply financially indebted for the billions of dollars in military aid they had received from the U.S., and this debt was not about to be forgiven (Hudson, 2003, Ch.1). The United States bled its former European allies to enrich itself. It was now emerging as a leading world power with its own sphere of hegemony in all of Latin America and with emerging global interests.

The industrial development of the United States drew cheap resources from Latin America and manufactured these in its industrial centers to be sold back at tremendous profit. The government acted to control market relations and the wealth-producing process in its own interest. The U.S. military routinely interfered in Latin American countries to protect "U.S. interests" there. In the late nineteenth and twentieth centuries, it intervened in Nicaragua alone six times, including invading and running the country for a period of thirteen years (Harris and Levy, 1975)

After the nations of Europe, along with Japan, again exhausted themselves in the carnage of World War Two, the United States emerged as the undisputed world economic, imperial, and military power. Even the developing Soviet Union could never begin to match the economic and military power of the U.S. Nevertheless, U.S. Cold War propagandists routinely inflated the power of the USSR in order to serve their own imperial interests. These imperial interests were no longer Western Hemispheric. They were now truly global, from Middle East oil to the tremendous natural resources of Southeast Asia.

After the Second World War, however, former colonies of the old imperial powers were anxious for freedom. Dozens of new countries were formed and joined the United Nations during the 1950s and 1960s. The United States favored de-colonization of the periphery of the old colonial powers, but it had no intention of creating a world of "free and equal sovereign nation-states" as the Charter of the United Nations professed to do. Physical colonial occupation was replaced by economic, political, and military manipulation and domination from abroad.

Military bases were constructed all over the world from which U.S. military power could be projected at a moments notice. Leaving aside a network of secret bases not publicly acknowledged, Pentagon statistics for 2002 tell us there are 725 such bases, with a replacement value of 118 billion dollars, and with close to 300,000 U.S. military personal stationed in 153 countries. All this, along with billions of dollars in secret operations, is directed to monitoring and controlling the economic, military, and political movements of every country on Earth (Johnson, 2004, pp. 153-161).

But the military is only an adjunct to a system of inequality of rights structured into law. Trade laws, intellectual property laws, private property laws, laws regulating financial institutions, laws regulating stocks and bonds, and laws awarding control of the airwaves to gigantic private interests all together create the global system of exploitation. The entire nexus of modern law consists in "inequality structured into law" through the legal creation of what economist J. W. Smith calls "subtle monopolies" (2005a).

Today the United States largely controls the World Bank and the International Monetary Fund (IMF). It promotes international trade agreements through the World Trade Organization and uses its immense political, economic, and military influence to coerce nations into signing agreements such as the North American Free Trade Agreement (NAFTA) or the Free Trade Agreement of the Americas (FTAA). Inequality is structured into law under the propaganda slogan of promoting "free trade." The beneficiaries are never the poor nations who find that their wealth is transferred by billions of dollars each year to the imperial centers of capital, leaving them more underdeveloped, more impoverished, more illiterate, more diseased, and more desperate with each passing year (Rich, 1994). As of 1998, the ratio of wealth flowing north on the globe to wealth going south was 7 to 1. Seven dollars flowed to the imperial centers for every one dollar flowing to the poor majority of the world's population in the south (Smith, 2005a, p. 20).

Global capitalism interlinked with the system of "sovereign" nation-states is part of one, integrated system of exploitation. As Stan Goff expresses this:

> Think colonizer and colonized. Think parasite and host. Interdependent polarities.... The ceaselessly expanding accumulation regime that defines the global structure of society has a shorter definition. Capitalism. Like a shark, it can never stop doing what it does or it will die. What it does is accumulate and expand value. What it eats are workers, and women, and colonies, and the biosphere. (2004, pp. 194-195)

It is the nation-state system (where nations inevitably act in their own perceived self-interest), in league with the global system of exploitative monopoly capitalism, that has created this economic nightmare for the majority of humanity. Both these institutions must be transformed into the unity-in-diversity of democratic world government under the *Constitution for the Federation of Earth*.

Under democratic federal world government, the prosperity of all nations and peoples is the constitutional goal. The elimination of poverty, illiteracy, misery, and disease worldwide is the goal. The preservation of the global environment for future generations is the goal. Demilitarization of the world is the goal. And the institutions will be in place (for the first time in history) that can meet these goals quickly and efficiently.

Once equality is structured into law through conversion of the present system of exclusive titles to nature's wealth changed to conditional titles (first recognized as necessary by American economist Henry George), these horrific systems of subtle exploitation will come to an end. Once property laws are based on the common interest of all human beings in using nature's resources to a create decent life for everyone, economic efficiency and genuine sustainable development will take place rapidly.

This cannot be done under the system of sovereign nation-states, since the system is predicated on the fragmentation of the absolute self-interest of these states, never on the good of all. It cannot be done by "fair" trade agreements or by the United Nations for the same reason. Real equality of opportunity structured into law requires real, enforceable world law. Again, we find ourselves confronting a revolutionary situation as we realize there is no way to a general economic prosperity for the majority of human beings without democratic world government under the *Earth Constitution.*

Both dominant institutions of the modern world ensure that inequality (poverty for the majority of nations and peoples) is structured into law. Both dominant institutions of the modern world are transformed with the adoption of the *Earth Constitution.* Both our political and our economic systems must be based on the principle of unity-in-diversity.

The *Earth Constitution* contains many explicit provisions concerning world trade and the conservation of world resources for the good of all. In addition, implicit in the *Constitution* are the economic principles described in the *Manifesto of the Earth Federation* below. Both exploitative capitalism and "sovereign" nation-states are fragmented institutions incapable of creating a just and prosperous world order. We require nothing less that a world revolution through world law.

7. The "Normalization" of Evil

Some authors speak of the "normalization of evil" that has afflicted our consciousness and is promoted by the world's corporate mass media (Goff, 2004). The unspeakable horror of the lives of the poor is ignored, marginalized, not mentioned, not brought to attention. This is intentional on the part of the ruling elite of imperial societies. Those who control the media and those who benefit from the world system in all the imperial and former imperial nations want the horror of poverty and of war to be acceptable to society, when it is not entirely invisible at least to be normal, inevitable, and "natural."

Some philosophers and economic theorists tell us that the horrific condition of the world is "normal" or "natural," given human nature. Some religious fanatics tell that the condition of the world is the inevitable product of some "original sin." Other such fanatics tell us that we are destined to face an "Armageddon" that is a consequence of this sin. They tell us that the destruction of the environment and building of weapons of mass destruction should be encouraged because it will hasten the second coming of God. Such philosophies and cheap theologies serve the purposes of the power-elite in "normalizing" or "naturalizing" what any decent, sane human being must surely recognize as not only mad, but evil.

Under the dominant system that produces this horrific world disorder, people must not be allowed to see what is plainly in front of their faces: that the fragmented institutions by which we organize life on Earth are

the source of this horrific evil. If the evil is not normalized, if it were recognized for the obscene and shocking thing that it is, then people would
inquire into the reasons for this immense suffering endured by the world's
poor or the insane institutions of militarism and war.

They would become upset and angry. Upset and angry people do not
make good self-indulgent consumers of goods that destroy the environment or are manufactured in horrible third-world sweatshops. If this state
of affairs were not "normalized," people would begin to see the system
of domination and exploitation for the intentionally maintained and ruth-
lessly protected system that it is. They would act to transcend both the
nation-state system and global monopoly capitalism.

This same process of normalization has operated throughout the modern period to justify the savagery of the imperial dominators. When I was
in Ghana in June 2002, our hosts took us to a series of "castles" that have
been preserved as museums up and down the entire coast of West Africa.
These castles, built and fought over by the Portuguese, the French, the
Dutch, and the British, were used to collect the slaves who were crammed
into dungeons awaiting the slave ships that would arrive to take them further into the nightmare of bondage to whomever could afford to purchase
them.

We saw the horrific tortures devised by the troops who ran the castles
to punish recalcitrant slaves. We saw horrible, dehumanized conditions
under which the slaves were kept awaiting transport in the even more horrible holds of slave ships. We saw the systems of rape of the women and
girls devised by the officers of each castle.

We learned of the perhaps 40 million human beings who were trans-
ported and of the massive death, disease, and suffering they endured in
transport through this slave system. To us, this was horrible, not normal.
Looking back on a former era from the distance of the early twenty-first
century, we guests were able to see these practices for what they were. To
the slavers and the imperial troops who were essential in maintaining the
system of domination and exploitation, the situation was "normal." They
bestialized and dehumanized their victims and rationalized their domination to the point that it became "natural" and "normal."

Today, the imperial center of the empire spreads its tentacles of torture,
murder, suffering, and massive destruction throughout the world – from
Vietnam to El Salvador, to Guatemala, to Somalia, to Columbia, to Hai-
ti, to Yugoslavia, to Afghanistan, to Iraq, and beyond (Blum, 2000). The
same psychic techniques of dehumanization and bestialization are used.
Vietnamese men, women, and children were slaughtered indiscriminately
in "free-fire zones" (comprising most of the country) by the invaders of

their homeland. Any U.S. soldier showing the slightest compassion for a Vietnamese civilian, even a child, was belittled as "a gook-lover" (Goff, 2004, p. 16).

But they were not simply slaughtered from both the air and land forces, they were raped, tortured, and mutilated by American forces. This savagery is essential to the logic of empire and not the result of accident or a "few bad apples." U.S. military training is training in the dehumanization of other peoples and the concomitant of that training is savage treatment – bestializing imprisoned captives in Guantanamo or Abu Ghraib prison in Iraq, driving sharpened stakes into the vaginas of women in Vietnam (Goff, 2004, p. 20), devising exotic tortures for the U.S.-sponsored, CIA-supervised death squads of Columbia, El Salvador, or Guatemala (Chomsky, 1996).

This must be "normalized" for those involved and covered up for those who do not wish to know the truth. Citizens of the empire must be taught to "support our troops." Mass media must report in sanitized, neutral language in such a way that the "enemy" is dehumanized while imperial troops are humanized and glorified. Propaganda reports from the Pentagon must be repeated uncritically as objective "news." The system is amazingly successful. The citizens of the imperial center of the empire are numb to any sensitivity to the suffering of "non-Americans." They cooperate with the corporate media, intentionally blocking their own consciousness of the rest of humanity. "Comfortable white America will kill to protect its illusions" (Goff, 2004, p. 19).

They normalize reports of massive death tolls of "enemy" people, pigeonholing them as "subversives," "terrorists," or "insurgents." They care only for the death toll of Americans. The huge numbers of dead and maimed are just a number, a cipher, a neutral statistic from which no imaginative account of human suffering is derived. The reports of U.S. soldiers indiscriminately shooting women, children, and old people in Iraq are not printed in the corporate owned media. Photographs revealing the agony of non-Americans are suppressed by the mass media. Like the imperial soldiers of the age of slavery, they have normalized and sanitized the hideous treatment of other peoples in the service of the system of domination and exploitation.

The "logic of empire" can tolerate nothing less. The U.S. army training of Latin American military officers at what was called the "School of the Americas" in Fort Benning, Georgia, has produced dozens of horrible torturers and mass murders, while the Army claims it teaches them "human rights." In 1992, a training manual was smuggled out of the school which taught people torture and assassination as political tools (Hodge and Cooper, 2004).

The policy is not simply reflected at this school, however. Explicit U.S. foreign policy is built in part on the training of foreign military personnel worldwide in techniques of "counter-insurgency warfare." This is warfare within nations directed to preserving the horrors of the status quo on behalf of those who benefit from the current world system. This means, in covert foreign policy terms, techniques of terrorizing and brutalizing their own populations.

It is important to realize that the use of torture is not just for extracting information. Its use is integral to the primary necessity of empire – to create terror in subject populations. The official line of the U.S. military is that torture does not work because the victim will say anything and the information is not "righteous." However, the torturers are experts in discerning what is "righteous" from what is not.

But that is not the main point. When the tortured just names the names of everyone he or she knows, this is valuable as well. The U.S.-supported dominators – in El Salvador, Guatemala, Chile, Argentina, Indonesia, East Timor, South Vietnam, and elsewhere – have routinely arrested, murdered, or brutalized everyone named. Similarly, human rights organizations have estimated that 70 to 90 percent of the brutalized inmates at Abu Ghraib prison were innocent of resisting the U.S. invasion of their country. (Let us dwell for a moment on the irony of that statement: "innocent of resisting the U.S. invasion of their country.") The target is not just "subversives." It never has been. It is necessarily the general population – who are required to live in terror (Chomsky 1996).

Edward S. Herman in *The Real Terror Network* describes the "institutionalization" of torture as U.S. foreign policy in the 1960s and 1970s. And Noam Chomsky and Edward S. Herman chart the specific relationships between the U.S. and the use of torture worldwide in the first half century after World War Two (1979). It has been a systematic feature of covert foreign policy for decades. When tortured and maimed bodies were regularly found by relatives in garbage dumps in El Salvador or Guatemala, when tortured people were released in East Timor to tell their story, when photographs of extreme humiliations were taken in Abu Ghraib prison, this has real political effectiveness in the service of covert foreign policy.

Empires, indeed, require cruelty "to subdue restive foreign populations." And they require their troops to treat the victims as non-humans, sub-humans, very much like the *Untermenschen* of the Nazis. The majority of the world's population suffering from the misery of extreme poverty and subject to the "grand strategy" of U.S. world domination, must be forced into a condition of political apathy and hopelessness in which they do not attempt to make change (Chomsky, 2003, Ch. 2). Their constant awareness of the incredible brutality to which they will be subjected if there is even a hint of political activity on their part is essential to keeping them in this condition.

The purpose of empires is always economic. (For a revealing description of the economic side of the empire read David Korton's *When Corporations Rule the World*, Michael Chossodovsky's *The Globalization of Poverty*, J.W. Smith's *Economic Democracy,* and John Perkins' *Confessions of an Economic Hit Man*.) The purpose of the U.S. empire is that the poor and wretched of the world should accept U.S.-owned sweatshops paying starvation wages, and U.S. corporations extracting the resources and wealth from their pliant countries while they remain in poverty and misery.

Without terror, people would never accept the brutal conditions of death, deprivation, misery, hunger, and disease that most of the people in the "grand area" endure for their entire lives. Today, the top 18 percent of the world's population owns 83 percent of the world's wealth. Each year untold billions of dollars in wealth are transferred from the poorest 60 percent of humanity to the wealthy imperial centers of capital. The rules of world "free trade" are formulated to ensure this transfer. Imperial military policy is formulated to protect and promote this system.

If the rights of the poor were respected – political rights and human rights – then they would organize and defeat the empire at will. They would take steps to use the resources of their countries to benefit their own people. This is exactly what empire cannot allow. Formerly secret Washington documents give this as the explicit reason for overthrowing the governments in Iran, Guatemala, Chile, and elsewhere. Only terror keeps subjugated peoples accepting the horror of their present lives of unspeakable poverty. Terror and its corollary torture are absolutely essential to U.S. foreign policy, as it is to the imperial logic of the system of "sovereign" nation-states.

Economic domination and exploitation by imperial nation-states can only be ended through effective democratic world government granting enforceable economic and political rights to all people on Earth and making economic exploitation illegal. Empires cannot be abolished from the Earth without creating a new world order that makes their existence impossible. The underlying assumptions of the United Nations and the current world order are two: the system of so-called sovereign nation-states and globalized monopoly capitalism.

A world order based on these premises makes empires inevitable. The systematic use of terror and torture by the imperial nation-states in their defense of empires can only be ended through enforceable democratic world law under nonmilitary world government. Mere political or military resistance to the empire from within has been going on for as long as the empire has been going on. In nearly every case, the empire has won and millions (literally) have lost their lives resisting it. It won in Vietnam as well: destroying three to four million lives and creating an economic basket-case of a nation, stultified by an ongoing economic boycott, and riddled by chemical poisons, massive birth defects, and high cancer rates.

Resistance and criticism to these horrendous practices are not enough. The empire's propaganda machine is immense and will always be able to convince the majority in the imperial center that "these abuses do not reflect the true goodness of the American people." The multi-billion dollar budget allocated to "covert operations" has the cover-up of this system from the American people as one of its primary goals. Career CIA agent Ralph McGehee, who defected and extensively studied CIA archives, describes the propaganda machine as follows:

> The CIA is not now nor has it ever been a central intelligence agency. It is the covert action arm of the President's foreign policy advisors. In that capacity it overthrows or supports foreign governments while reporting "intelligence" justifying these activities. It shapes the intelligence...to support presidential policy. Disinformation is a large part of its covert action responsibility, and the American people are the primary target of its lies. (1983, p. 192)

The goal of empire is not only to establish a hegemony with client governments to dominate the politics and economics of exploitable countries. If this goal does not succeed, victory for the empire can still be salvaged by destroying any viable alternative to its system of domination.

Hence, the massive destruction of the civilian infrastructure through savage bombing that took place in Vietnam in the late 1960s to early 1970s, Iraq in 1991, and Yugoslavia in 1999. Alternative victory can also be secured through economic blockades preventing recalcitrant countries from becoming economically successful. This strategy has been used against Cuba, Libya, North Korea, Vietnam and many other countries with significant success. The fact that millions of innocent civilians suffer and die from these practices is irrelevant to the aims of empire.

Struggle for justice must be informed by a positive vision of a transformed world order. That is the function of this little book. It contains the seeds of a transformed world order, the core of nonviolent world revolution. As a reader, you are warned that you are holding dynamite in your hands – the very real and practical possibility of a new world order that is available to the people of Earth here and now. The changes needed are not difficult, nor impractical. But they are indeed fundamental.

The "Declaration of the Rights of People," the *Manifesto*, and the *Earth Constitution* together in this volume provide all that is necessary to establish this new world order. The framework for the new order is practical, simple, and common sense. It does not require 1,000 page U.N. reports or ten-year studies from some blue-ribbon "Commission on Global Governance." All that is required is the political will to take action now. Any normally intelligent person can see the common sense of the solutions put forth in these documents.

The option of violent revolution within the oppressed regions of the world is not viable. Such action only reinforces of logic of empire. In the imperial center, the justification is made for bigger imperial military budgets, more sophisticated weapons of immense destruction, and more training of torturers and murderers for "counter-insurgency warfare." In North Vietnam, every building over one story high had been destroyed by the time the invaders withdrew. Even if the resistance "wins," the people lose. Meanwhile, the immense evil of the empire is "normalized" in the eyes of the imperial population, who are told there are violent enemies everywhere.

Afghanistan will never recover in our lifetimes the immense damage done to it even if it throws out the imperial invader. Iraq is poisoned forever by a significant quantity of depleted uranium in its soil and water (with a radioactive half-life of 4.5 billion years). The Cuban people have endured 44 years of crushing poverty enforced by a vicious economic blockade of their country. The only option for the oppressed majority of humankind is to establish the genuine rule of democratic law on Earth. The only option is to change the terms of the equation, abolish the institutions that perpetuate such horror, and found a truly civilized world order on the principle of human unity-in-diversity for the first time in history.

No nation or people is inherently evil. Neither the Portuguese, the Dutch, the Spanish, the French, the British, the Germans, the Italians, the Japanese, nor the Americans are inherently evil. Their behavior is the product of the institutions that shape them and encourage their complicity in the maintenance and "normalization" of these perverse practices. If we change the institutions, we will change the world order of domination and exploitation with its inherent logic of torture and dehumanization of victimized peoples.

The institutions of the modern world that have created this horrific world disorder are the nation-state system integrated with the system of exploitative monopoly capitalism. These two systems have worked hand in glove with the wealthy holders of capital controlling the policies of nation-states in their own interests and the rulers in imperial nation-states promoting and protecting the private wealth and power of the capitalist class. At one time, the soldiers of the empire maintained the "castles" where slaves were collected, raped, and tortured as part of a system promoting the private profits of corporations – independent slave trading companies. The U.S. military today destroys the poor and their aspirations worldwide on behalf of the rich and their system of trans-national corporations. Only by changing both these institutions (the nation-state and monopoly capitalism) can we truly transform our world order into one of peace, justice, equality, and prosperity.

The *Earth Constitution* lays out the framework for this new world order, based, as its Preamble says, on the principle of "unity-in-diversity." The *Manifesto* elaborates the new economics implicit in the *Constitution* and outlines the practical steps by which the world can move to a new, truly human, truly peaceful and just era. The long nightmare of domination and exploitation is nearly at an end. It is up to you, the reader of these documents, and all others of good will and good faith, to establish the new premises for a just world order: the unity-in-diversity of all peoples and nations.

8. Revolution and Legitimacy

Revolutionary change is justified when institutions that govern human interactions become unable to fulfill their promise of peace, prosperity, justice, equity, and freedom for citizens. At one time national governments might have been able to make this promise with some hope of fulfillment. At one time proponents of the world's dominant economic system may have been able to make this promise without hypocrisy. But those days are gone forever.

Today, the promises of nation-states to provide peace, prosperity, equity, and freedom, like the promises of the economists in the World Bank or the dominant universities of the imperial centers of capital, ring of propaganda and hypocrisy (see Perkins, 2004). More and more thoughtful people are realizing that neither governments as we know them nor the dominant economic system can fulfill their promises. These institutions have become illegitimate.

They are not illegitimate because of corrupt people in power. Rather, the institutions themselves tend to place corrupt people in power. The nation-state and global capitalism are illegitimate because they cannot fulfill the purposes for which they supposedly exist. The very logic of this system destroys the possibility of the realization of these ideals. And the very hypocrisy of this situation invites corruption (Goff, 2004; Perkins, 2004).

Global poverty, disease, and misery are increasing worldwide. Global violence and social chaos are increasing worldwide. Global democratic institutions and respect for human rights are declining worldwide. Global wealth and power have steadily been concentrated in fewer and fewer hands throughout the twentieth century. The hope of global security and peace has steadily disappeared (Renner, 1996).

With the development of super-sonic weapons, space-based weapons, nuclear, chemical, and biological weapons, depleted uranium weapons, stealth weapons, cruise missile weapons, inter-continental ballistic delivery systems, nuclear submarine weapons systems, and other forms of technological means of destruction, no nation is able any longer to guarantee security for its population. Attempts to create security under the system of "sovereign" nation-states have led to more and more militarism, greater and greater governmental secrecy, and the development of "national security states." This has meant the giving up of aspirations to democracy, freedom, governmental openness, and protection of civil liberties, while simultaneously decreasing real security. It has meant the destruction of democracy in nations large and small worldwide.

With the development of globalized economics, economic decisions taken in foreign centers of capital impact the livelihood of people in entire nations or regions of the world. The promise of governments to promote the prosperity of their people becomes a chimera. The central banks of many debtor nations have been taken over by the World Bank and structural adjustment has been forced upon helpless governments in which the economy of the country is reoriented to pay off international debt while services to the poor majority are slashed or privatized to exploitative multinational corporations. The economic health and stability of nations is not in the hands of the governments of nations (Chossudovsky, 1999; Caufield, 1996; Rich, 1994).

Legitimate government is government that can promote the security, peace, freedom, and prosperity of its people. By these criteria, no government on Earth is today legitimate, for globalized weaponry, globalized economics, and global interdependence have placed control of these goods beyond the scope of any government, even the most powerful.

Today, there is no force that can protect the global environment. There is no force that can regulate the global economic system on behalf of the prosperity of all the people on Earth. There is no one who can control global militarism, weapons proliferation, or the manufacture of weapons of mass destruction. The economic and political institutions of the modern world have become obsolete and, in turn, illegitimate. As Philip Allott writes, "A legal system which does its best to make sense of murder, theft, exploitation, oppression, abuse of power, and injustice, perpetrated by public authorities in the public interest, is a perversion of a legal system" (1990, p. xvii). (For a more detailed examination of this issue, see my Introduction to *Emerging World Law,* Almand and Martin, eds., 2005.)

This makes all human beings into what Richard Falk calls "pilgrim citizens" in search of a legitimate world order within which to be citizens (1992). It means that such a world order is yet to be established. Yet citizens of the world are not without the resources to accomplish this. Our impediments are lack of will, lack of revolutionary courage, and lack of the necessary information – because our options are excluded from view by the global propaganda system in the service of the illegitimate institutions of the past.

Thousands of citizen pilgrims and visionaries have acted to address this situation by creating the *Constitution for the Federation of Earth* and the Provisional World Parliament. The *Constitution* has been translated into twenty-two languages and sent throughout the world. It is premised on the principle of unity-in-diversity and designed to address all the global problems that are beyond the ability of nation-states to handle. Adopting it as the supreme law of the Earth can easily give us a world of security, peace, freedom, and prosperity within a relatively short time, perhaps twenty years.

Adopting the *Constitution* and federating all the nations of Earth under the House of Nations will also restore legitimacy to the nation-states. They will no longer be "sovereign," that is, in complete control over all affairs and entirely independent in "foreign policy." All nations in the Earth Federation will have to obey world law – environmental law, human rights laws, and laws against possessing military machines and weapons of mass destruction.

The harm now done by the principle of "sovereignty," where big states impose a system of domination and exploitation on weaker states, will come to an end. The harm now done by global economics, where trade relations bring immense profits into the imperial centers of capital while world poverty and misery continues to grow, will come to an end. There is no other way to transform the system as a whole except through enforceable world law.

The *Constitution* gives us legitimate government – government capable of bringing security, peace, freedom, and prosperity to all peoples on Earth. But the *Constitution* has not yet been ratified by the people and nations of Earth according to the procedures set forth in Article 17. The

Constitution outlines a morally legitimate democratic world government, but it does not yet have the legitimacy of effective enforcement of world law that can only come with ratification.

This is another reason why our situation is a revolutionary one. It is our moral duty as pilgrim citizens to create a decent world order under the rule of enforceable world law. The current governments of the world are illegitimate without democratic world government under the *Constitution*. We are obligated to act to create a nonviolent revolution through world law.

One way to do this is to become a personal ratifier of the *Constitution* and begin work to get the people and nations of Earth formally to ratify the *Constitution*. You can begin by copying the Pledge of Allegiance to the *Constitution* at the end of this book, signing it, and mailing it to the offices of the WCPA along with your address, e-mail, etc. By personally recognizing the legitimacy of the *Constitution* as world law, each person so doing is taking a revolutionary stance, one morally required by our crisis situation at the beginning of the twenty-first century. I declare that I will henceforth recognize the *Earth Constitution* as the supreme law of the Earth, superseding all merely national laws.

The situation is somewhat parallel to the one I found myself in as a young man in college facing possible draft into the Vietnam War. I had taken a world history course my freshman year. We studied one war after another in that course, one invasion after another, one empire after another, for the past 2,500 years. I realized something about the tragic history of human beings on this planet. And I realized that every empire and every nation attempted to justify its wars in the eyes of its population.

The Nazis justified their invasion of Europe just as the U.S. government declared it was "fighting Communism" in Southeast Asia. I understood that this war system that perpetuated itself throughout history was illegitimate. And I made a revolutionary decision. The buck would stop with me. They could imprison me, persecute me, even kill me, but there was nothing they could do to make me fight as part of their illegitimate system of death and destruction.

Today, we face the illegitimacy of the global economic and political systems of modernity. And we have before us a founding document that creates legitimate government for the Earth and restores the legitimacy of the national governments once they have become members of the Earth Federation. I can passively refuse to act out of self-interest (being personally comfortable within the current world order) or out of cowardice (for social stigma or other penalties will possibly come from both government and the dominant social conformity).

Or I can take the revolutionary act of signing the *Earth Constitution* and stating that the buck stops with me. Whether the rest of the world signs or not, I have had the courage to say that I will not live without legitimate government. I will be a citizen of the Earth Federation. They can imprison me, persecute me, even kill me, but they cannot take away the fact that I have publicly chosen to live under legitimate government.

The war system may continue, even though I am a conscientious objector to this horrific and diabolical system. The system of "sovereign" nation-states may continue, even though I have personally ratified the *Constitution*. However, my act contributes to the ground-swell of persons who have chosen to live their lives on authentic moral principles. My act is a powerful one feared by the dominant elites who require control over the public mind to ensure their horrific system.

My act also frees me in many ways from their system of corruption, domination, and death (not entirely, of course, for no one is entirely free of the dominant system). I refuse to go along with their system and have taken the revolutionary decision to live under the rule of legitimate law applied equally and fairly to all persons who live on Earth.

All over the world today there are courageous people recognizing the illegitimate, unjust nature of laws, policies, or systems and engaging in acts of nonviolent civil disobedience. To commit civil disobedience in the face of this illegitimacy is often a heroic and noble act that risks jail or worse forms of repression. But the act places those who perform it in a "no man's land" of life without government (based only on their moral principles). We are citizens of the world first, and our rights derive from our humanity, our sovereignty as world citizens (Davis, 2004, pp. 22-24).

My civil disobedience declares that I have a moral right nonviolently to violate the laws of this illegitimate system and its governments. People doing civil disobedience to illegitimate systems are now living in an anarchy in which their moral principles may disagree with those of others and there is no ground for the equal treatment of everyone under the rule of democratically enacted universal laws. They are in danger of appearing to disrespect all laws (Zinn, 1990, Ch. 6).

They have rejected the present-day hypocritical claim that they are living under "democracy" as a lie. Conceptually speaking, they are now living in a "no man's land" beyond the framework of legitimate government. This vacuum must be filled by a complementary *act of civil obedience*. The decision to respond with civil disobedience to illegitimate governments and institutions is complemented by a voluntary decision to submit oneself to the rule of law under the sovereignty of the people of Earth.

Combining civil disobedience to illegitimate government with the supreme act of *civil obedience* to the *Earth Constitution* means that I have not rejected the principles of legitimate government in committing civil disobedience. I have only rejected what is no longer legitimate. This is the key to world revolution through world law.

As Garry Davis never tires of saying, each of us is a world citizen first and foremost, born on spaceship Earth, and the governments that claim us as a member of some pitiful territorial segment of the Earth are entirely illegitimate (1984). We need to act out of the dignity and sovereignty of our world citizenship which is what is truly real about us, and not out of cowardly subservience to these corrupt, imposter nation-states.

We must work to expose the illegitimate nature of all governments and their dominant economic institutions today. We must make the supreme act of *civil obedience* ourselves, whether or not we engage in civil disobedience. We must also show our present governments that *their legitimacy can only be restored* through federating under the *Constitution for the Federation of Earth*. We do not want to abolish national governments but restore their legitimacy.

As democratic guardians of their respective peoples through nationwide territorial laws, and federated within a world government that deals with global issues and the needs of all the Earth's citizens, nation-states are legitimate. As so-called "sovereign" nations, independent of the rest of the world, claiming some "ownership" of us prior to our world citizenship, they are illegitimate. If they want our *civil obedience*, our governments themselves must choose the moral act of civil obedience to the *Earth Constitution*.

Otherwise they are hypocritically demanding our obedience to their laws while themselves refusing to live under the rule of law. Our governments today insist on the anarchy of claiming they are autonomous individuals ("sovereign" nation-states) with no genuine, enforceable law above them. We are supposed to obey their laws, but they are unwilling to live under the rule of law themselves. Without this choice of *civil obedience*, they remain immoral and illegitimate. Without our own act of civil obedience, our own personal choice to live under the rule of world law, our personal lives also remain immoral and hypocritical.

The *Constitution for the Federation of Earth* has greater legitimacy than any other document today. Other constitutions have been proposed, and many have been written. But none has been created by four Constituent Assemblies of world citizens, none has been translated into twenty-two languages and distributed worldwide, and none has created organizations that are actually building the institutions of democratic world government within the shell of the old world system. There are no other real options.

No other constitution has actually created District World Courts that have taken genuine legal actions, and none has founded a Provisional World Parliament that has done extensive work in elaborating an excellent body of provisional world law (see Almand and Martin, 2005). Through these actions, we are actually building the emerging Earth Federation. We are inviting all people and nations to join the emerging Federation of Earth!

By recognizing the *Constitution* as the legitimate law for the people of Earth, I am taking a stand for a transformed world order based on the rule of universally enforceable democratic laws. In a world of international chaos, imperial domination, and global economic exploitation, this is a revolutionary act. It is also a fundamental moral act, as we have seen, to take a stand for human security, peace, freedom, justice, and prosperity.

It is not an act on the political left or the political right. It is an act that is in front, premised on a real future for human beings on this planet. It is an act that demands a similar stance from all human beings. We find ourselves in a revolutionary situation on planet Earth, and we are required to act in the face of that situation.

The Earth Federation Movement is a movement of all people of Earth. It cannot be defined by the "political spectrum" of left or right. It seeks no power for itself. It seeks only to enfranchise the disenfranchised people of Earth through the *Earth Constitution*. The people and nations of Earth can then elect whom they want to represent them. We do not have a political platform but rather an urgent moral mandate to represent all the citizens of Earth. We are the suffrage movement for all the people of Earth.

However, many persons interested in creating a decent world order are not ready to question their own privileged position within the imperial centers of power. They encourage mere *reform* of the world order toward democratic world "governance" (many of them speak only of "governance," not government) and do everything they can to criticize those who affirm genuine world government under the *Earth Constitution*. (For our published response to some of these reformists, see *Toward Genuine Global Governance,* Harris and Yunker, 1999.) Our revolutionary commitment (like all such commitments) involves an implicit criticism of their timidity and inaction. E-volution is not the same as Re-volution.

E-volution of the present world system of "sovereign" nation-states and global capitalism will not and cannot give us a substantially better world. For one thing, there is simply no time for this, since the world condition is one of global crisis and daily getting worse. Secondly, the very nature of these systems, as I have shown above, will forever subvert attempts to modify them toward a better order. International law and worthwhile U.N. agencies need not be abolished. They can easily be converted to valuable tools of world law by founding them on legitimate premises.

Only a founding document, presenting for the world a set of principles for a decent world order from the very beginning, can give us hope. A founded society is not an evolved society, which can only be a hodgepodge of conflicting forces, conditions, and claims. A founded society under the *Constitution* is structured for a just world order from the very beginning (Martin, 2005, chs 12 and 13).

This founding document gives us the premises of unity-in-diversity under the sovereignty of the people of Earth. The present system can easily be converted from its current absurd and unjust premises ("sovereign nation-states and exploitative monopoly capitalism") to legitimate premises. With this simple conversion, a new world order would have truly begun.

We sign the Pledge of Allegiance to the *Constitution* and the "e-volutionists" claim that the *Constitution* is "only legitimate in the eyes of its ratifiers." Others claim "the *Constitution* was not sufficiently democratically created." We need decades, they say, to involve all the people of Earth in writing a *Constitution*. One wonders how the more than one billion people now starving to death on the planet feel about this. Some others, comfortably embedded in wealthy first-world institutions, claim that those who affirm the *Constitution* are "the lunatic fringe of the world government movement."

To take a truly nonviolent revolutionary stance in today's world requires courage, integrity, and the capacity for real moral decision and action. It also requires a clear seeing of the absolute need for world government promised on a founding document. It is not for the timid and faint-hearted who cling to their harmless "idealism." "Oh wouldn't it be nice if the world were a place of security, peace, freedom, and prosperity," they say. "Let us hold another conference about it." Let us "dialogue." Let us have "participatory democracy" in our ineffectual NGOs.

Anything but real government. Anything but taking on ourselves the responsibility for creating genuine government for the Earth. Anything but making a revolutionary commitment to the principle that "the buck stops with me, and the decision to live under real, legitimate government begins with me." Anything but a genuine act of *civil obedience*. In this, they are like the nation-states who also refuse to live in a world of enforceable law.

Like the nation-states, they refuse to take responsibility for governing themselves. We citizens of the Earth Federation deeply respect the often genuine motives of people in the movement to create a decent global world order. We cooperate and network with them as much as possible, but we cannot let their largely ineffectual idealism corrupt the revolutionary purity of our commitment to world revolution through world law. We must begin to govern ourselves. However, such idealism has its place.

It may do some good through educating people to be concerned about global issues. It may make some incremental changes in the United Nations system or other global "governance" institutions. But ultimately, only those with the courage to choose world revolution through affirming practical and concrete world law in the here and now are going to be effective. It must begin someplace, and that place must be me.

It is up to each of us in the world, poor and rich, of every race, religion, and culture, to create a decent world order for future generations. Governments are trapped in a network of economic, political, and military corruption and are not likely to lead the way to a just and free world order. The rich are often trapped in the corrupt system that generates their wealth and are not likely to lead the way. We must mobilize ourselves as world citizens to pressure our governments to act to ratify the *Constitution for the Federation of Earth*. The ratification process in Article 17 of the *Constitution* requires both people and nations to participate.

The Earth Federation will be a true federation with effective government at all levels. Local city and town governments will still operate. Regional governments and national governments will be vital. The revolutionary difference is that under world government they will all be working together rather than in competition and hostility to one another. All levels of the federation will have to obey world law that requires respect for the rights of not only their own citizens but all other citizens worldwide.

All that is necessary is twenty-five nations who become fed up with the vampire of the present world system sucking the life and blood from their peoples and perpetuating forever immense human suffering, disease, death, and despair. All it takes is the leadership of twenty-five nations who are not hopelessly corrupted by their masters in the imperial centers of capital in the global north. How this process can easily work is described below in section seven of the *Manifesto* entitled "Common Sense Economics Under Democratic World Government."

In a very short time, with only a little courage and political will on the part of oppressed nations of the global south (in cooperation with world citizens from every nation), the foundations of a decent and prosperous world order can be established. The cornerstone (the *Earth Constitution*) is finished and ready to be placed. All that is required is a few decent, courageous, and honest national leaders and their citizen supporters.

But ordinary people must also act to educate, and to build the Earth Federation from within, regardless of the response of governments. These governments are no longer fully legitimate and their legitimacy can only be restored through joining the Earth Federation. The future of the world and humanity is in our hands, not in the hands of governments. We represent legitimacy, not them. We must act now: boldly, intelligently, and decisively. The *Constitution* also allows for direct ratification by people.

To sign the Pledge of Allegiance to the *Constitution for the Federation of Earth* is a truly transformative act. To create a chapter of the *Earth Federation Movement,* in which every member has signed the Pledge, is not just to create another organization working for some ideal. It is a practical decision and a commitment to take one's stand on a truly new world order in the here and now. Protest marches taking place everywhere on Earth often chant "What do we want? Justice. When do we want it? Now." It is this "now" that is at the heart of revolutionary nonviolent morality.

This "now" is what Mahatma Gandhi took his stand on. He insisted that we should all live our "utopias" every day of our lives, in the here and now. For they are not merely "utopias," but the common sense of the way human beings should be living on this Earth. Gandhi insisted that "we must be the change we want to see in the world" (1987, pp. 458-460; Jesudasan, 1984, p. 32). The right time to demand justice is now. And justice can only exist if it is institutionalized within a founding document.

The world will not and cannot "evolve" toward justice, at least not on the level I am addressing here. Justice is an ethical decision, a decision that can be made by nations, corporations, groups, and individuals. It is not a slowly evolving organic life-form. It is not an impractical "ideal" to be postponed indefinitely into the future. It is a choice, a decision, capable of transforming our world in the here and now. But the transformation requires an institutional framework, the *Earth Constitution* as the basis of a *founded,* just, world government.

The here and now of the decision to live one's life as a citizen of the Earth Federation is a gigantic and powerful one. It not only confers ever-greater legitimacy on the *Constitution for the Federation of Earth.* It confers a powerful moral legitimacy upon our own lives. To sign the Pledge is not the end of our work. It signals the beginning. As citizens of the emerging Earth Federation, we have much work to do. Tomorrow will be too late. The time for world revolution through world law is now.

Chapter Two

Declaration
of the Rights
of the People of Earth
to create and ratify
a World Constitution
and hold sessions of the
Provisional
World Parliament

Unanimously ratified at the Eighth

Session of the Provisional World

Parliament, August 2004

We, the citizens of the Earth, have the right and duty
to establish a viable world government capable of maintaining the Rule of
Law among all nations in place of the disastrous anarchy now prevailing
among sovereign states, to abolish massively destructive armaments and
end all wars, to protect the global environment for future generations, and
to create economic justice and prosperity for all the citizens of our planet.

1. *These are the times the world will not soon forget.* Future histori-
ans will wonder how a few of us maintained our sanity and dignity in the
face of the global breakdown of world order. Never in history have so
many people been starving to death on Earth. Never have so many people
lacked clean water or sanitation. Never has there been so much poverty
and misery.

Never in history have so many people possessed so many weapons
and engaged in continuous mutual slaughter of one another – in Columbia, Afghanistan, Sudan, Uganda, Chechnya, Iraq, and elsewhere. Never
have human beings everywhere on Earth been so insecure. Never has the
average person anywhere on Earth felt so afraid and the future seemed
so hopeless. Fifteen years after the collapse of the USSR, the threat of a
global nuclear holocaust remains in place, while the superpower continues
to develop space-based and tactical nuclear weapons.

Nowhere in previous history has the world faced a possible breakdown of its planetary ecosystem. Never has the ozone layer that protects
the Earth from the sun's deadly radiation been threatened. Never have the
ocean fisheries been collapsing from over-fishing, never before has grazing land been turning to desert on a global scale from overgrazing, never
has agricultural land disappeared at the astonishing rates that we see today.
Never before has the world's fresh water supply been endangered.

2. *Some people in every age of historical crisis have been the visionaries, the civilizers, the advanced thinkers* who see the way forward
beyond the narrow assumptions and petty issues of their day. Some people
in every age have spoken for universal principles, for justice and human
dignity, for equality and freedom among nations, peoples, and individuals of the Earth. These are the civilizers; these are the voice of legitimate
creativity. These are the ones who establish new institutions and give
renewed hope for the future.

The legitimacy of an action is not always whether it is approved by
some majority. Very often in history the majority have represented reac-

tion, intolerance, and injustice. The legitimacy of an action is whether it moves history forward toward greater universality. The innovators within history, like the writers of the French Declaration of the Rights of Man or the U.N. Universal Declaration of Human Rights, have always been a tiny minority.

The legitimacy of their work derives from its universality. The movement of history, the extension of rights, is from the tribe to the clan to the territory to the nation to the entire planet. The ultimate universality is the sovereignty of the people of Earth. New eras of legitimacy in history have been initiated by those who extended human rights and freedom to ever greater numbers of people and to those who promoted the just rule of law in human affairs.

The criterion of legitimacy in human affairs is moral universality. The core of democracy is not majority rule but the protection of minorities from both majorities and tyrants. It is equal rights for all under just laws. Nor is legitimacy derived from either power or existing institutions by themselves. Gigantic systems of power have existed historically from the Roman Empire to the many European Empires, to the present American Empire. The fact of military, bureaucratic, or institutional power does not lend legitimacy.

The only criterion is whether human rights, dignity, freedom, and justice prevail because of these institutions. This is why democracy is the ultimate criterion of legitimacy, democracy defined as any system that promotes rights, dignity, freedom, and justice in human affairs. Only global democracy represents the sovereignty of the people of Earth.

3. *The present institutions of the world are failed institutions.* The global economic system has not led to prosperity for most of the Earth's citizens, but to starvation, poverty, disease, and misery for the majority. The present global political systems of the world, called territorial nation-states, have not led to a just or peaceful world order, but to endless wars, destruction of peoples and cultures, imperial domination and conquest, and global systems of exploitation of the weaker by the stronger.

The United Nations has not led to a world where the many rights listed in its Universal Declaration of Human Rights have been extended to the Earth's citizens, but to denial of those rights for the majority and continuous increase in war, poverty, social chaos, and environmental destruction. By the criterion of legitimacy set forth in this document, these institutions have made themselves illegitimate. Citizens of Earth have the right and duty to create new institutions that represent the people of Earth.

4. *The sovereignty of the people of Earth is represented in those who seek universal human political, social, and economic rights.* The sovereignty of the people of Earth is represented in those who seek universal economic justice and the common good of all who live on Earth. The sovereignty of the people of Earth is represented by those who promote the rule of law on Earth and an end to the barbaric rule of militarized force and violence. The sovereignty of the people of Earth is represented by those who seek global democracy in the form of federal world government.

It is irrelevant whether the people of Earth elected representatives to write the *Constitution for the Federation of Earth.* What matters is that the people of Earth have the opportunity to ratify the *Constitution* and begin the rule of just law in the world. It is irrelevant whether delegates to the Provisional World Parliament were elected by their countries as representatives to the Parliament. What matters is that the delegates promote universal human rights, justice, freedom, and prosperity.

Those who represent the people of Earth in this quest are not self-appointed partisans of special interests. Such self-appointed demagogues are easily identifiable by their programs that always deny rights and dignity to those they oppose. Delegates to the Provisional World Parliament are appointed, under Article 19 of the *Constitution*, by the universal principle of morality on which the *Constitution* is based that is the criterion of legitimacy in human political and economic affairs. Their work includes all persons on Earth, and excludes none.

5. *At this juncture of world history,* no nation can have a fully legitimate democracy. For the very existence of "sovereign" nations means that the rights of those outside their borders are ignored or betrayed. At this junction of world history, no nation can protect the environment for future generations. For the destruction of the planetary ecosystem is beyond the scope and effectiveness of any nation-state.

At this juncture of world history, no nation can create economic justice. For in today's globalized economy, prosperity for individual nations always involves exploitation and poverty for other nations. The nation-state system is dead. Only those representing global democracy through federal world government can possibly represent legitimacy in human affairs.

The present world system not only embodies failed institutions but it is also built on morally illegitimate institutions. Every human being is morally required to live under democratically legislated universal laws. Without the rule of law, human affairs are always in a *defacto* state of war in which the stronger or more clever will be able to take advantage of the weaker.

Genuine law legislates equality, freedom, and the principle of justice for all. Yet in the world system today there is no genuine law, for nations are all victims to the social, military, and economic chaos that characterizes international affairs and afflicts all persons living within particular nation-states. The unenforceable pronouncements of the treaty-system that constitutes the United Nations is a travesty of genuine "international law." We are morally required to live under universal democracy and federal world government representing all persons on Earth equally and creating the just rule of enforceable law on Earth.

6. *In the face of our world condition in the past five decades, world citizens had every right to create the Constitution for the Federation of Earth.* In the face of the global chaos resulting from monopoly capitalism and the system of sovereign nation-states, these world citizens also had a duty to write a *Constitution for the Federation of Earth.* We do not characterize these acts as the noble actions of do-gooders contributing to the human project. We describe here the universal duty of every person on Earth to live under the rule of enforceable world law.

Our work is not only more legitimate than that of politicians within nations who pass legislation excluding the majority of humanity from the laws they write. Our work is absolutely obligated by the demand for universality in human affairs and by the need to protect future generations from the lethal consequences of present institutions. It is with this understanding that we affirm our right and duty to hold future sessions of the Provisional World Parliament, to work unceasingly to activate the fledgling institutions of democratic world government, and to communicate to every citizen on Earth the absolute need to ratify the *Constitution for the Federation of Earth.*

*   *   *   *   *

Commentary:
A Democratically Created Constitution
and a Founded World Order
Glen T. Martin

The above historic declaration of the Eighth Session of the Provisional World Parliament echoes a similar declaration pronounced by the hundreds of world citizens who assembled at the Hotel Rannmuthu in Colombo, Sri Lanka for the Third Constituent Assembly in January, 1979. The people of the world have the right to act on behalf of a decent world order! This is not difficult to comprehend.

Declarations of human rights such as the French Declaration of the Rights of Man, the U.N. Universal Declaration of Human Rights, and the U.S. Constitution and Declaration of Independence all agree that human rights reside with human beings *prior to the creation of government.* Human rights are natural rights. These documents agree that sovereignty belongs to people prior to any and all government. We are human beings possessing this immense human dignity living on this tiny spaceship Earth.

Why do we put up with the madness of governments claiming they are "sovereign" and usurping that concept into a mad territorial system that divides the planet into approximately 191 armed camps called "nation-states"? Why do we put up with the madness of individual governments, in the places where we happen to be accidentally born, claiming our total allegiance *to the exclusion of the rest of our planet and the rest of humankind?* Why do we not act on our true and prior world citizenship that is not given to us by any government but, so to speak, by God?

We know that our problems cannot be solved by the absurd system of territorial nation-states, each claiming autonomy from all the others, each claiming the "right" to an independent military and foreign policy over and against the rest of humanity. We know the Earth is being destroyed environmentally and that they are building ever-more weapons that will destroy our children and their future. We know the population of the Earth is out of control and global poverty and misery increase daily.

We know the Earth is being divested of its topsoils, its grazing lands, its ocean fisheries, and its forests at a terrifying rate. Then why do we not act on our dignity as human beings with rights and sovereignty prior to governments? Why don't we withdraw our allegiance and cooperation from this mad and illegitimate system that is destroying the Earth?

The Declaration of the Rights of Peoples affirms this dignity and sovereignty. We citizens of the Earth have the right and duty to create a *Constitution for the Federation of Earth* and to act now to save a future for our children and our planet. Some thousands of world citizens have done just that by writing the *Earth Constitution* and creating the Provisional World Parliament and the beginnings of democratic world government representing all the Earth's citizens.

Yet over and over I hear the question "who are these 'people of the world,' and why do they have the right and authority to act?" "Certainly," we are told, "none of us as individuals has the right to act on behalf of the people of Earth. For only a democratic majority can take such actions." Again, they say, "what right do these few have to impose a top-down constitution on the rest of us?"

"Perhaps," some say, "if we created a Global Peoples' Assembly, and set up mechanisms for the participation of people from all nations and many NGOs, then such a body could claim that it has the right to act on behalf of a decent world order." However, this Global Peoples' Assembly would likely have no authority but would only be advisory to the U.N. General Assembly, itself merely an advisory body to the U.N. Security Council. The Global People's Assembly could then act by speaking its mind on behalf of the people of Earth. Of course, its speech would have no legislative power and, if ignored, no effect. But this might be a small step forward, they tell us, toward creating a decent world order by the people of the world.

"Perhaps," others say, "we should begin by creating participatory democracy on-line in a provisional global democracy forum." We could eventually bring in more and more people who could discuss and begin voting on provisions that they would like to see in a constitution some day. Of course, we can only include those human beings with access to email, leaving out the bottom 80% of humanity. But, even if this process took a very long time, at least we would be acting "democratically" with respect to the few thousand who might be interested in such a discussion and have access to email. The rest of the six billion on the planet? Well, perhaps if we wait long enough we will be able to patiently develop a "grass-roots" democracy. *But such timidity and indecision as this will mean the destruction of our planet and a future for all the world's children.*

In every religion on Earth human beings are (in one way or another) children of God, our destiny is linked to God, and our call to action is a command from God. In every religion, human beings have an absolute dignity, beauty, and divine calling that arises from the very foundations of the universe. In the great secular philosophies created by philosophical humanists like Karl Marx, Jean Jacques Rousseau, John Dewey, William James, or Erich Fromm, there is a corresponding insight into the dignity and responsibility of being human. And in the emergent evolutionary visions of such thinkers as Sri Aurobindo, Nicholas Berdyaev, Errol E. Harris, Pierre Teilhard de Chardin, and Alfred North Whitehead our human destiny emerges toward a "superhuman" level of energy, purity, unity, and awakening to the very depths of the universe.

In every case, the great thinkers and spiritual leaders of humankind emphasized the greatness of our human destiny. This is different from my personal fate in terms of my tiny individuality, my personal likes and dislikes, my little hopes and fears. The visionaries of humankind understood that each of us participates in another dimension in which we are all ONE.

We are all human beings first! This dimension is our humanity (Immanuel Kant called it our "dignity" beyond all calculation, beyond all "price") that comprises what is most fundamental about each of us. Each is infinitely valuable, each has inalienable "human rights," precisely because each is human. Is it possible for each of us as individuals to speak and act from this trans-personal greatness of our human destiny?

Is it possible for groups like the Eighth Session of the Provisional World Parliament, in union, solidarity, and like-mindedness, to speak from this greatness of our human destiny? Take an example from the Bible, accepted as revelation by the Jewish, Christian, and Islamic traditions. The English word "prophet" comes from the Greek, meaning "to forecast." But the Hebrew language in which the first part of the Bible was written uses the word *navi,* which means "a speaker, one who can speak."

A prophet is one who can speak authentically because the prophet (*navi*) is in touch with the depth dimension of human existence. It is said that God speaks through the prophet on behalf of the dignity and greatness of our human destiny. We are called to respond, to "stand upright."

"Standing upright" (*omed*) is another fundamental theme of the Bible. God commands Ezekiel, "Son of man, stand upon thy feet..!" (Exekiel 2:1) We are commanded to "stand upright" and accept our immense human destiny to create a world of peace, justice, freedom, and dignity upon the sacred Earth. Our human destiny arising from the depths of the world (understood by great humanists and evolutionists as well as followers of the sacred scriptures of the world) is to build the "kingdom of God" on Earth.

In secular terms, we are tasked to create a world of peace, justice, freedom, and dignity. Yet many who want peace ask, "who are we to speak for all humanity?" And many religious people take refuge in their prayers, rituals, temples, and solemn chants. But the God of the Bible booms forth: "What are your endless sacrifices to me? says Yahweh.... You may multiply your prayers, I will not listen. Your hands are covered with blood, wash, make yourselves clean. Take your wrong-doing out of my sight. Cease to do evil. Learn to do good, search for justice (*mispat*), stop the oppressor; do justice to the widow, plead for the orphan." (Isaiah 1:10-20) In the world system of today, where first world fossil fuels and first world clothing and consumer goods come from the sweat-shops and from the bombed and oppressed societies of the global South, each of us is implicated. Each of us is "covered with blood."

Those who speak for what is universal and what is right have the duty and the moral right to speak for humanity. "A tree is known by its fruit," says Jesus of Nazareth (Matthew 12:33). It is not difficult to distinguish those who speak for what is truly universal from those who speak from personal, class, racial, gender, or other special interests. Who was Mahatma Gandhi to speak for the people of India and the world? He was not elected. But this is why they called him "Mahatma," because he spoke form the depths of his existence. And he urged all of us to do the same.

Who are we to create a *Constitution for the Federation of Earth*? Who are we to speak for the people of Earth? Is such action democratic? Has it been the result of the democratic participation of the people of Earth? Everyone is called to act from what is truly real and profound in his or her existence. What is profound is the very depths of our own humanity and our own existence. When we speak from these depths we are like the *navi*, speaking from what is true and universal. "By their fruits you shall know them."

It is important to distinguish between humility and cowardice. Cowardice is the unwillingness to "stand upright" and speak from the depths of what is universal within each of us. Cowardice wants to be politically correct, to be "democratic" in the sense of never standing for universal truth but always letting "the group" decide. Cowardice is lost in the merely personal and relative. It refuses to see its way clear to the deeper truth within each of us.

Humility, on the other hand, is not incompatible with taking a stand upon the gigantic truth of universal human rights, our common humanity, and the sovereignty of the people of Earth. But it does not confuse universal truth with the personal ego. The personal ego must get out of the way for truth to emerge. The universal is truly that. We must not confuse it with what is merely personal and private about each of us.

For the past ten years I have worked very hard for nonmilitary democratic world government under the *Constitution for the Federation of Earth*. As is well known, the World Constitution and Parliament Association (in association with the Institute On World Problems) promotes ratification of the *Constitution* and holds Provisional World Parliaments in locations around the world to promote the development of world law and world democracy. Since I am a professional philosopher by training, many of the articles I have written about this attempt to articulate the philosophical basis behind the *Constitution* and the reasons why it should be supported. In December 2003, at the Seventh Session of the Provisional World Parliament, the Executive Cabinet appointed me to the post of Secretary-General of WCPA.

In the course of this work, I have traveled to many countries in these ten years giving lectures and seminars about the need for democratic world government under the *Constitution*. In developing countries, many people that I speak with immediately see the arguments why we need to work for ratifying the *Constitution*. In the developed countries, on the other hand, some world federalists and other people sympathetic to the idea of democratic world government raise the issue of whether the *Constitution* has been "democratically created."

They often believe that the world must wait until people and nations get together and decide to create a democratic constitution for the Earth, starting, perhaps, with a Global Peoples' Assembly as part of the U.N. A few people, they say, do not have to the right to do this and speak on behalf of all humanity. Any world constitution must be "democratically created."

I believe this point about the *Constitution for the Federation of Earth* not being a "democratically created document," misses not only the history of constitutions of nation-states that have been written so-far and the context of our present world-situation. It also misses what I attempted to address in the above remarks and what the Declaration of the Rights of People addresses: our right and duty to speak out of the depths of our unimaginable human dignity and destiny on this planet. We admire Mahatma Gandhi, Martin Luther King, Jr., Albert Einstein, and others who have spoken from the universality of their humanity. But we refuse ourselves to "stand upright" and "to speak" through accepting our immense dignity as human beings and acting from that source.

What is "democracy" except the institutionalized recognition of this immense dignity as residing in every single human being? "Democratic" is whatever nonviolently brings such institutional recognition into being. "Undemocratic" is whatever defeats the goal of history in the name of profit, power, special privilege, or cowardice. Democracy does not simply mean "majority rule," for a possible "tyranny of the majority" is just as dangerous as the dictatorship of the few. Democracy must institutionalize protections against both forms of tyranny, and this can only be done through institutionalization of human dignity along with carefully designed checks and balances. Such dignity is institutionalized not only though guaranteed political and economic rights, but through built-in safeguards to protect nations, individuals, and minorities from both majorities and minorities.

To think that democracy can only be created or maintained through a process of always letting the majority decide in any situation is a tragic mistake. No majority can decide to remove our inalienable human rights. Only rarely do majorities decide to do what is morally right and to institutionalize what is truly universal in human life.

Democracy occurs when individuals are institutionally empowered to act from universal principles. As Mahatma Gandhi expressed this: "The rule of the majority has a narrow application, i. e., one should yield to the majority in matters of detail. But it is slavery to be amenable to the majority, no matter what its decisions are. Democracy is not a state in which people act like sheep. Under democracy individual liberty of opinion and action is jealously guarded" (1972, pp. 132-133).

It is probable that no national constitution ever written, including the U.S. Constitution, was truly "democratically created." The U.S. Constitution was written by a few elite visionaries, mostly by James Madison and a few others. Democracy is what can follow from a founding document. It cannot exist without an institutional framework and a founding set of rules for how democracy is to operate. The U.S. Constitution, like the "Declaration of Independence," was written by leaders determined to institutionalize "inalienable rights" and the truth that "all men are created equal."

In the situation of today's world when time is very rapidly running out, what would a "democratically created constitution" look like? A few elite world federalists perhaps getting together? A few world-parliament NGOs? And out of these, how few would actually do the writing? Hundreds of millions in the world cannot even read or write! To be "democratically created" a world constitution would have to consult the majority of the Earth's population, per impossible. There would have to be some mechanism already in place to allow their participation. But this is precisely what is not in place. In this context, the phrase "democratically created" lacks meaningful content, since there are no world democratic institutions to provide the format for democratically creating something. Hence, the arguement of these critics is spurious.

The *Constitution for the Federation of Earth* provides the format. Like all innovations in human history, there most be a first, put forward by a few visionaries and nonviolent revolutionaries, to provide the institutional framework for later democratic processes. As I described in the Introduction to this book, the four global Constituent Assemblies in 1968, 1977, 1979, and 1991 each had world citizens from all over the world participating. They discussed every paragraph of the *Constitution*, voted on each change or addition, and then on the entire result.

After the initial draft was written by a committee elected at the 1968 Assembly in Interlacken, Switzerland and Wolfach, Germany (according to guidelines laid down by the Assembly), the draft was circulated worldwide for comments (for 9 years) until the Second Assembly in Innsbruck, Austria. All these comments were received in Lakewood Colorado, collated, and taken into consideration in the revisions of the draft.

At Innsbruck the 125 delegates from dozens of countries and six continents went over the document paragraph by paragraph. And then it was again circulated worldwide and the same process was followed twice more in 1979 and finally in 1991 at Troia, Portugal. Under the circumstances of today's world, it is very unlikely that any process could be more "democratic" than this, since there is no institutional framework to define "democracy" for any such project.

Even if the U.N. General Assembly sat down and wrote and ratified such a document (per impossible), it would be no more democratically created than this one since the representatives in the General Assembly do not represent the peoples of the world, but elites, dictatorships, oligarchies, corporations, lackeys of the Superpower, etc. Under these circumstances, the idea of a "democratically created" document becomes meaningless obfuscation, delaying, perhaps until it is too late, the need for immediate action for a new world order.

Like all good constitutions, the *Constitution for the Federation of Earth* contains one Article that is used only once, the article for ratification. This is the source of the democratic validity of the *Constitution*, not the red herring of who wrote it or how many they were. It was the same with the U.S. Constitution, drafted by about thirteen people. Who wrote it is irrelevant if it is ratified by the people. Article 17 gives the criteria for ratification and legitimacy. It must be ratified by the people of the Earth according to strict democratic procedures.

No other constitution of the 150 or so written so far has gone through a process even similar to this. This *Constitution* is known worldwide, has been translated into 22 languages, and in the face of the shortage of time before global collapse or totalitarianism descends, it is indeed the only viable option we have. What I mean by the words "only option," of course, is not strict logical possibility, but the only practical option if we are to survive much longer on this planet and if the world's children are to have a decent future at all.

If we live and act from what is universal in ourselves, rather than remaining lost in the petty and personal, we will speak and act on behalf of a transformed future for humanity and the possibility of a founding document, a real decision on the part of humanity to create a new and decent world order for the first time in history. To live and act from what is universal in ourselves requires the courage to stand forth from that universality. Too often the assertion that we must be "democratic" becomes simply a subterfuge for lack of courage, for unwillingness to step out of ones petty individuality and take action on behalf of humanity.

This is why every Provisional World Parliament has been a momentous historic occasion, and not merely another of endless peace conferences. At these Parliaments we do not forever talk about the need for a better world. We do not discuss ideals and values of peace, disarmament, or human rights, but rather participate in the founding of a new world order! That is why those days are different from all other days and why our movement and these sessions of Parliament are different from all other events. We are not just talking. We understand that the time for endless talk is past. We are doing it. We are the vanguard, the advanced front, the visionary servants of humanity's effort to become civilized.

For we realize that the world cannot wait any longer for the slow evolution of its forces of power, chaos, greed, and fragmentation to create a decent world order before it is too late. It is already too late! The global environment is already in the process of collapsing! Global poverty and misery are already of gigantic proportions and getting worse daily. Global militarism is already destroying civilized living around the world. The global water supply is shrinking. Global farm lands are disappearing. Global fisheries are collapsing. Tomorrow is too late!

We assemble at these Parliaments because the world already has a *Constitution for the Federation of Earth.* Those of us who are delegates have personally ratified this *Constitution* and recognize it as the supreme law of the Earth, superceding all merely national constitutions. We are not only building on the brilliant work of those predecessors who realized in 1958 that the world needed a constitution and a founded world order more than anything else. We are here to continue the building of that world order under the authority of Article 19 of the *Constitution.*

The Earth Federation has begun! It was begun at the initial ratification of the *Constitution* at the Second Constituent Assembly in Innsbruck, Austria in June, 1977. We are the visionaries and laborers who are building the new world order outlined by the *Constitution for the Federation of Earth*. But insofar as we have ratified the *Constitution*, we are also citizens of the Earth Federation who have begun the new world order within the husk of the old decaying and rotten world disorder. As citizens of the Earth Federation, we speak and act from what is truly universal in ourselves, that which we have in common with all humanity.

As such, at each historic session of Parliament we will continue to elaborate the mission and vision for the actualized world parliament once the *Constitution* has been ratified by the people and nations of Earth. And we continue to develop the body of provisional world law, building on the previous sessions of the provisional parliament, which will serve as a model and set of guiding principles for the actual world parliament once the *Constitution* has been officially ratified under Article 17 of the *Earth Constitution*. We are not just talking about a new world order, we are actualizing it. We are helping to create it with courage and integrity. How dare the timid ones of the world accuse us of not being democratic!

The new world order is not an evolved world order but *a founded world order* – founded on the *Constitution for the Federation of Earth*. This distinction is utterly important. First, in a founded world order, everything begins anew within the framework of universal law premised on a world of equality, justice, and freedom for all. The framework of universal, enforceable law provides the matrix and the principles necessary for a rapid transformation of the present unjust, unequal, and unfree world order.

An evolved world order can do none of this. In an evolved world, beginning in a situation of injustice, inequality, and unfreedom, those who are powerful and wealthy will work to ensure greater advantages for themselves and legal universal equality for all will never be achieved. The forces that influence the evolution of world society are never simply those of justice. The central evolutionary determinants are undemocratic economic, political, and military forces.

The evolutionary process incorporates the plethora of competing interests and forces and will never result in a world order based on truly universal principles before it is too late and we witness global environmental collapse, global totalitarianism under one nation, or global military holocaust. A merely evolved world order will never achieve enforceable, truly universal laws. Fragmentation will continue and chaos will result.

Second, a founded society is established upon ethical principles. Democracy is the only ethically legitimate form of government and world democracy is the only from of democracy that gives all human beings their birthright to live in peace, freedom, and equality. A founded society is a moral decision by humanity to live under universal principles and the rule of law. This is the only truly legitimate form of human social and political life – all human beings subject to the same democratically legislated laws and participating in the creation of those laws.

The *Constitution for the Federation of Earth* embodies the ethical principle of the sovereignty of the people of Earth (for this is, and morally can be, the only true sovereignty). It embodies the ethical system of practical, democratic decision-making for human affairs, for there is no other morally legitimate form of human decision-making at the world level. Finally, it embodies the two extensive bills of human rights (Articles 12 and 13) that articulate in detail the ethical principles, rights and duties, that apply to every person on Earth.

An evolved society will always compromise these ethical principles in the face of the "realities" of political and economic power, hegemony, and inequality. Only a society founded on universal ethical principles can create a truly civilized world order. An evolved society will always and forever compromise, always cater to power and influence, will never quite reach its vague ethical ideals. The world can ill afford such a haphazard and ill-conceived method of developing a better world order. Human rights are universal; human dignity is universal; the demand for freedom and justice is universal. No evolved society can even begin to fulfill these ethical demands that are inherent in our human situation from the very beginning.

Third, the optimal situation is already embodied in the basic principles of a founded world society. The principles of justice, prosperity, equality, and freedom are there from the beginning for all to see. This means that citizens of the Earth Federation can work to transform the world rapidly in the direction of freedom, prosperity, justice, and equality using the *Constitution* and its clearly defined rights as a universal standard and goal. The optimal situation is embodied in the founding principles rather than serving as some vague ideal that people must struggle for into an uncertain future.

An evolved society has no such set of goals or universal standards that serve as a key for transformation to a just and peaceful world order. In an evolved society, the goals themselves are in dispute and there is a chaos of forces moving history in this direction and that. The evolutionary process also includes major forces that are trying to prevent the moving of history toward a decent world society. The powerful and rich (whether nation-states, individuals, world banks, or corporations) want to build into the evolutionary goal special advantages for themselves.

In a founded society as embodied in the *Constitution for the Federation of Earth,* the initial premise is equality and justice for all and the social task of transforming the world to conform to this premise is much more coherent, certain, and achievable. The founding principles serve as a standard and a goal that makes a coherent, civilized world order possible for the first time in history. Social conflct is guided by the founding principles.

There are already some examples of founded societies in history, although none are truly universal in scope. The United States was a founded society, a decision of many people to live under a founding constitution according to ethical principles. As Karl Marx points out, this was a great step forward in world history. Even though its *Constitution* was never intended to create economic democracy, it created a limited political democracy in which the abolition of slavery and the political equality of women were implicit and inevitable.

The greatest flaw in the assumptions behind the U.S. Constitution, as with most national constitutions, was that it established political democracy only in one nation, leaving the world in a system of power struggles, economic, and political rivalry among sovereign nation-states. As the U.S. Supreme Court determined in 1936, the U.S. Constitution does not apply to foreign policy (Zinn, 1990, pp. 124-125). In foreign policy, human rights or human life need not be respected. The result is the monster that we all see today. The Constitution of India, with its Article 51, may be unique in this regard, allowing for India to be one day part of a founded democratic world government.

The attempt to evolve the United Nations into a governing body for the world will inevitably also give us some sort of monster. Beginning with a number of absurd (literally absurd) premises upon which the U.N. system is based, many well-meaning people believe they can evolve that body in the direction of a decent world order. What are these absurd premises? First, the system of sovereign nation-states itself, which the U.N. charter says it is there to protect and preserve, which is a war system, a power-struggle system, a security and espionage system, and a profoundly undemocratic system.

This stupid and brutal way of organizing human affairs cannot be reformed or evolved but can only be transcended by genuine world government (with the valuable agencies of the U.N. being integrated into that government). The second absurd premise involves the global economic system of private monopoly wealth exploiting the land, resources, and poor of the world to make the super-rich ever richer at the expense of the rest of us, the environment, and future generations. The U.N. is up to its ears in neo-liberal global (so-called "free trade") economics run by vast undemocratic economic and political forces. It has been colonized by forces that will forever resist evolution in the direction of a just world order.

Third, the U.N. is founded on the international war system. The U.N. is premised on using military force "to keep the peace" whatever this explicit contradiction can possibly mean. This war system is perhaps the ultimate madness of human beings. In the war system, social organizations, usually nation-states, attempt to systematically exterminate and destroy one another, devoting a large portion of their economies to developing the capacity to perform this slaughter, while systematically researching and manufacturing ever more diabolical technologies to further enhance their ability to destroy. This fine system, itself integral to the system of nation-states and the present global economic system, is a founding principle of the U.N. Charter in Articles 2, 25, and elsewhere.

Finally, the U.N. is profoundly undemocratic. It was never intended to be a democracy or to approximate world democracy since it was founded by the victors in World War Two with the intention of creating their domination in world affairs. It is merely a treaty system of so-called sovereign nation-states controlled, like all such systems, by those that are bigger and more powerful. To try to evolve his nightmare system, starting with these absurd principles, and contending with the immense forces that resist evolution in the direction of a decent world order, is not "practical realism" as those trying to reform the U.N. system claim. It is to be completely out of touch with the deep structures and meanings of our present world order.

At each session of the Provisional World Parliament we are not trying vainly to evolve anything! Neither are we talking endlessly about peace or human rights as they do in one peace conference after another worldwide. We are engaged in founding a new world order, not in evolving one. We are taking our stand on the principles of universal enforceable law, universal ethical principles, and universal founding ideals that serve as a standard for the transformation to a decent world order. We are elaborating the principles and laws of that new world order under the authority of Article 19 of the *Constitution for the Federation of Earth*. We continue working to get the peoples and nations of Earth to ratify the *Constitution*. The *Constitution* is the founding document of this new world order.

We are the seed, the embryo, the vanguard, of the Earth Federation. We are the pioneers of a founded and just world order. This is a time not only of pioneer struggle and work but of great celebration and joy. For we have made the profoundly ethical decision to speak and act from what is truly universal in ourselves and all humanity. We are no longer cowardly private individuals asking "what can a tiny individual like me do in the face of the immense forces of injustice in the world?" We are not lost in the delusion of a self-proclaimed "realism" that thinks the futile attempt to evolve this profoundly unjust world system is somehow practical and commonsensical. The profoundest realism is to live and act from our deepest humanity and our infinite dignity as human beings, from that depth which is within all of us. From the bottom of my heart, I ask you to join me in celebrating the birth of the Federation of Earth!

Chapter Three

Century Twenty-One: Humanity at the Crossroads

The Manifesto of the Earth Federation

Glen T. Martin

Unanimously ratified

as an official statement

of the Provisional World Parliament

at its Seventh Session,

Chennai, India, December 2003

Foreword

This manifesto summarizes, as briefly as possible, the multiple crises our world is facing and the kind of response necessary if we are to survive the twenty-first century. It demonstrates on every page why federal world government under the *Constitution for the Federation of Earth* is necessary in the very near future. In 1995, the report of the blue ribbon "Commission on Global Governance" outlined many of the global crises we confront today and stated that "the present generation knows how close it stands to cataclysms." This manifesto shows this claim to be false.

The present generation insists on remaining in denial and willful ignorance. Yet the arguments for federal world government are compelling and decisive. They are presented on nearly every page of this manifesto. Those who have ears to hear and eyes to see, need to listen and look. This manifesto is intentionally as short as possible so that it may be easily read and understood. It deals with the issues of terrorism, war, the environment, social movements, the U.N., the system of nations, and global economics. It may well be one of the most significant documents you will ever read.

The Prologue below describes the final crossroads that human beings face today. We can reap the insights of twentieth-century science showing the holism and interdependency of every aspect of our universe. Or we can continue in fragmentation, division, and mutual destruction. Our world of war, terror, massive poverty and misery, and environmental destruction cannot endure much longer. Human beings must become politically and economically whole or we will perish. The choice is clear and simple, and the momentous consequences at stake are not difficult to discern.

Part Two, what the Earth Federation has accomplished to date, reviews the momentous legacy that we inherit from the generations who created the *Constitution* and the Provisional World Parliaments. A tremendous movement has emerged around the *Constitution for the Federation of Earth*. It has been translated into many languages and people in nearly every country are beginning to rally around the banner of the Earth Federation. Much excellent work is already accomplished. We do not have to invent the wheel. We are in a position today to set the wheel in motion.

Part Three, humanity poised at the crossroads between destruction and liberation, expresses the reasons we are at a crossroads for human existence on this planet. It considers global economics, the nation-state system, the United Nations, and global social movements. It shows the interdependence of all these movements in the nexus of crises that we face on Earth. It shows the role of our major world institutions in creating and deepening these crises. We must choose for a civilized world order today, with a clear choice and decisive action, or we will surely destroy the Earth for ourselves and for all future generations.

Part Four, failure of the United Nations, considers the United Nations, its history, its structure, and its failure to transform our world into a world of peace with justice. It lays out the facts for all who are willing to see and hear, and shows clearly why the U.N. has failed. It details how the many worthwhile agencies of the U.N. could really do their job if they were incorporated into the Earth Federation and, for the first time, had adequate funding and authority.

Part Five, the dead end environmental hopes of Rio and Johannesburg, looks at the Environmental Summits at Rio de Janeiro in 1992, at Johannesburg in 2002, and other treaties such as the Kyoto Protocol. It documents the failure of the nations to live up to their environmental agreements (leading to ever greater planetary catastrophe) and why they do not and cannot act to save the global environment. It shows that the very structure of our world system, which is historically outdated and manifestly unjust, is preventing humanity from saving the planetary environment.

Part Six, the condition of our world at the dawn of the twenty-first century, considers the nexus of global crises that we confront at the outset of our new century. It provides the latest scientific facts documenting all these crises: the crisis of fresh water, the crisis of poverty, the crisis of arable land and viable fisheries to feed the people of Earth, the environmental crisis, the population crisis, the crisis of sickness and disease, the crisis of education, the crisis of global economics, and the crisis of global militarism.

It demonstrates in what ways these crises are all interdependent and interrelated and underlines how they all stem from the fragmented world system of so-called sovereign nation-states and global monopoly capitalism. It makes clear for each crisis why federal world government is the only viable solution. It specifies exactly how these problems are addressed by the *Constitution for the Federation of Earth*, including how the *Constitution* specifically addresses the problems of militarism, terrorism, and war.

Part Seven, common sense economics under democratic world government, outlines the intelligent and fair economics that are being developed by the Earth Federation to create a world of prosperity and equity rather than one of scarcity and misery. The seven economic innovations outlined in Part Seven are readily understood and easily implemented. It makes clear that a world of plenty and justice is not merely a utopian dream but a very real possibility under the *Constitution for the Federation of Earth*. All reasonable people can understand the rationality and simplicity of these options. Another world is truly possible.

Finally, Part Eight, where do we go from here? addresses the actions we must take at this historical crossroads to create a sustainable, just, and prosperous world order. These actions are common sense and based on clear, compelling arguments, and extensive factual evidence. Part Eight appeals to the poor majority of people on Earth to act on their own behalf and on behalf of a future for their children.

But it points out that we are all made poor by the present world order of injustice, misery, and war. We are all citizens of the Earth under the *Constitution*, and today we are all made poor by the wretched conditions that the old rotten system perpetuates into the future. It calls for all citizens of the world to unite under the Earth Federation. If many citizens of the Earth were to stand up on behalf of a decent world order at this crossroads of history, a world of sanity, peace, and prosperity would be just around the corner.

1. Prologue

1.1. Human history on planet Earth has reached its final crossroads. Human beings can continue on the road to imminent perdition, or we can rise to a new level of civilization for the Earth. This manifesto clearly describes that crossroads for all who care to see and hear. Our message is not a confused and sentimental longing for a better world as is so often heard today from groups seeking to protect human rights, or advance democracy, promote peace, or address poverty and disease. Our message is clear, precise, and specific. The reasons we are on the road to imminent perdition can be easily understood. And the reasons for the Earth Federation are clear, compelling, and decisive. This manifesto is about that choice. Time is running out when this choice will be available to us. The time for firm decision is now. There is no other time.

1.2. This choice is not an arbitrary or irrational one. For the concept of holism (unity) emerges as the fundamental insight of every twentieth-century revolution in science. The Einstein revolution showed that nature and the cosmos must now be understood holistically. And Quantum physics has shown this to be true on the sub-atomic level. On both the macro and micro levels, our universe exhibits unity as a seamless, interdependent field of space/time/energy/matter. Ecology and the biological sciences have also demonstrated holism at every level of living nature, including the encompassing ecosystem of the Earth.

1.3. The major sphere where fragmentation, division, and reductionism remain is the sphere of human social life in the system of territorial nation-states and the global economic system of violence, greed, and non-cooperation. It is no accident that Einstein was an outspoken advocate of planetary federal government. He understood the inescapable holism of the world we live in. The choice before us is to convert our thinking to holism (the unity and interrelatedness of all persons on the Earth) or to continue into destruction with our fragmentation and violence. This holism is embodied in the *Constitution for the Federation of Earth* through a dynamic and comprehensive relationship of unity-in-diversity. We must immediately choose the holism of federal world government or we may soon perish from the Earth.

1.4. Today, a creative groundswell in the movement for a sane federal world order is making the current lords of the Earth tremble in their corruption and fragmentation. The people of the world are awakening to the lies and distortions of the media, their subservience to power, and the corrupt interests defending the old rotten order while destroying the Earth for future generations. We citizens of the Earth Federation are spokespersons of this new world order predicated on wholeness, democratic values, and the common good of all persons on Earth. They may imprison or kill us as individuals, but the groundswell of awakening among the people of the Earth is unstoppable. We are poised at a crossroads for humanity. We must choose wisely – for humanity – or we may perish from the Earth.

2. What the Earth Federation has accomplished to date

2.1. We citizens of the Earth Federation, gathered at this historic Seventh Session of the Provisional World Parliament, recognize that we are building on the collective efforts of thousands of world citizens who worked tirelessly since 1958 (and throughout the twentieth century) to bring us the great legacy that we inherit today. They are to be honored and revered as prophets and designers of the Earth Federation that is destined to create truly civilized life on planet Earth for the first time in human history.

2.2. Our predecessors, some of whom are among our leaders yet today, gave humanity, first and foremost, the *Constitution for the Federation of Earth*. This document, one of the great milestone documents of human history, was forged to the finest quality by the effort of hundreds of world citizens in four Constituent Assemblies from Wolfach, Germany in 1968 to Troia, Portugal in 1991. Today, it has been distributed worldwide and translated into twenty-two languages.

2.3. The *Constitution* is recognized by many people around the world as the supreme law for Planet Earth, superseding all laws passed by the approximately 190 territorial entities that today call themselves "nation-states" and claim the false right to pass laws for their territories not accountable to the rest of humankind. We understand today that no merely territorial entity has the right to claim absolute sovereignty for its laws unaccountable to the universal principles of equity, justice, freedom, and peace embodied in the *Earth Constitution* and widely endorsed universal declarations of rights and responsibilities, including the Earth Charter. True sovereignty resides with all the citizens who live on Earth, not within limited territorial entities.

2.4. The *Constitution* creates a parliamentary system that will not be subject to subversion and corruption as has turned the so-called liberal democracies into "national security states" dominated by executive branch secrecy and arbitrary power. There will be no need for executive secrecy and arbitrary power when all nations are demilitarized under the rule of democratically legislated laws. The world parliament has three houses (a House of Counselors representing all humanity, a House of Nations representing every nation on Earth, and a House of Peoples with proportional representation from 1000 electoral districts worldwide). The main branches of government under this Parliament (the World Judiciary, the World Executive, the World Police and Attorneys General, and the World Ombudsmus) are all directly accountable to the Parliament and have no power to suspend the *Constitution*, withhold spending of the budget, violate human rights, create a military apparatus, or otherwise subvert the universal guarantees given to all nations and peoples by the *Constitution*.

2.5. By recognizing the sovereignty of the people of Earth and universal economic and political rights for all citizens, the *Constitution* ends once and for all the power-politics of nation-states that struggle for economic advantage, control of resources, military hegemony, and spheres of influence. This struggle continues to destroy the rights and the lives of millions around the globe, as it has for centuries. It mandates equitable use of the Earth's essential resources for all people, making possible a truly civilized world order under the rule of democratically legislated law for the first time in history.

2.6. Will there be "opposition parties" within the Earth Federation? Of course. Unlike the pseudo-diversity of today's two party systems, a genuine diversity of voices is the heart and soul of democracy. Under today's common one or two party systems, the group in power attempts to suppress, silence, co-opt, or eliminate its opposition. There is a lack of that mutual respect and unity necessary to legitimate the diversity of genders, cultures, religions, ethnicities, or political viewpoints.

2.7. Sheer diversity without authentic unity results in conflict, violence, and the rule of the most powerful. The Earth Federation is predicated on "unity in diversity." Diversity is protected and encouraged precisely because it is encompassed by the unity of the universal rule of law and universal citizenship. Everybody has a voice and a stake in the welfare of the whole and of everyone else. A genuine plurality of voices listening to one another (rather than trying to suppress and drown one another out) is here made possible for the entire Earth.

2.8. The second great accomplishment of our predecessors was to take many active steps to actually initiate democratic world government under the *Constitution*. They have given us a body of provisional world law that has been carefully developed since the first Provisional World Parliament met in 1982, and they have begun elaborating the ministries necessary for the functioning of world government. Since 1982, the Provisional World Parliament has met in six different locations around the world, the Sixth in Bangkok, Thailand in March 2003, the Seventh in Chennai, India in December 2003, and the Eighth in Lucknow, India in August 2004.

2.9. Today, the world inherits from our predecessors a body of quality planetary law that serves as a model and a beacon for all humanity lighting the path by which we can move from a world of chaos, war, and imminent disaster to a world of peace, freedom, equity, and justice. The Sixth Provisional World Parliament established a Commission for Legislative Review to codify and professionalize this body of world law. When the first operative stage of World Government has begun, and the official World Parliament has been constituted, this body of law will serve as a tremendous gift to humankind, and available to the Parliament for review, modification, or immediate ratification.

2.10. Those of us worldwide who have personally ratified the *Earth Constitution* are now ambassadors and spokespersons for the Earth Federation, voices crying in the wilderness of global chaos, violence, and fragmentation, but also prophets speaking for the future of civilization and the greatest hope for humanity. The Earth Federation lives at the moment through us until the day when it will become recognized and embraced by all of humanity. On that day we will be honored and revered as courageous pioneers who selflessly struggled against tremendous odds on behalf of our precious planet Earth, universal justice, and a decent life for future generations.

3. Humanity poised at the crossroads between destruction and liberation

3.1. Recognition of our great movement is happening everywhere among the poor and dispossessed majority of the world. Recognition that all the tired options of the past have long been exhausted and that the present world order is kept in place not by hope and vision for a better future but by institutionalized force and violence. This poor and dispossessed majority are the great hope for humanity and the Earth Federation.

3.2. Monopoly conditions dominated by global corporations and imperial governments enforce upon the world's poor majority a global system of economic exploitation and domination. The World Trade Organization, the International Monetary Fund, the World Bank, imperial governments, and the heads of multinational corporations work in secret forums to effectively eliminate all opposition to their criminal pillage of the planet and its resources. This system is one of planetary institutionalized violence, forcing unnecessary death and disease on untold millions who are victims of the rape of the planet by the rich and powerful. This system is enforced by the overt violence of strategically placed global weapons sales, counterinsurgency military training provided to dominant elites in poor countries, political manipulation, threats of economic sanctions or punishment, and outright invasions or bombings of countries that attempt to take an independent course.

3.3. Yet with the failure of the United Nations to prevent genocide against the Iraqi people culminating in the 2003 invasion of their country, and the total failure of the U.N. to prevent the complete devastation of Afghanistan over the past twenty years, it has become clear to the poor nations and peoples of the world that the U.N. is a false prophet and an ideological cover for the preservation of the system of global exploitation and domination. The recently created "International Coalition Against Terror," illustrates the impotence and irrelevancy of the U.N. This coalition creates a permanent, global war system largely comprised of the wealthiest nations, most of whom have a history of colonial domination of other countries, who today produce most of the world's weapons, including weapons of mass destruction.

3.4. Independent people's movements, like the World Social Forum, have sprung up globally, determined to create a more just and equitable world order. There are also many non-governmental organizations working to protect human rights, relieve poverty, preserve the environment, or promote health-care throughout the world. They speak of "resistance" to the dominant order, of restoring "living democracy" to the planet, empowering the poor, canceling international debt, or "food first" for the world. Yet they offer no clear means for achieving these goals within a world system predicated on war, national imperialism, and power politics, only vague ideas about making economics and politics more democratic, more just, or more responsive to the needs of the poor.

3.5. The Earth Federation does not want to be "more responsive to the needs of the poor." The Federation provides the means for eradicating poverty from the Earth. We do not work to make the existing institutions of power, domination, and exploitation (the "sovereign" nation-state and global capitalism) "more democratic." There is no way to make the flawed and fragmented power-based institutions of today's world "more democratic." They are inherently totalitarian and undemocratic, whatever their ideologies may claim, and have produced a living hell for those unfortunate enough to be their victims.

3.6. The metaphor of hell is apt, for the institutions of the "sovereign" nation-state and their global economic system have created a living hell on Earth for the past five centuries through their policies of merciless conquest, genocides of indigenous peoples, brutal systems of slavery, vicious colonialism, endless colonial wars, world wars, and militarized neocolonial domination of today. Presently, for at least 1.5 billion citizens on this planet, and for the poor majority of the world, they truly represent the rule of hell on Earth. We understand that these institutions must be replaced by genuine federal world government and by an economic system premised on rapid sustainable development and the welfare of all the Earth's citizens.

3.7. The key to solving the terrible global crises confronting humanity is the creation of global institutions capable of planetary action and premised on creating a world of equity, freedom, justice, and peace. There are no such institutions in the world today. Only democratic world government is capable of dealing with global crises on a planetary level. Gradual modification of the present flawed institutions of the world is a prescription for planetary suicide.

3.8. Approximately 150 years ago, another manifesto announced that a "specter was haunting Europe," the specter of violent revolution and expropriation of the stolen wealth of the rich. We announce that a peaceful revolution is at hand, more far reaching than that earlier manifesto could have imagined. We announce that there is no need to expropriate the wealth of the rich to create global equity, freedom, justice, peace, and prosperity.

3.9. Our revolution is more far reaching because it is planetary in scope and because humanity is at the final crossroads. The earlier revolution was premature, for humanity had not yet reached its final crossroads. Our revolution for the first time in history creates planetary institutions that represent all the world's people based on the principle of unity-in-diversity. No one is excluded. For the first time in history, the needs, rights, and interests of the whole of humanity are taken into account by democratic, truly planetary institutions.

3.10. The choice today is between certain chaos, barbarism, and destruction or democratic world government under the *Earth Constitution*. Our revolution abolishes not only the worst features of capitalism and monopoly corporate pillage as did that earlier manifesto. It also abolishes that other demon from hell that has wreaked havoc on the Earth for the past five centuries: the absolute "sovereignty" of nation-states. The so-called "sovereign" nation-state is a fragmented, irrational, and dangerous institution that has divided the Earth into approximately 190 competing territorial entities. Its very existence denies the sovereignty of the people of Earth. We must not only eliminate the worst features of capitalism. We must also eliminate the warring, imperialistic, and greedy institution of the absolute sovereignty of nation-states.

3.11. Since nation-states call themselves "sovereign," and recognize no authority of law above themselves, they are always in a relation of chaos, struggle, and *defacto* war with one another. This fact was pointed out by Thomas Hobbes, Baruch Spinoza, Immanuel Kant, G.W.F. Hegel, and many other political thinkers. In this situation, action for the common good of humanity and the Earth is in principle impossible. The only authentic and legitimate sovereignty is that of all the people who reside on Earth. And the *Earth Constitution* embodies that sovereignty in effective world government in which all people and nations live under the rule of democratically legislated law for the first time in history. The holism of nature and the ecosystem of Earth is for the first time realized also in human affairs. The common good of the Earth and future generations can for the first time be effectively addressed.

3.12. The old order is dead and dying. The world is at its final crossroad. We can sink further toward imminent destruction of the Earth and its inhabitants led by the rich and powerful corporations, governments, and financial institutions concerned only to preserve their system of exploitation and domination as long as possible into the ever darkening future. Or we can move to a higher level of human dignity and civilization on planet Earth by uniting in one world under the *Constitution for the Federation of Earth*.

4. Failure of the United Nations

4.1. Many nations and many well-meaning people in the world, however, have not embraced a truly new world order under the *Earth Constitution* but have followed the U.N. system based on the failed institutions of the past five centuries of the modern era. The United Nations was created by the victors of the Second World War in order to ensure their continued dominance in the affairs of the world. This has been illustrated in its sad history of veto upon veto, preventing the majority of nations in the world, representing the majority of the people of the world, from altering the world order in the direction of equity, freedom, justice, or peace.

4.2. The ideals embodied within the U.N. Charter, such as preventing "the scourge of war" are belied by its undemocratic organizational structure and its underlying assumptions. According to the U.N. Charter, the "scourge of war" is to be prevented in the last resort by the Security Council going to war. Such absurdities of our present world order permeate the document. The U.N. Charter is based on "the sovereign independence" of its member states, reaffirming the flawed and false principle of territorial sovereignty. For this reason also imperial nations can ignore the U.N. when they choose, and go to war at will entirely outside of the U.N. system.

4.3. In practice, for the past five centuries, this doctrine of "sovereign independence" has meant that the powerful nations dominate and exploit the weaker nations. It has meant that the global north has become rich through exploiting the global south. Today, this system continues through the GATT system of the U.N., the World Bank, International Monetary Fund, and the World Trade Organization. The global south (Africa, Latin America, South Asia) is poorer, more exploited, and more miserable today than ever before in history. The wealthy elite in the global north is richer today than ever before in history.

4.4. The United Nations has failed to prevent war. There have been some 130 wars since the advent of the U.N. resulting in some 25 million war-related deaths, most of them civilians. The U.N. has failed to create security for the people of the world. It has allowed rampant world militarism with ever faster and more destructive weapons created and deployed at the staggering figure of approximately 850 billion U.S. dollars per year. Not only has military insecurity increased worldwide, the people of the world are today faced with an every growing number of insecurities connected directly with the failure of the United Nations.

4.5. Food insecurity has increased worldwide, as has water insecurity, insecurity with respect to health care, and insecurity of educational opportunities. Under the U.N., millions have been displaced from their rural lands and been forced into horrible slums in gigantic third world cities to be faced with community chaos and insecurity in the form of drugs, prostitution, violence, and crime.

4.6. The U.N. has failed to eradicate poverty. Global poverty is significantly greater today than when the U.N. was created. Today, largely under domination by the United States with its shameless promotion of multinational corporations dedicated to pillaging the planet of its resources and cheap labor in the service of private profit, the U.N. is turning more and more to "private solutions," making deals with private, profit making corporations to supply education, water, electricity, health care, vital drugs, farming, or transportation to so-called developing countries.

4.7. Dozens of countries around the world have seen their essential infrastructures and services that served the people privatized and destroyed by employee cutbacks, profit gouging, and holding poor populations hostage to their monopoly control of essential services. The bottom line is that the concept of "developing countries" is a misnomer, for most of the world remains merely a colonial service area to supply cheap resources, labor, and quick profits for the wealthy corporations and their sponsor governments. Under the present system, there is no hope and no real intention of these countries ever "developing."

4.8. In addition, the U.N. has failed to limit the exploding global population that today is in excess of six billion persons and growing by eighty million new persons each year, numbers of people that the finite resources of the Earth cannot possibly support. Finally, it failed to protect the disintegrating environmental integrity of our planet despite holding huge conferences on the environmental crisis in Rio de Janeiro in 1992 and Johannesburg in 2002.

5. The dead-end environmental hopes of Rio and Johannesburg

5.1. The June 1992 Earth Summit at Rio de Janeiro was a milestone in a clear understanding of our human condition on planet Earth. The documents produced at Rio show the understanding that the global crises are all interconnected and interrelated. We cannot protect the environment without simultaneously eliminating poverty, eradicating war and militarism, controlling population growth, and restricting the drive for economic gain through acting on universal principles of what sustains and protects the common good of the planet and its future.

5.2. By the time the 35,000 delegates met at the Earth Summit in Rio, it was clear that all development on the Earth must be "sustainable," for the planet could not much longer survive a model of development treating the finite resources of the Earth as an unlimited cornucopia for exploitation. Nor could the limited ability of the planet to absorb waste materials and pollution be treated any longer as an infinite cesspool, where industrial development indiscriminately externalized its costs and its wastes into the water, air, and soil. The people at the Rio Summit understood that sustainable development means meeting the needs and improving the quality of life in the present without sacrificing the ability of future generations to meet their own needs while living lives of quality and dignity.

5.3. The delegates at Rio created one of the great documents of the twentieth century: "Agenda 21." This document understood that workers and farmers in developing countries had to be empowered and protected, that protections and opportunities for women and children worldwide had to be strengthened, that education had to be disseminated to all peoples of the developing world. In short, sustainable development must necessarily mean reducing population growth, eliminating poverty, providing the education necessary for development. Agenda 21 also made it clear that definite, rigorous goals had to be set for the reduction of greenhouse gasses and ozone depleting gasses by nations and their industries, and that global fisheries, farmlands, grazing lands, and forests had to be preserved and restored. Many nations signed Agenda 21 and promised to achieve the goals set for them by the document.

5.4. The subsequent Earth Summit at Johannesburg, South Africa in August-September 2002 represented a widespread recognition of the failure of Agenda 21 and the hopes of Rio for bringing the world back from the brink of disaster. There was nothing wrong with the Agenda 21 plan itself. The nations of the world simply did not honor the commitment and demand to reduce greenhouse and ozone depleting emissions, to empower the developing world in ways that provided education, eliminated poverty, and reduced population growth, and to create a sustainable and integrated world economy and more equitable world order.

5.5. Why should any one of the 190 competing territorial units, each with its own internal problems and self-interest in mind, act for the common good of the Earth and future generations? The very assumption that they might do this was hopelessly naive. Why should any of the multi-billion dollar corporations now pillaging the Earth act for the common good of humanity and future generations? Familiarity with their actions around the world demonstrates that these organizations are often criminal in nature and run by criminals. Several of the books in the bibliography to this manifesto document in detail the worldwide criminal interrelationships between multinational corporations, banking institutions, governments, and even global terrorism. How naive for the people at Rio to believe that any hope for the environment was possible under the current world system!

5.6. Many at Johannesburg recognized that governments alone (of which the U.N. is officially comprised) cannot save the world from disaster. Many governments are not representative of their own people: many are dominated by big business interests, some are dominated by religious extremists or criminal thugs (dictators), many are under the thumb of the big imperial powers or the structural adjustment programs of the World Bank. For this reason, many world citizens struggled at the Johannesburg conference to get a voice for the non-governmental organizations at the decision-making tables.

5.7. They argued that governments (and their corporate partners) alone are not capable of representing the interests of the future, the people of the world, or the planet itself. Some progress was made in getting NGOs recognized as a voice in the dialogue about the future of the world, and some people, sadly, believe this represents a success of Johannesburg. But in reality it only illustrates the complete failure and hopelessness of the U.N. process.

5.8. Agenda 21 failed not because its goals were incorrect or unrealistic, but because it was a product of a United Nations Conference recognizing the "sovereign independence" of each of the 190 territorial entities on the planet and affirming a global economic system of crass greed and pillage. Agenda 21 was merely a treaty, like the subsequent Kyoto Protocol on the environment, like the United Nations Millennium Declaration of the year 2000, and like whatever agreements emerged from Johannesburg. Subsequently, corporations and imperial nations acted to destroy the Kyoto Protocol from within by creating a system for "pollution credits" or, as they call it, or "global emissions trading." This system has allowed them to continue trashing the environment while claiming that they are conforming to "free market" environmentalism.

5.9. The structure of the world system is deeply flawed and absolutely inadequate to the vital needs of the world to end poverty, war, population growth, environmental degradation, and social chaos. A system of 190 territorial entities all claiming sovereignty over some piece of land cannot possibly produce universal equity, freedom, justice, or peace in the world. A world economic system based upon the unbridled greed and self-interest of nations and corporations cannot possibility create sustainable development and save the planet from impending disaster.

5.10. 'To bring new voices of NGOs to the discussion table may push governments and public opinion towards recognizing existing injustices. International groups of doctors and others have prompted resolutions about land mines, an international criminal court, and the environment. However, naively assuming that this produces adequate and responsible remedies is a recipe for total disaster. NGOs, like world citizens, have a healthy democratic function but not a right to speak for all humanity apart from world government. The nations of the U.N. do not speak for all humanity but only for themselves and their sovereign interests. Neither are such NGOs elected by the people of the Earth to represent their interests.

5.11. The U.N. system is as undemocratic and unjust as any set of institutions could possibly be. The U.N. failure to protect the global environment and create sustainable development is not the result of a lack of understanding of the problems we face. It is a result of an organization premised on the particularized and inadequate institutions nearly five centuries old (the nation-state and global capitalism) and entirely inadequate to address universal needs and interests.

5.12. To add a powerless "peoples' assembly" to the already powerless General Assembly of the U.N., or to add the voices of a few NGOs to the dialogue about the world's future, may seem to some a giant step, but it is a feeble gesture towards a democratic rule of law among nations. It is to ignore the living hell that is the world we live in for a good portion of humanity. It is to ignore the impending cataclysms nearly upon us of global population increase, global epidemics, global water shortage, global starvation, global collapse of fisheries and farmlands, global warming, global flooding of coastal lands, global ozone depletion, global war, and global social chaos.

5.13. Democratic world government is the only rational option, the only possible vehicle that can represent universal and global needs and interests. The *Constitution for the Federation of Earth* is directed explicitly to the global crises faced by our planet: population, poverty, militarism, health care, education, and environment. It gives the elected representatives of the sovereign people of Earth the legal authority and the mandate to create sustainable development for the entire Earth and to transform the world to one of equity, freedom, justice, and peace. No other force on

Earth can accomplish this task within the limited time available to us.

5.14. Replacing the U.N. Charter with the *Earth Constitution* does not mean dismantling many excellent U.N. organizations and their worthwhile infrastructure that can be used as a basis for the agencies of world government concerned with health care, the welfare of children, the rights of women, sustainable development, education and cultural exchange, labor standards, international shipping, postal regulations, meteorology, environmental standards, and other important fields. Many U.N. agencies do excellent work in all these areas despite the impediments placed in their way by sovereign nations and global economics. The Earth Federation will immediately increase the funding and global scope of all worthwhile U.N. agencies, converting them to ministries of the Federation. Many agencies of the U.N. are valuable and should be preserved. It is the U.N. Charter with its flawed assumptions that must be replaced.

5.15. The failed United Nations system is bringing the world ever nearer to complete disaster, as was recognized by many at Johannesburg. To invest more time and energy into that system is mad and even suicidal. We are one world, one humanity, one global ecosystem, one system of information and communication. We are deeply interdependent and interrelated with every other person on the planet. Yet we have failed to create any global institutions based on this truth. The *Constitution for the Federation of Earth* is the only viable document based on this understanding. Its Preamble states that "Humanity is One," and that the principle of "unity in diversity is the basis for a new age when war shall be outlawed and peace prevail," and "when the Earth's total resources shall be equitably used for human welfare."

5.16. The *Earth Constitution* represents, for the first time in human history, planetary institutions, planetary vision, planetary responsibility, and democratically guided planetary planning for sustainable development and the welfare of future generations. This is the only truly viable, widely publicized option presently available as we face the crossroads of the early twenty-first century. Shall we continue on our disastrous course of attempting to deal with planetary crises through fragmented and divisive institutions nearly five centuries old?

5.17. Or shall we move to a new level of existence on this planet, perhaps fulfilling the very meaning of our historical pilgrimage on Earth? Shall we at last create planetary institutions representing all the people of Earth, all the living creatures of Earth, and the welfare of future generations? The Seventh Provisional World Parliament (who ratified this Manifesto), along with the many thousands of planetary citizens who have ratified the *Earth Constitution* worldwide, recognize that we are the prophets and harbingers of a truly new world order premised on the universal principles of equity, freedom, justice, and peace. Our responsibility is correspondingly great. We must continue activating a global movement among the peoples and nations of Earth to ratify the *Constitution* and initiate truly democratic, federal world government before it is too late.

6. Condition of our world of at the dawn of the twenty-first century

6.1. The crisis of fresh water. There is a growing shortage of fresh water worldwide. Every person living needs approximately thirty gallons of clean water daily. Yet hundreds of millions of people live on less than ten gallons daily. As the population of the planet continues to increase by eighty million persons per year, so does the need for water. Yet underground aquifers from which most water comes are receding at an alarming rate. Four decades ago groundwater levels could be found a few meters below ground. Today in many places special wells and pumping systems are required to access water 180 meters or more beneath the Earth.

6.1.1. The size of the giant underground aquifers on which people depend for irrigation and to supply cities with water are steadily shrinking. The aquifer under the Midwest of the United States is half the size it was less than one hundred years ago. In addition, unsustainable industrial development has poisoned water systems around the world so that many groundwater systems are polluted with heavy metals and other toxins from mining, oil drilling, or manufacturing.

6.1.2. Governments of the world have also not acted to preserve the water that falls in the form of rain. They have not acted to preserve the forests that retain fresh water over the land and serve as a conduit to move the water inland from the sea. Irrigation systems, accounting for seventy percent of the world's fresh water use, irresponsibly waste immense amounts of water, often because of the drive to maximize profit rather than preserve the Earth for future generations. Meanwhile, drip irrigation systems are available that could conserve a tremendous volume of fresh water.

6.1.3. How is the global water crisis to be handled if not by democratic world government? Nation-states alone have no ability to deal with this global phenomena. Water patterns are global. Global warming is changing these patterns worldwide, creating droughts in some places and floods and hurricanes in others. Sources of water cross borders, as for example the sources of water in Bangladesh, with its immense problems of flooding, lie largely in India. Currently, water systems in many nations have been privatized, placed in the hands of global corporate criminals. Water prices have skyrocketed, while purity and protection of clean water supplies have evaporated. Only the World Parliament operating under the *Earth Constitution* can create a workable water policy for the entire planet.

6.2. The crisis of poverty. Poverty is greater and far more extensive today that ever before on Earth. 1.5 billion people, or close to twenty percent of the Earth's population, live on less than one U.S. dollar per day. This means a large portion of the Earth's population go to bed hungry each night. It means millions of malnourished children and immense human potential for creativity and development lost because malnourishment often leads to retardation or diminished intellectual capacity.

6.2.1. It is often truly said that there is enough food grown globally to feed all people currently on the Earth. But the global economic system distributes that food to those who can pay, to the wealthy first world nations, leaving hundreds of millions of people in the developing world hungry. Poverty cannot be eliminated through giving resources directly to hungry people. Charity is not development.

6.2.2. Poverty can only be eliminated through extensive programs of education, health care to eliminate the many diseases and diminished potential that go with poverty, non-exploitative finance capital to activate local and regional economies, and infrastructure development to enhance the economic multiplier effect that can come from widespread circulation of money between producers and consumers throughout the developing world.

6.2.3. There are no Earthly institutions that can accomplish all these goals in an effective and timely manner. To accomplish these tasks would take immense resources, planning, coordination, and oversight to provide education, health care, nonexploitative finance capital, and a high quality infrastructure throughout the developing world. Only world government representing the Earth Federation could do this. Without effective world government, there is no hope of eliminating poverty and misery from the Earth.

6.3. The crisis of resources for feeding the people of Earth. There are at least four features of the Earth that humans and animals depend on for food and survival: farmlands, grazing lands, ocean fisheries, and forests. All of these resources are being degraded and destroyed at alarming rates.

6.3.1. Farmlands lose many billions of tons of topsoil every year to wind and water erosion because of unsustainable farming methods. Farmlands worldwide are also being over-planted, leading to soil exhaustion and deterioration. Every year millions of acres of agricultural land are become unusable and are lost to human food production.

6.3.2. Grazing lands, where herds of goats, cows, sheep or other animals are pastured, are becoming degraded and diminished through overgrazing. Overgrazing eventually destroys the land itself, leading to growing desertification worldwide. Deserts, increasing in size worldwide, are largely waste that cannot support human or animal life. By some estimates, fifty percent of the land in Asia and Africa is now useless for supporting life.

6.3.3. Third, ocean fisheries are dying due to over-fishing and perhaps to the rise of ocean temperatures from global warming. The tonnage in fish harvests is diminishing each year. In some cases, such as the once rich North Atlantic fishery, the entire fishery has collapsed, costing the world millions of tons of protein once supplied by those fish each year.

6.3.4. Finally, we are losing the forests of the world. Forests hold the soil from eroding, store fresh water and move it inland, moderate the climate, provide a habitat for the Earth's wild creatures, and provide a wealth of biological materials for medicine and human well-being. They are also "the lungs of the Earth," since they bind the carbon dioxide given off by most human industrial processes and give off oxygen to replenish the atmosphere. As with agricultural lands, grazing lands, and fisheries, forests are disappearing from our planet at an alarming rate. The world loses approximately thirty million acres of rain forest per year.

6.3.5. As with the other crises listed here, the causes of this are well-known and understood. And as with the other crises, the factors are intertwined with the factors causing all these crises. Global militarism at 850 billion U.S. dollars per year obviously wastes immense resources that should be used for education and development. Global militarism produces immense amounts of toxic wastes, and war itself creates environmental havoc. Global poverty contributes to the destruction of forests since most people in the developing world use wood for cooking.

6.3.6. In addition, the global economic system of unregulated greed and self-interest unsustainably logs these forests for private profit. Global population pressures lead to over-farming, over-grazing, and overfishing, and hence destruction of the very basis for feeding future generations on this planet. Industrial pollution and the continued production of greenhouse and ozone depleting gases daily diminish the planet's ability to support life in the future.

6.3.7. What institutions in our world possess the ability to mount a coordinated, carefully thought-out, well-financed, and strategically designed plan for dealing simultaneously with all these interdependent and interrelated crises? There are none, least of all the United Nations which we have seen is predicated on the fragmented institutions of the past and committed to the barbaric and outmoded systems of "sovereign nation-states" and corporate pillage.

6.3.8. What is needed is not merely a coordinated policy of conservation, what is needed is a dynamic policy directed toward reversing the tremendous damage already done and restoring the Earth to ecological health. Only a World Parliament, representing all the people of Earth as well as future generations, with the authority and resources to carry humanity over the crossroad from possible extinction to a new world order of equity, freedom, justice, and peace, can provide the solution to these otherwise insurmountable problems.

6.4. The environmental crisis. The crisis of resources for feeding the people of Earth, like the water crisis, are part of a multi-dimensional breakdown of the planetary ecological systems. Depletion of the ozone layer that protects living things from the deadly ultraviolet radiation of the sun, destruction of the forests and phytoplankton in the oceans, exhaustion of fresh water supplies, and dumping of millions of tons annually of toxic wastes into the air, water, and soil, all constitute substantial disruptions of the health of the planetary ecosystem and portend eventual environmental collapse.

6.4.1. Global warming is a widely recognized scientific fact that has already resulted in massive weather pattern changes, increased melting of the polar caps, and unprecedented "superstorms." And it is widely recognized that global warming will inevitably bring rising oceans and flooding of the coastal lands of Earth, displacing more than a billion people and submerging a good portion of the Earth's remaining farmland. Yet little is being done to change this nightmare scenario. We are told that the demand for oil (a chief cause of global warming) will increase by thirty percent in the next ten years. And today the nations and multinational corporations of the world are fighting (economically, politically, and militarily) to ensure the "stability" of countries housing old oil reserves and to control vast regions of Asia in the light of the new reserves soon to be available from the Caspian Sea basin.

6.4.2. Under the current world system such madness (with the power and profit that the control of oil brings) is inevitable. Only a federation representing the entire Earth could have the political will and authority to convert the world to solar, wind, water, and hydrogen power, find ways of recycling and minimizing toxic waste, really protect the ozone layer, and restore the other essential features of Earth necessary for a quality human life for all persons.

6.5. *The population crisis.* The teeming slums and social chaos of Mumbai, Dhaka, Mexico City, or Rio de Janeiro spread diseases like Malaria, Cholera, Tuberculosis, and AIDS. They create pollution from cooking on innumerable charcoal fires, and they crowd more people into tiny areas than can possibly live on the resources available there. Such teeming slums in hundreds of cities around the world, create immense sanitation and water problems. They create social chaos, crime, drug and alcohol addiction, and they damage the environment simply because there are too many human beings in too small a space.

6.5.1. All over the world, overpopulation is causing havoc. It is crowding more and more people onto agricultural lands and villages that cannot support them. Desperate for income and work, millions are being driven into the vast slums of monstrous cities where a nightmarish life of suffering and deprivation await.

6.5.2. Eighty million persons per year are added to the population of the Earth. Many scientists estimate eight or nine billion persons on our planet by the year 2025. Yet even the current population cannot be sustained by the finite and diminishing resources of Earth. Ninety percent of the eighty million children born into the world each year are born into extreme poverty. Every new person requires another thirty gallons per day of potable water. Every person requires food, educational, health care, and infrastructural resources. Every person produces waste and pollution that must be absorbed by the environment.

6.5.3. While some governments have had limited success in reducing population, the problem is global, not territorial. Reducing population growth in Kenya will little affect the world's bleak future if the planet continues to add eighty million new persons each year to its limited carrying capacity. Only democratic world government has the authority and resources to promote the health of the whole planet.

6.5.4. The remedies are as simple as they are impossible under the system of territorial nation-states. Elimination of poverty, education, support for family planning programs, if done on a global scale with adequate resources and organization, can quickly reduce the birth rate on the planet. Some estimate that the Earth can only sustain reasonably well about 2.5 billion persons. Under the present world system, the goal of reducing the Earth's population to this level is a mere chimera. Under the Earth Federation, a significant reduction in the planetary birth rate is a sensible and rational possibility and can be achieved within fifteen to twenty years of the inception of world government.

6.5.5. The net result will not be costly for the people of Earth. Population reduction through education, family planning programs, and the elimination of poverty will add to the world's human resource potential, eliminate the cost of rampant diseases and the spread of AIDS, eliminate the costly effects of pollution generated by an unsustainable population, and free up the resources of the Earth for the prosperity of future generations.

6.6. *The crisis of sickness and disease.* Overcrowding, lack of basic sanitation, poor water quality, shortage of fertile land, inadequate nutritious food, environmental pollution all are causes of disease and crippling health limitations among the poor of the world. Fifty percent of the population of the world lack adequate sewage and sanitation systems. The sewage runs into local streams and rivers, and into the puddles in the dirt roads where children play and adults walk. Poor sewage systems threaten sources of clean water, compounding the risks and sources of possible disease.

6.6.1. Waterborne diseases like cholera and typhoid are common. These diseases have been eliminated in developed countries because we understand their causes and how to eliminate them through sanitation and clean water systems. The problem is not lack of knowledge and understanding. The problem is today's world system that makes providing clean water and sanitation to the poor countries of the world a virtual impossibility.

6.6.2. Anyone traveling in South Asia, South America or Africa is struck by the number of crippled and maimed people living in every city, town, and village. Polio and other preventable crippling diseases are common. People unnecessarily crippled by these diseases often become less productive and less useful to the economic potential of their societies. Early death and a drain on the health care systems of poor countries also comes from such common diseases as tuberculosis, malaria, or AIDS. Tuberculosis is on the increase worldwide as is AIDS. Yet dealing with these diseases requires dealing with all the other global crises outlined in this manifesto. It requires effective sanitation systems for all, clean and adequate supplies of water for all, education and adequate health care systems for all, and nutritious, adequate food supplies for all.

6.6.3. The transformation to a decent world order required is not a luxury or a utopian dream. It is an absolute necessity if the world is to have a future at all. More than a century after microbiology discovered the causes of most disease, many decades after the development of the technologies of water purification and sanitation, many decades after the development of antibiotics and drugs adequate to control most diseases, unnecessary sickness and disease are still increasing worldwide.

6.6.4. This epidemic of preventable sickness and disease among the world's poor is a shame upon the humanity of us all. It cannot be dealt with apart from democratic world government under the Earth Federation. The *Earth Constitution* mandates health care for everyone, education for everyone, clean and sanitary environment for everyone, not just for those who can pay, not just for those who now dominate and exploit the rest for their own benefit.

6.6.5. The AIDS epidemic alone requires vast resources and coordinated efforts across the world. Yet these are not forthcoming under the present world system. The entire continent of Africa is being ravaged by AIDS, with an estimated 28 million cases in this year, 2003, as well as the other diseases mentioned here. Only the Earth Federation with the resources, authority, and coordinated planning to deal with simultaneously with global sanitation, poverty, disease, pollution, militarism, land degradation, global warming, human rights protections, and universal education can adequately address the AIDS epidemic or the problems of preventable sickness and disease.

6.7. The crisis of education. Universal quality education is absolutely fundamental to sustainable development, just as it is to the elimination of poverty, the prevention of disease, and the control of population growth. In the developing world, some 120 million children do not even go to elementary school. Even where schooling is available, many millions of poor children throughout the world must go to work at an early age to help themselves and their families survive.

6.7.1. Eight and nine year old children in bare feet, with no parents anywhere to be seen, beg pennies from automobiles at stoplights in Managua and Mumbai. The AIDS epidemic in Africa alone may leave twenty million children orphans within the next few years. These children, and others in similar desperate poverty throughout the developing world, have little chance of becoming literate, let alone gaining enough education to become effective agents in the transformation of global society towards equity, freedom, justice, and peace.

6.7.2. Poor nations, strangled by international debt to the World Bank and wealthy First World financial institutions, are being forced through structural adjustment programs to sell off public educational systems, transportation systems, water systems, health care, and other systems to private, profit making enterprises. As a result education is becoming ever more elitist in the developing world as those who can afford to pay for private schooling get the tools necessary for success or escape from their native country to the first world, while the vast majority who are extremely poor are deprived of any opportunity for a decent education. Those who can afford an education often immigrate and this "brain drain" diminishes the number of skilled and educated people necessary for sustainable development.

6.7.3. Education, while absolutely essential to development, is not a priority for those remaining who struggle simply to survive from day to day. As with the other features of our planetary crises, education is not possible without eliminating poverty, without developing sanitation and clean water systems, without developed infrastructure from roads to computer terminals and telephone lines. Education is not possible while poor countries waste their resources on purchasing ever more sophisticated weapons from the first world arms merchants. Education is not possible when the Earth is adding eighty million new persons to its population each year. Education is not possible in the face of ever increasing food shortages and water shortages.

6.7.4. To create an educated population capable of energetic and creative solutions for sustainable development requires the complete transformation of our present institutions and an integrated solution to the interrelated nexus of global crises. Only federal world government under the *Earth Constitution* would have the resources, universal vision, and integrated, global approach necessary to solve the world's problems through putting education at the center of a global policy of sustainable development. Educated and energetic people can solve their own local sanitation and water problems, address the waste of their own governmental bureaucracies, initiate development projects, and control population growth.

6.7.5. The airwave communications spectrum supporting radio, television, telephone, and internet must be used by the people of developing nations for free education of their populations concerning sanitation, family planning, agricultural methods, control of disease, and development projects. There is tremendous potential for real institutional transformation through education that is next to impossible under present global institutions.

6.7.6. Corporations are interested in private profit, not education for fundamental change. Governments are often interested in militarism and staying in power rather than in fundamental change. Only world government under the *Earth Constitution* can solve the crisis of education and make possible a quality education for every citizen of Earth. Only world government under the *Constitution* is unafraid of fundamental social change, since its mandate is precisely fundamental change to a world of equity, freedom, justice, and peace.

6.8. The crisis of global economics. The vocal protests at World Bank meetings and meetings of the World Trade Organization (WTO) around the world emphasize the elitist nature of the global economic system, controlled by multinational corporations, First World financial institutions, and powerful First World governments. This economic system, despite the rhetoric of "free trade" or "development" is designed, as were its colonial predecessors, to benefit the powerful financial players of the world and to ignore the consequences for the rest of humanity and future generations.

6.8.1. Corporations have gained extraordinary power in the last few decades. Even to the limited extent that territorial governments can deal with multinational corporations with more assets than many governments themselves, the corporations have taken steps to ever more exempt themselves from the environmental or social consequences of their practices. Corporations can now sue governments before secret WTO tribunals if, for example, environmental laws interfere with the profit margin of corporations doing business in those countries. Global economic regulations are formulated in secret by the powerful and imposed upon the weaker majority of the nations of the world. They are not formulated with the common good of human beings or the planet in mind, but for the prosperity and profit of private financial institutions.

6.8.2. Who is to regulate corporations and the powerful governments that support them? Who is to speak for a rational, democratically planned, and equitably designed economic system directed toward universal sustainable development? Clearly the U.N. has been colonized by these very multinational corporations as well as dominated by the powerful governments that represent these corporations, primarily the United States. Clearly the World Bank and the IMF serve these same interests.

6.8.3. The present global economic system has destroyed jobs in mass on the local level worldwide. It has created a race to the bottom where many poor countries compete to sell off their precious natural resources or other export products to the lowest bidder. It has destroyed effective environmental regulations everywhere. It has led the economies of entire nations to crash and burn in a chaos of poverty, social disintegration, and unemployment. Some examples of this (out of many) are the destruction of the economies of Somalia, Rwanda, Tanzania, Indonesia, Bolivia, Equador, and Argentina, with the ensuing horrific violence and social disintegration in each case.

6.8.4. A decent economic system for the world promoting universal prosperity and ending exploitation and domination in the service of private interests is impossible without federal world government under the *Constitution for the Federation of Earth*. Only enforceable world laws, applicable to all individuals (whether heads of corporations or heads of governments), can give us sufficient democratically guided economic regulation and activation to eliminate poverty and create genuine sustainable development worldwide.

6.8.5. The principles of a decent global economic system are rational, common sense, and easily attainable. Some of these will be described below. At this point we wish to make clear that there can be no dealing with the numerous global crises outlined here without an equitable and thriving planetary economic system. Only democratically legislated and enforceable world law can create such a system.

6.9. *The crisis of global militarism.* Global militarism has not decreased with the end of the Cold War. Weapons sales worldwide have only increased, as has the amount most nations of the world spend upon their military establishments. Neither has the world been able to create effective treaty bans on land minds, antipersonnel weapons, depleted uranium weapons, nuclear weapons, intercontinental missiles, or space-based weapons. Chemical and biological weapons are still being researched and developed by many nations.

6.9.1. Powerful forces have tremendous economic and imperial interests in preventing any progress towards arms control or demilitarization. We have seen that the world currently spends approximately 850 billion U.S. dollars per year on militarism and war. It is sometimes said that only half this amount spent annually for the next two decades could transform the world into one of equity, prosperity, and environmental integrity.

6.9.2. Yet to make this claim is to say little or nothing in the face of the immense forces of the world arrayed against arms limitations or demilitarization. To make this claim without challenging the global institutions promoting war – the system of so-called sovereign nations and the global economic system that makes war and militarism extremely profitable for a few powerful corporations – is to state a merely utopian dream.

6.9.3. Nothing can control the militarism of the world under the present world system, not NGOs, not the U.N., not individual nation-states. Under the present system of militarized "sovereign" nation-states, there is a nearly inevitable temptation, within both large and small nations, to try to impose military solutions on what are essentially economic, social, and political problems. The result is inevitably disaster, spawning immense human rights abuses, devastation of civilian infrastructures, environmental destruction, rebellion and social unrest, radical terrorist groups, religious fundamentalism, and a host of other problems. The result of thinking in terms of violence and coercion (which is what all military thinking does) is that nations are involved in a complex and corrupt global power game that even leads them to arm and support some terrorist groups while trying to suppress others.

6.9.4. Extremist terrorist movements flourish under the conditions of a militarized, violent, warring world order. Such terrorist movements are an inevitable response to state terrorism. And nearly every military action by nations amounts to exactly this: state terrorism. The standard definition of terrorism (the illegal use of violence and coercion to achieve social or political goals) fits the military actions of nations as well as those of extremist groups. The solution to both extremist group terrorism and state terrorism is to legally abolish all terrorist and military activities worldwide. They are two sides of the same coin.

6.9.5. World government under the *Earth Constitution* abolishes all military and concentrates on the economic, social, and political problems that breed extremism and social unrest. It encourages political, religious, and cultural pluralism so that all groups feel their voices are heard rather than suppressed. It addresses the roots of terrorism which involve the suppression of political participation, poverty, exploitation, and domination of the many by the few. By doing so it will break the cycle of violence forever.

6.9.6. Without effective world government under the *Earth Constitution*, there is no possibility of reaping the almost unimaginable benefits of converting the nearly one trillion dollars per year now wasted on world militarism to sustainable development and human welfare. The *Constitution* prohibits the world government from having a military of its own in any form. Therefore, no resources of the Federation will be wasted on militarism. Under the *Earth Constitution*, nations joining the Federation (and they will join in droves once they see the incredible benefits of uniting) are required by law to demilitarize under the careful supervision of the World Disarmament Agency.

6.9.7. Each nation joining the Federation is required to give half its last year's military budget to the Federal Government and may keep the other half of this amount for its own purposes. Nations joining the Federation would immediately have not only innumerable benefits from a federal world government now very well funded with former wasted military money, but would reap the benefits of retaining for useful purposes half their own funds formerly wasted on militarism.

6.9.8. Here is the key to creating a decent and civilized world order and addressing all the crises outlined in this manifesto. The money for transforming the world order to one of equity, freedom, justice, and peace is readily available. This one source alone can provide 850 billion dollars per year. But there is no way to tap this cornucopia of now wasted wealth without the authority and legitimacy of democratic world government. The U.N. has failed miserably in this regard, for one cannot defend the integrity of the nation-state system, base global economics on the Western model of greed, financial exploitation, and corporate self-interest, claim that peace can be preserved by going to war, create U.N. armies called "peacekeeping" forces, and expect at the same time to diminish the insane militarism of the world.

6.9.9. Under the *Earth Constitution* all nations are disarmed and the world federal government itself is nonmilitary. All weapons of war and of mass destruction are carefully and systematically destroyed. Disarmed governments without armies and weapons do not invade one another or attack one another. Extremist groups do not emerge as "blowback" against military suppression. Disputes are handled by the World Court system designed to create a just and equitable world order and through political participation of everyone in the World Parliament. An independent branch of government is created (the World Ombudsmus) to represent those who believe their rights under the *Constitution* have been violated. The world police possess only weapons necessary to apprehend individuals, for only individuals (and not entire nations) commit crimes.

6.9.10. Crimes (whether in the form of manufacturing weapons, human rights violations by heads of state, or environmentally destructive policies by corporations) are committed by individuals, and a global society under the rule of law has the authority and means to arrest and prosecute individuals. The madness of attacking the people of an entire nation for the supposed crimes of a few is ended forever under the *Earth Constitution*. There will be no more bombings of the good people of Yugoslavia because their President is suspected of crimes, no more bombings of the good people of Afghanistan because it is suspected there are terrorists in their midst, no more invasions of the innocent people of Iraq because their leader is suspected of crimes.

6.9.11. The madness of the current world system of sovereign nation-states where an entire nation must be militarily attacked or economically punished because of the suspected crimes of a few must be abolished forever. The only way to abolish this mad system is to create a demilitarized Earth Federation where all individuals on the planet are equally subject to the rule of democratically legislated law. The powerful heads of corporations or imperial nations will no longer be exempt from arrest and prosecution as they currently are. Terrorists and violators of human rights will no longer be able to hide behind the borders of so-called sovereign nations as they often do today. For the first time in human history, universal justice and equity will be possible on our planet.

7. Common sense economics under democratic world government

The economics of a decent world order under the Earth Federation can be summarized in seven simple, yet fundamental principles. Once the official World Parliament is elected, it will have the authority to implement a global economic policy based on these principles.

7.1. First, extensive lines of credit in Earth Currency and nonexploitative loans will be made immediately available to individuals, businesses, and governments for purposes of sustainable development. The great lie of the present world order is that only those who possess wealth can loan money or create lines of credit. But real wealth is a product of natural resources, capital, and human labor. The world government can create immense lines of credit in Earth Currency to be used for rapid, sustainable economic development wherever this is needed within the Federation.

7.1.1. With the creation of real wealth from development, these lines of credit can be repaid for only an additional small accounting fee. There will be no exploitative interest rates. And the value of Earth Currency will not be predicated on the global financial institutions that now devalue currencies of poor countries and manipulate the "convertible currencies" to continue to enrich themselves.

7.1.2. The first twenty-five nations to ratify the *Constitution* (comprising a large portion of the Earth's population, resources, and collective technological know-how) will form a substantially autonomous economic unit. The Federal government will immediately begin extending lines of credit for development, not merely to the already wealthy elites within these countries but to the poor or whoever has a sustainable, nonmilitary project in mind that would create wealth as well as benefit society. Individuals, businesses, and governments will have ample lines of credit available to them for only the cost of an accounting fee. Governments could reasonably focus on rapid development of infrastructure (roads, schools, hospitals, sanitation, communications), while businesses focused on goods and services.

7.1.3. Every poor nation knows that it is watched carefully by the imperial powers to ensure that it does not deviate from its subordinate role within the global system of domination and exploitation. Every nation knows that if it ratified the *Constitution for the Federation of Earth* alone, it would be economically punished for this by withdrawal of investments, recall of loans, or economic sanctions. Witness the forty-three years of suffering that has been imposed on the Cuban people because their government attempted to take an independent course that cared about its own poor and dispossessed citizens.

7.1.4. For this reason, a number of governments in the developing world must coordinate their efforts and plan to simultaneously ratify the *Constitution*. World government can easily begin with perhaps twenty-five nations simultaneously joining together to create the initial Earth Federation. Immediately such a group of nations ratifying the *Constitution* would become a substantially autonomous economic unit, using Earth Currency and receiving extensive lines of credit for development from the newly created federal government. Withdrawal of investments, recall of loans, or threat of sanctions would not matter. The federal government would assume all international debt of these nations to be paid back in a reasonable manner at nonexploitative interest rates.

7.1.5. Approximately twenty-five nations would immediately enter into dynamic cooperation in the use of their resources, technologies, educated leaders, and development initiatives. Their debts would be removed under the current world order and they would receive extensive lines of credit for sustainable development based on the ability of their people to produce real wealth using finance capital, labor, and natural resources. Corporations or industries within these nations that refuse to cooperate in the conversion to Earth Currency would be nationalized or mundialized, whichever is most appropriate. The simple but liberating economic principles outlined in this manifesto would immediately take effect. The increase in prosperity, creative energy, and hope would be immediately evident and contagious.

7.1.6. There is no mystery about how to create prosperity. Place a great deal of money in the hands of people who wish to develop projects, employ workers, procure the necessary natural resources, and buy and sell locally and regionally. Money gets into the hands of ordinary people who then recirculate it through increased consumption and the purchase of services. There is no reason to take anything away from the already rich or oppose the policies of the World Bank or corporations operating outside the initial Federation.

7.1.7. Those who are rich may retain their wealth. What is eliminated is their ability to exploit others to make themselves richer. The World Bank may continue to offer its development loans to poor countries of the world. But who will want these loans when immense lines of credit are available to individuals, nations, and businesses at the cost of only an accounting fee? Exploitative interest rates are eliminated and with it the ability of those already rich to exploit and dominate the poor who need money for development purposes.

7.2. Second, large scale technology transfer and infusion of fertile ideas and techniques for sustainable development can be activated through common sense revisions of current intellectual property rights laws. As the writings of economists Michael Chossudovsky, David Korton, Vandana Siva, J.W. Smith and others have shown, one of the ways the wealthy world retains neo-colonial monopoly control on the global economy is through intellectual property rights, which have become a fundamental tenant in WTO regulations. The simple device of allowing any patented idea to be used for the payment of a reasonable royalty fee would make all ideas and techniques available to humankind for sustainable development purposes.

7.2.1. Through its system of absolute intellectual property rights, the current world system keeps the developing world in a low tech condition, forcing them to sell their natural resources to the wealthy world to be there manufactured and sold back to the developing countries at a profit. It keeps monopoly control over marketable ideas and innovations, thereby belying its ideology of "free trade." Versions of this policy have been going on since the advent of colonialism. They keep life saving drugs from reaching the AIDS stricken countries of Africa. They keep seeds and key agricultural necessities profitably expensive while poor farmers starve worldwide.

7.2.2. The simple change of allowing any idea to be used if a reasonable royalty is paid, eradicates these intellectual property rights monopolies and liberates the poor of the world for efficient, rapid development. This modified system of intellectual property rights would also activate the regional economies of the world with a tremendous influx of new techniques and ideas. Scarcity would be ended and prosperity rapidly created.

7.3. The third simple principle for rapidly creating global equity and prosperity involves massive programs of education and empowerment of populations throughout the world through use of airwaves and other forms of communication for free global education on behalf of rapid sustainable development. Just as the present world system involves a monopoly on money creation and lending, and a monopoly on advanced technologies and techniques, so the present world order involves a monopoly on media and communications. The governments of the world have given away the airways and media for communication to private, profit-making interests. The electromagnetic spectrum from TV to radio to satellite communications is largely used for commercial purposes, for enrichment of private, profit making corporations, and for propaganda on behalf of the current world system. These should be used for sustainable development and global free education that this requires.

7.3.1. We have seen that a massive worldwide educational effort is essential to rapid sustainable development and the elimination of poverty and unsupportable population growth. The technologies and means of communication are available to achieve this. All that is required is government that serves the needs and interests of all the world's citizens and not government, as in the United States, that serves the needs and interests of the big corporations.

7.3.2. Use of the available technologies and means of communication for rapid sustainable development would activate regional and local economies. People would learn sanitation techniques, family planning techniques, literacy, foreign languages, water purification techniques, techniques for generating nonpolluting forms of energy, techniques for increasing their income and quality of life. This simple change in the use of the world's airways and means of communication would serve as a third major step for creating universal prosperity and sustainable development.

7.4. Fourth, simple legal steps would be taken fostering the empowerment of regional and local economies where money is retained within the locality and not siphoned off to foreign banks or corporations. Regions would produce as many goods and services for themselves as reasonably possible and economically feasible, and import only what is necessary to complement the local economies. The amazing waste of energy and resources that now occurs in transporting goods around the world that could just as well be produced locally would cease. Regions would employ many at good wages creating a population capable of buying good and services and businesses would develop in response to these demands.

7.4.1. In the United States, when a multinational "superstore" moves into a town, many local businesses begin to fold. They cannot compete with the ability of the superstore to procure cheap clothing, food, drugs, shoes, housewares, furniture, sporting goods, hardware and nearly everything else. The superstore may employ a few people at low wage jobs, but its profits do not remain in the community. They are sent back to corporate headquarters and to distant investors. The economy of the local community begins to die. Small businesses close up and unemployment increases.

7.4.2. This same phenomena also happens on a global scale. A soft drink or medical drug from a multinational corporation in a developing country may be able to undersell a domestically produced soft drink or drug. But the profits from the multinational soft drink or medical drug return to wealthy first world investors and are not recirculated within the local or regional economy. Very often, the developing country is even prevented from producing its own drink or medical drug by intellectual property rights regulations. These global monopolies strangle regional economies.

7.4.3. The principle of health for economies, and for sustainable development of prosperity in developing countries, is to activate regional and local markets. This includes raising wages, producing locally whatever can be produced to supply the needs of the population, and creating a healthy interchange of supply and demand that keeps money circulating within the region.

7.4.4. The Earth Federation is not opposed in principle to "globalization." Converting the world system to democratic federal world government is maximal globalization. But globalization of economics without the globalization of democratic world law has simply extended the current system of chaos and violence worldwide. Without world law, imperial nations and gigantic corporations exploit and dominate the poor of the world in their own self-interest. We need global planning for the future, global monitoring of the environment, and global trade where appropriate for the benefit of everyone involved. Globalization without democratic planning, regulation, or concern for the common good will necessarily result in the viciousness and corruption that we see everywhere in today's "globalized" economy.

7.4.5. Today, the "anti-globalization movement" is providing vital resistance to this world system of economic domination and exploitation. Many of the individuals and organizations that participate in this movement are committed to democracy, justice, the ending of poverty, environmental protection, and human rights. They play a vital role in exposing the terrible legacy of economic globalization with respect to all these issues. However, the central focus of this movement is that it is against globalization.

7.4.6. To be against all "globalization" is to be against planning for the future of the Earth. It is to be against the universal rule of law on Earth. They are "anti," without having a clear vision of how the world can be transformed into a civilized world order. Vague notions of justice, democracy, or protecting human rights without a global, democratic, legal mechanism for achieving these are futile. The *Earth Constitution* gives humanity the specific political and economic means to achieve these goals.

7.5. Fifth, the market may be an efficient way of determining prices for many things, but certainly not for wages. There must be equal pay for equal work at good wages throughout the Earth Federation. Economist J. W. Smith points out that the rate of advantage of equally productive but unequally paid workers doing the same work is exponential, not arithmetical. Take the example of a worker in the developing world paid one U.S. dollar an hour for producing an item that is identical to the item produced by a first world worker making ten dollars per hour. Since the cost of labor largely determines the prices of these items, the developing world item sells for one dollar while the first world item for ten dollars. How many of the developing world items can the first world worker buy after working ten hours? How many items of the first world worker can the developing world worker buy after working ten hours? The rate of advantage in this simple example is 100 to 1 (Smith 2005a, Chapter One).

7.5.1. Under this rate of advantage there is no possibility of the developing world ever catching up with the first world through activation of its economies or sale of natural resources. The exponential rate of advantage ensures what has in fact been the case for decades: billions of dollars in wealth are transferred annually from the poorest segment of humanity to the wealthiest segment of humanity. The poor under our current world order are getting poorer and the rich are getting richer.

7.5.2. Markets have a useful but limited role in human economies. They are not and cannot be the solution to all problems as the imperial economic ideology has it. Markets can produce many (not all) goods and services efficiently. But essential services like water, electricity, and health care are much better served by good government. Nor can markets ensure just or equitable distribution of services or wealth. And they cannot ensure sustainable development that involves conceptions of the common good and the welfare of future generations.

7.5.3. Markets are blind to all noncommercial values such as community, human rights, sustainability, equity, justice, and peace. Markets, as we know so well, will produce weapons of war if there is a profit to be made from this, or weapons of mass destruction. Markets (like big business) are morally blind and must be tempered by democratic, non-commercial values that are necessarily built into good government. Markets are not based on the moral principle of unity-in-diversity.

7.5.4. The principle of equal pay for equal work at decent, living wages will place cash in the hands of the poor in the developing counties and will produce an activated local economy while at the same time increasing global equity. As we said earlier, there is no need to appropriate the accumulated wealth of the rich to solve the global crises facing humanity. All that is necessary is to eliminate the means for the rich to continue to accumulate more wealth through exploiting those already poor. The exploitative, monopoly features of the current system listed here perpetuate both the wealth of the rich and the poverty of the poor and make global equity and sustainable development an impossibility.

7.6. Sixth, economically stable and equitable laws will be enacted to promote worldwide land reform so that the land and its wealth can be returned to the people of Earth. The exploitation of the poor by the few who now control the quality land and resources of the world will rapidly come to an end. In general, land and resources will be recognized as belonging to the people of the Earth and need to be legally protected for the common good. Land and resources will be seen as the global commons and private property will be recognized for land use by individuals, governments, and businesses. That is, property rights will be converted from "absolute rights" to "conditional rights."

7.6.1. Land is provided by nature, not built by labor, thus all natural resources are nature's heritage for all. Applying Henry George's concept of exclusive title to nature's wealth restructured to conditional title (society collecting the landrent) instantly collapses those exclusive (monopoly) values to zero. The price of homes are the cost of building a house and the price of businesses will be the facilities themselves. Monopoly values have been converted to use-values owned by true producers. Just as with land, today's technology, money, and communications monopolies are subject to the same efficiency gains. [This paragraph, not submitted at the 7th Session of Parliament, will be expanded and submitted to the 9th Session.]

7.6.2. The effectiveness of careful organic farming, with composting, crop rotation, and ecologically sound planting and harvesting has been repeatedly demonstrated. These farming methods produce many times the food per acre now produced by commercial agribusiness while conserving the soil and eliminating the pollution cased by chemical fertilizers. They are best done by small farmers who own and care about their own land and have a stake in its preservation. Even with the diminished quality farm land in the world today, a global program of population reduction, effective farming methods, and activated local economies can easily end hunger and create a world sufficient for all.

7.6.3. Such programs of land reform have been attempted in individual countries such as Guatemala in the early 1950s, Chile in the early 1970s, Nicaragua in the 1980s, Cuba in the 1970s, 80s, and 90s, and Venezuela at the beginning of this century. In every case the United States has destroyed or attempted to destroy the government promoting the land reform. This has been a global policy of the imperial center since the Second World War.

7.6.4. All good examples of economic health and common sense must be destroyed so that the world believes there is no alternative to global economic monopolies dominated by multi-billion dollar corporations and protected by the military might of First World nations. The lethal combination of the our present world system of sovereign nation-states (dominated as always by the imperial centers) and ruthless global corporations cannot but act to enforce a regime of global domination and exploitation. These consequences are built into these global institutions of the past five centuries.

7.6.5. Only democratically legislated law, enacted by a World Parliament representing all the people and nations of Earth, can formulate and effectively carry out a planetary policy of land reform. Such reform is badly needed not only to activate the local and regional economies of the world, but to end exploitation of the poor by the rich, to conserve the soil while reducing erosion and pollution, and to increase food production, rapidly ending hunger on Earth.

7.7. Seventh, the federal world government will engage in large-scale employment of the unemployed or underemployed millions in developing counties in a multitude of projects directed toward sustainable development and the activating of regional and local economies. These projects will certainly include replanting the depleted forests of the Earth, restoring the soil and grazing lands to integrity, building schools and health care centers, creating efficient, low cost sanitation and water systems, converting military installations and weapons factories to the production of peaceful goods and services, and converting the energy sources of the world to sustainable, non-polluting forms of water, wind, solar, and hydrogen energy.

7.7.1. The condition of the developing world today is similar to that of the United States during the great depression of the 1930s. There is massive unemployment and hence no money to circulate within economies. The U.S. government had the vision to create vast public works projects and put hungry people back to work.

7.7.2. The Earth Federation will undertake similar initiatives, thereby not only putting people to work and activating their economies, but creating the infrastructure necessary to a prosperous sustainable development. The nexus of global crises are too advanced and the threat to the future of the world too extreme to sit passively by and hope for private development efforts alone to succeed. The world needs sanitation and water systems now. It needs to restore the damaged environment now. It needs to deal with the crisis of sickness and disease now. It needs to restore soil, grazing land, fisheries, and forests now. It needs family planning and population reduction efforts now. It needs education for the masses now. It needs to employ the unemployed millions now.

7.7.3. As one of the great speeches before the 1992 Rio Environmental Summit expressed this principle: "tomorrow is too late." The global crises outlined here are upon us and action must be taken immediately to create a decent, prosperous, and equitable world order. We are at the crossroads of human existence. One road leads to certain disaster. The other to an equitable, free, just, and peaceful world order.

8. Where do we go from here? A call to the people and nations of the Earth

8.1. That earlier manifesto of 150 years ago demanded that "workers of the world unite!" The manifesto of the Earth Federation demands that the poor, the disenfranchised, and all decent people of the world unite. The problem is not simply exploitation and dehumanization of workers, although today this continues in sweat shops, extensive use of child labor, and starvation wage employment practices worldwide. The problem is the nexus of global economics and sovereign nation-states that continues the global system of domination and exploitation from generation to generation.

8.2.   At least a billion human beings fall outside this system of worker exploitation. They are not "workers" needed by the profit-seeking institutions, and are of no use to the imperial nation-states, and therefore are considered extraneous, useless, mere surplus to be allowed to rot and die in their hell of poverty or to be slaughtered as acceptable "collateral damage" through carpet bombings of their countries. The poorest of the world are of no concern to the world order as it now exists. It is they who are uniting for a new world order. It is the poor majority who are the hope of the world.

8.3.   The poor majority who are the central hope for the world -- and those caring and awakened people and nations who act in solidarity with them in their struggle to create a decent world order for themselves and their children.   We are all made "poor" by the current world order. We are all degraded, manipulated, and shamed through our complicity with the rule of corrupt wealth and power. We are all faced with the historical, practical, and moral demand to save the Earth from further destruction and create a decent, sustainable world order before it is too late.

8.4.   Why do the wealthy of the world and their minions in government fear us so much? They know we are not interested in taking their wealth from them. We are only interested in simple changes that remove global monopolies and eliminate the ability of private organizations and nations to continue to enrich themselves at the expense of the poor. Yet this very fact fills them with dread.

8.5.   The thought of a world of equity and justice, where the few have lost their ability to dominate and exploit the rest, terrifies those who have never worked for a living but have only ruled, dominated, and exploited. They are mortified by the thought of civilized world order where the rich actually have to live in equity and justice with the poor, where special privileges have been abolished, where freedom and peace mean there can be no more military domination of the powerful over the rest, where no more profits can be reaped from selling weapons, pillaging, or defrauding the poor in a world of chaos and violence.

8.6.   It is difficult for the average decent person to imagine how corrupt are most of the captains of industry, military, and government in today's world. The ruling elite in business, military, and government know only power relations, influence pedaling, and corrupt deals with super-rich corporate executives, arms merchants, drug kingpins, regional warlords, dictators, torturers, shady financial investors, or slimy politicians. They have only contempt for the poor or ordinary decent people. The chaos of the political and economic worlds is so deep under global capitalism and the nation-state system that any talk of a decent world order based on universal values sounds like naive gibberish to their ears. Yet they fear us because they know that decent people everywhere respond positively to the *Earth Constitution* designed to create planetary justice, peace, and prosperity.

8.7. Is "human nature" so corrupt that government, military, or business will always attract to themselves twisted people who without remorse are willing to destroy human beings, our environment, and the welfare of future generations in their lust for wealth and power? Most ordinary human beings are honest and decent. The corruption is fostered by the institutions dominating our world. Fragmented institutions often attract fragmented and corrupt human beings to positions of power. Both the system of territorial nation-states and the global economic system are founded on immoral self-interest, the drive for domination, and structures of greed and exploitation. They cannot in principle be reformed to create a decent world order for they are fragments predicated on naked power, chaos, and violence.

8.8. Fragments result in unredeemed conflict and power relationships. The *Constitution for the Federation of Earth* is founded on the fundamentally different principle of unity-in-diversity. Diversity (of interests, races, ethnicities, religions, nations, cultures, and individuals) is protected and legitimated through the moral unity recognizing all equally as citizens and members of the Earth Federation. Diversity within the moral unity created by the Earth Federation does not corrupt persons into violence and greed as does fragmentation.

8.9. We are all one as citizens of the Earth Federation and members of the human race. We have historical, practical, and moral obligations to one another, to our Earth, and to future generations. Under the Earth Federation, this unity-in-diversity is both a moral and a legal category creating, for the first time in history, government and business operating according to morally legitimate principles. Who will lead humanity into a new, morally decent world order premised on the principle of unity-in-diversity?

8.10. Solidarity with the Earth Federation is not likely to come from the comfortable classes of the First World nations who are conditioned to be passive, self-interested consumers and without compassion or concern for their fellow human beings around the planet. Solidarity with the Earth Federation will not come from the imperial nations or the multinational corporations who now dominate the world in their ignorance and corruption. Unity with the Federation can only come from the poor, those in solidarity with the poor, and those rare governments who have some concern for their own people and the future of the Earth.

8.11. The poor of the world must organize under the banner of the Earth Federation! They must educate themselves, raise funds for educating others, send delegations to their leaders, write editorials, get on radio shows, hold town meetings, and hold ratification campaigns. Localities, villages, towns and cities may commit to the Earth Federation. There must be active pressure placed upon the governments of poor countries, and upon all decent governments. Chapters of the World Constitution and Parliament Association must be organized and members must join the rapidly growing Earth Federation. The *Constitution for the Federation of Earth* must be studied and translated into ever more languages.

8.12. We must urge poor nations and their populations (and those nations and world citizens in solidarity with them) to work together and coordinate a simultaneous ratification of the *Constitution* by many nations. The effect on the world would be electrifying. Before the imperial powers and the multinational corporate criminals could even think in terms of blockades or sanctions, other poor nations would be clamoring to join the Federation. A truly new world order recognizing the equality and right to prosperity of all human beings would be unmistakable and irresistible.

8.13. The majority of countries would immediately see that they have nothing to lose and everything to gain from joining the Earth Federation. Soon the entire world would perceive that at last true liberation for humanity and the Earth was at hand. The tiny minority of powerful imperial leaders, bankers, and corporate executives who oppose this order would be overwhelmed by public pressure and before long the final operative stage of the Earth Federation would be reached and there would be peace, prosperity, freedom, and justice on the Earth. We do not mean a "utopia." We mean a practical, workable, decent world order for the first time in history.

8.14. It is important to see that the first twenty-five nations ratifying the *Constitution* would not be forming another power block like North America or the European Union. If there were to be an African Union within the current world order, this would change nothing. It would simply create another military and economic block to struggle with Europe, Japan, China, the U.S. or other power centers. The world would remain in fragmentation and chaos. However, an African Union, or a Latin American Union, could easily be magna-regions within the Federation of Earth.

8.15. The initial Earth Federation is something truly new in human history, for it invites in all and excludes no one. It recognizes every human being as a citizen of the Earth Federation, and invites every nation to be a member of the Federation with all the rights, privileges, and benefits that apply under the *Constitution*. It would take nothing from those already rich and oppose no one militarily or economically. It would end exploitation of nation by nation and person by person. And it would be clear to the world that the Earth Federation was the only institution that could address the nexus of global crises that threaten our extinction on Earth.

8.16. Our task is to communicate this message to the world. Our task is for the poor nations and peoples of the world to unite and organize behind the Earth Federation. The Federation is not an ideal we are promoting but a dynamic reality from which we live. Our every thought, breath, and movement must emanate from the living reality of the Earth Federation. Every human being must know and ratify the *Constitution*.

8.17. The poor majority of our planet must take the initiative to liberate themselves and their world. They must ratify the *Constitution* personally and collectively. The poor nations of the world (and those nations in solidarity with them) must act in unison and ratify the *Constitution* collectively. The Earth Federation will grow like wildfire until there is one citizenship, one system of justice, one World Parliament, one bill of rights, and one world order of peace with justice. Then, and only then, can the religious or the nonreligious affirm the final meaning of history as one world under God, Allah, Brahman, the holy cosmos, this sacred Earth, or this just world order.

8.18. All people on Earth are already citizens of the Earth Federation. For the only sovereignty is that of the people of Earth. We are already members of the new world order of equity, freedom, justice, and peace. If we act from this living reality, we will successfully pass the crossroads of imminent death and destruction. To unite under the banner of the Earth Federation is to act for the liberation of humanity, this precious Earth, and future generations.

8.19. The poor, the dispossessed, and all decent people of the world must unite! We have nothing to lose but our misery, our chains of economic and political domination! For we are all victims in this present world of injustice and violence. We are all made poor and disenfranchised by this current world order. We are all already citizens of the Earth Federation! In the darkness of these times, we know that tomorrow is too late, and the time is now. A new dawn is rising for the world. Liberation for humanity is at hand. Citizens of the world unite!

Long Live the Earth Federation!!!

Chapter Four

A Constitution

for the Federation

of Earth

As Amended at the

World Constituent Assembly

in Troia, Portugal, 1991

NOW BEING CIRCULATED

WORLDWIDE

FOR RATIFICATION

BY THE NATIONS

AND PEOPLE OF EARTH

PREAMBLE

Realizing that Humanity today has come to a turning point in history and that we are on the threshold of an new world order which promises to usher in an era of peace, prosperity, justice and harmony;

Aware of the interdependence of people, nations and all life;

Aware that man's abuse of science and technology has brought Humanity to the brink of disaster through the production of horrendous weaponry of mass destruction and to the brink of ecological and social catastrophe;

Aware that the traditional concept of security through military defense is a total illusion both for the present and for the future;

Aware of the misery and conflicts caused by ever increasing disparity between rich and poor;

Conscious of our obligation to posterity to save Humanity from imminent and total annihilation;

Conscious that Humanity is One despite the existence of diverse nations, races, creeds, ideologies and cultures and that the principle of unity in diversity is the basis for a new age when war shall be outlawed and peace prevail; when the earth's total resources shall be equitably used for human welfare; and when basic human rights and responsibilities shall be shared by all without discrimination;

Conscious of the inescapable reality that the greatest hope for the survival of life on earth is the establishment of a democratic world government;

We, citizens of the world, hereby resolve to establish a world federation to be governed in accordance with this constitution for the Federation of Earth.

CONSTITUTION FOR THE FEDERATION OF EARTH

Article 1. Broad Functions of the World Government

The broad functions of the Federation of Earth shall be:

1. To prevent war, secure disarmament, and resolve territorial and other disputes which endanger peace and human rights.

2. To protect universal human rights, including life, liberty, security, democracy, and equal opportunities in life.

3. To obtain for all people on earth the conditions required for equitable economic and social development and for diminishing social differences.

4. To regulate world trade, communications, transportation, currency, standards, use of world resources, and other global and international processes.

5. To protect the environment and the ecological fabric of life from all sources of damage, and to control technological innovations whose effects transcend national boundaries, for the purpose of keeping Earth a safe, healthy and happy home for humanity .

6. To devise and implement solutions to all problems which are beyond the capacity of national governments, or which are now or may become of global or international concern or consequence.

Article 2. Basic Structure of World Federation and World Government

1. The Federation of Earth shall be organized as a universal federation, to include all nations and all people, and to encompass all oceans, seas and lands of Earth, inclusive of non-self governing territories, together with the surrounding atmosphere.

2. The World Government for the Federation of Earth shall be non-military and shall be democratic in its own structure, with ultimate sovereignty residing in all the people who live on Earth.

3. The authority and powers granted to the World Government shall be limited to those defined in this Constitution for the Federation of Earth, applicable to problems and affairs which transcend national boundaries, leaving to national governments jurisdiction over the internal affairs of the respective nations but consistent with the authority of the World Government to protect universal human rights as defined in this World Constitution.

4. The basic direct electoral and administrative units of the World Government shall be World Electoral and Administrative Districts. A total of not more than 1000 World Electoral and Administrative Districts shall be defined, and shall be nearly equal in population, within the limits of plus or minus ten percent.

5. Contiguous World Electoral and Administrative Districts shall be combined as may be appropriate to compose a total of twenty World Electoral and Administra-

tive Regions for the following purposes, but not limited thereto: for the election or appointment of certain world government officials; for administrative purposes; for composing various organs of the world government as enumerated in Article IV; for the functioning of the Judiciary, the Enforcement System, and the Ombudsmus, as well as for the functioning of any other organ or agency of the World Government.

6. The World Electoral and Administrative Regions may be composed of a variable number of World Electoral and Administrative Districts, taking into consideration geographic, cultural, ecological and other factors as well as population.

7. Contiguous World Electoral and Administrative Regions shall be grouped together in pairs to compose Magna-Regions.

8. The boundaries for World Electoral and Administrative Regions shall not cross the boundaries of the World Electoral and Administrative Districts, and shall be common insofar as feasible for the various administrative departments and for the several organs and agencies of the World Government. Boundaries for the World Electoral and Administrative Districts as well as for the Regions need not conform to existing national boundaries, but shall conform as far as practicable.

9. The World Electoral and Administrative Regions shall be grouped to compose at least five Continental Divisions of the Earth, for the election or appointment of certain world government officials, and for certain aspects of the composition and functioning of the several organs and agencies of the World Government as specified hereinafter. The boundaries of Continental Divisions shall not cross existing national boundaries as far as practicable. Continental Divisions may be composed of a variable number of World Electoral and Administrative Regions.

Article 3. Organs of the World Government

The organs of the World Government shall be:
1. The World Parliament.
2. The World Executive.
3. The World Administration.
4. The Integrative Complex.
5. The World Judiciary.
6. The Enforcement System.
7. The World Ombudsmus.

Article 4. Grant of Specific Powers to the World Government

The powers of the World government to be exercised through its several organs and agencies shall comprise the following:
1. Prevent wars and armed conflicts among the nations, regions, districts, parts and peoples of Earth.
2. Supervise disarmament and prevent re-armament; prohibit and eliminate the design, testing, manufacture, sale, purchase, use and possession of weapons of mass destruction, and prohibit or regulate all lethal weapons which the World

Parliament may decide.

3. Prohibit incitement to war, and discrimination against or defamation of conscientious objectors.

4. Provide the means for peaceful and just solutions of disputes and conflicts among or between nations, peoples, and/or other components within the Federation of Earth.

5. Supervise boundary settlements and conduct plebiscites as needed.

6. Define the boundaries for the districts, regions and divisions which are established for electoral, administrative, judicial and other purposes of the World Government.

7. Define and regulate procedures for the nomination and election of the members of each House of the World Parliament, and for the nomination, election, appointment and employment of all World Government officials and personnel.

8. Codify world laws, including the body of international law developed prior to adoption of the world constitution, but not inconsistent therewith, and which is approved by the World Parliament.

9. Establish universal standards for weights, measurements, accounting and records.

10. Provide assistance in the event of large scale calamities, including drought, famine, pestilence, flood, earthquake, hurricane, ecological disruptions and other disasters.

11. Guarantee and enforce the civil liberties and the basic human rights which are defined in the Bill of Rights for the Citizens of Earth which is made a part of this World Constitution under Article 12.

12. Define standards and promote the worldwide improvement in working conditions, nutrition, health, housing, human settlements, environmental conditions, education, economic security, and other conditions defined under Article 13 of this World Constitution.

13. Regulate and supervise international transportation, communications, postal services, and migrations of people.

14. Regulate and supervise supra-national trade, industry, corporations, businesses, cartels, professional services, labor supply, finances, investments and insurance.

15. Secure and supervise the elimination of tariffs and other trade barriers among nations, but with provisions to prevent or minimize hardship for those previously protected by tariffs.

16. Raise the revenues and funds, by direct and/or indirect means, which are necessary for the purposes and activities of the World Government.

17. Establish and operate world financial, banking, credit and insurance institutions designed to serve human needs; establish, issue and regulate world currency, credit and exchange.

18. Plan for and regulate the development, use, conservation and re-cycling of the natural resources of Earth as the common heritage of Humanity; protect the environment in every way for the benefit of both present and future generations.

19. Create and operate a World Economic Development Organization to serve eq-

uitably the needs of all nations and people included within the World Federation.

20. Develop and implement solutions to transnational problems of food supply, agricultural production, soil fertility, soil conservation, pest control, diet, nutrition, drugs and poisons, and the disposal of toxic wastes.

21. Develop and implement means to control population growth in relation to the life-support capacities of Earth, and solve problems of population distribution.

22. Develop, protect, regulate and conserve the water supplies of Earth; develop, operate and/or coordinate transnational irrigation and other water supply and control projects; assure equitable allocation of trans- national water supplies, and protect against adverse trans-national effects of water or moisture diversion or weather control projects within national boundaries.

23. Own, administer and supervise the development and conservation of the oceans and sea-beds of Earth and all resources thereof, and protect from damage.

24. Protect from damage, and control and supervise the uses of the atmosphere of Earth.

25. Conduct inter-planetary and cosmic explorations and research; have exclusive jurisdiction over the Moon and over all satellites launched from Earth.

26. Establish, operate and/or coordinate global air lines, ocean transport systems, international railways and highways, global communication systems, and means for interplanetary travel and communications; control and administer vital waterways.

27. Develop, operate and/or coordinate transnational power systems, or networks of small units, integrating into the systems or networks power derived from the sun, wind, water, tides, heat differentials, magnetic forces, and any other source of safe, ecologically sound and continuing energy supply.

28. Control the mining, production, transportation and use of fossil sources of energy to the extent necessary to reduce and prevent damages to the environment and the ecology, as well as to prevent conflicts and conserve supplies for sustained use by succeeding generations.

29. Exercise exclusive jurisdiction and control over nuclear energy research and testing and nuclear power production, including the right to prohibit any form of testing or production considered hazardous.

30. Place under world controls essential natural resources which may be limited or unevenly distributed about the Earth. Find and implement ways to reduce wastes and find ways to minimize disparities when development or production is insufficient to supply everybody with all that may be needed.

31. Provide for the examination and assessment of technological innovations which are or may be of supranational consequence, to determine possible hazards or perils to humanity or the environment; institute such controls and regulations of technology as may be found necessary to prevent or correct widespread hazards or perils to human health and welfare.

32. Carry out intensive programs to develop safe alternatives to any technology or technological processes which may be hazardous to the environment, the ecological system, or human health and welfare.

33. Resolve supra-national problems caused by gross disparities in technological development or capability, capital formation, availability of natural resources, educational opportunity, economic opportunity, and wage and price differentials. Assist the processes of technology transfer under conditions which safeguard human welfare and the environment and contribute to minimizing disparities.

34. Intervene under procedures to be defined by the World Parliament in cases of either intra-state violence and intra-state problems which seriously affect world peace or universal human rights.

35. Develop a world university system. Obtain the correction of prejudicial communicative materials which cause misunderstandings or conflicts due to differences of race, religion, sex, national origin or affiliation.

36. Organize, coordinate and/or administer a voluntary, non-military World Service Corps, to carry out a wide variety of projects designed to serve human welfare.

37. Designate as may be found desirable an official world language or official world languages.

38. Establish and operate a system of world parks, wild life preserves, natural places, and wilderness areas.

39. Define and establish procedures for initiative and referendum by the Citizens of Earth on matters of supra-national legislation not prohibited by this World Constitution.

40. Establish such departments, bureaus, commissions, institutes, corporations, administrations, or agencies as may by needed to carry out any and all of the functions and powers of the World Government.

41. Serve the needs of humanity in any and all ways which are now, or may prove in the future to be, beyond the capacity of national and local governments.

Article 5. The World Parliament

Sec. A. Functions and Powers of the World Parliament

The functions and powers of the World Parliament shall comprise the following:

1. To prepare and enact detailed legislation in all areas of authority and jurisdiction granted to the World Government under Article IV of this World Constitution.

2. To amend or repeal world laws as may be found necessary or desirable.

3. To approve, amend or reject the international laws developed prior to the advent of World Government, and to codify and integrate the system of world law and world legislation under the World Government.

4. To establish such regulations and directions as may be needed, consistent with this world constitution, for the proper functioning of all organs, branches, departments, bureaus, commissions, institutes, agencies or parts of the World Government.

5. To review, amend and give final approval to each budget for the World Government, as submitted by the World Executive; to devise the specific means for directly raising funds needed to fulfill the budget, including taxes, licenses, fees,

globally accounted social and public costs which must be added into the prices for goods and services, loans and credit advances, and any other appropriate means; and to appropriate and allocate funds for all operations and functions of the World Government in accordance with approved budgets, but subject to the right of the Parliament to revise any appropriation not yet spent or contractually committed.

6. To create, alter, abolish or consolidate the departments, bureaus, commissions, institutes, agencies or other parts of the World Government as may be needed for the best functioning of the several organs of the World Government, subject to the specific provisions of this World Constitution.

7. To approve the appointments of the heads of all major departments, commissions, offices, agencies and other parts of the several organs of the World Government, except those chosen by electoral or civil service procedures.

8. To remove from office for cause any member of the World Executive, and any elective or appointive head of any organ, department, office, agency or other part of the World Government, subject to the specific provisions in this World Constitution concerning specific offices.

9. To define and revise the boundaries of the World Electoral and Administrative Districts, the World Electoral and Administrative Regions and Magna Regions, and the Continental Divisions.

10. To schedule the implementation of those provisions of the World Constitution which require implementation by stages during the several stages of Provisional World Government, First Operative Stage of World Government, Second Operative Stage of World Government, and Full Operative Stage of World Government, as defined in Articles XVII and XIX of this World Constitution.

11. To plan and schedule the implementation of those provisions of the World Constitution which may require a period of years to be accomplished.

Sec. B. Composition of the World Parliament

1. The World Parliament shall be composed of three houses, designated as follows:

    a. The House of Peoples, to represent the people of Earth directly and equally;

    b. The House of Nations, to represent the nations which are joined together in the Federation of Earth; and

    c. A House of Counselors with particular functions to represent the highest good and best interests of humanity as a whole.

2. All members of the World Parliament, regardless of House, shall be designated as Members of the World Parliament.

Sec. C. The House of Peoples

1. The House of Peoples shall be composed of the peoples delegates directly elected in proportion to population from the World Electoral and Administrative Districts, as defined in Article 2-4.

2. Peoples delegates shall be elected by universal adult suffrage, open to all persons of age 18 and above.

3. One peoples delegate shall be elected from each World Electoral and Administrative District to serve a five year term in the House of Peoples. Peoples delegates may be elected to serve successive terms without limit. Each peoples delegate shall have o ne vote.

4. A candidate for election to serve as a peoples delegate must be at least 21 years of age, a resident for at least one year of the electoral district from which the candidate is seeking election, and shall take a pledge of service to humanity.

Sec. D. The House of Nations

1. The House of Nations shall be composed of national delegates elected or appointed by procedures to be determined by each national government on the following basis:

   a. One national delegate from each nation of at least 100,000 population, but less than 10,000,000 population.

   b. Two national delegates from each nation of at least 10,000,000 population, but less than 100,000,000 population.

   c. Three national delegates from each nation of 100,000,000 population or more.

2. Nations of less than 100,000 population may join in groups with other nations for purposes of representation in the House of Nations.

3. National delegates shall be elected or appointed to serve for terms of five years, and may be elected or appointed to serve successive terms without limit. Each national delegate shall have one vote.

4. Any person to serve as a national delegate shall be a citizen for at least two years of the nation to be represented, must be at least 21 years of age, and shall take a pledge of service to humanity.

Sec. E. The House of Counselors

1. The House of Counselors shall be composed of 200 counselors chosen in equal numbers from nominations submitted from the twenty World Electoral and Administrative Regions, as defined in Article II-5 and II-6, ten from each Region.

2. Nominations for members of the House of Counselors shall be made by the teachers and students of universities and colleges and of scientific academies and institutes within each world electoral and administrative region. Nominees may be persons who are off campus in any walk of life as well as on campus.

3. Nominees to the House of Counselors from each World Electoral and Administrative Region shall, by vote taken among themselves, reduce the number of nominees to no less than two times and no more than three times the number to be elected.

4. Nominees to serve as members of the House of Counselors must be at least 25 years of age, and shall take a pledge of service to humanity. There shall be no residence requirement, and a nominee need not be a resident of the region from which nominated or elected.

5. The members of the House of Counselors from each region shall be elected by the members of the other two houses of the World Parliament from the

particular region.

6. Counselors shall be elected to serve terms of ten years. One-half of the members of the House of Counselors shall be elected every five years. Counselors may serve successive terms without limit. Each Counselor shall have one vote.

Sec. F. Procedures of the World Parliament

1. Each house of the World Parliament during its first session after general elections shall elect a panel of five chairpersons from among its own members, one from each of five Continental Divisions. The chairpersons shall rotate annually so that each will serve for one year as chief presiding officer, while the other four serve as vice-chairpersons.

2. The panels of Chairpersons from each House shall meet together, as needed, for the purpose of coordinating the work of the Houses of the World Parliament, both severally and jointly.

3. Any legislative measure or action may be initiated in either House of Peoples or House of Nations or both concurrently, and shall become effective when passed by a simple majority vote of both the House of Peoples and of the House of Nations, except in those cases where an absolute majority vote or other voting majority is specified in this World Constitution.

4. In case of deadlock on a measure initiated in either the House of Peoples or House of Nations, the measure shall then automatically go to the House of Counselors for decision by simple majority vote of the House of Counselors, except in the cases where other majority vote is required in this World Constitution. Any measure may be referred for decision to the House of Counselors by a concurrent vote of the other two houses.

5. The House of Counselors may initiate any legislative measure, which shall then be submitted to the other two houses and must be passed by simple majority vote of both the House of Peoples and House of Nations to become effective, unless other voting majority is required by some provision of this World Constitution.

6. The House of Counselors may introduce an opinion or resolution on any measure pending before either of the other two houses; either of the other houses may request the opinion of the House of Counselors before acting upon a measure.

7. Each house of the World Parliament shall adopt its own detailed rules of procedure, which shall by consistent with the procedures set forth in this World Constitution, and which shall be designed to facilitate coordinated functioning of the three houses.

8. Approval of appointments by the World Parliament or any house thereof shall require simple majority votes, while removals for cause shall require absolute majority votes.

9. After the full operative stage of World Government is declared, general elections for members of the World Parliament to the House of Peoples shall be held every five years. The first general elections shall be held within the first two years following the declaration of the full operative stage of World Government.

10. Until the full operative stage of World Government is declared, elections

for members of the World Parliament to the House of Peoples may be conducted whenever feasible in relation to the campaign for ratification of this World Constitution.

11. Regular sessions of the House of Peoples and House of Nations of the World Parliament shall convene on the second Monday of January of each and every Year.

12. Each nation, according to its own procedures, shall appoint or elect members of the World Parliament to the House of Nations at least thirty days prior to the date for convening the World Parliament in January.

13. The House of Peoples together with the House of Nations shall elect the members of the World Parliament to the House of Counselors during the month of January after the general elections. For its first session after general elections, the House of Counselors shall convene on the second Monday of March, and thereafter concurrently with the other two houses.

14. Bi-elections to fill vacancies shall be held within three months from occurrence of the vacancy or vacancies.

15. The World Parliament shall remain in session for a minimum of nine months of each year. One or two breaks may be taken during each year, at times and for durations to be decided by simple majority vote of the House of Peoples and House of Nations sitting jointly.

16. Annual salaries for members of the World Parliament of all three houses shall be the same, except for those who serve also as members of the Presidium and of the Executive Cabinet.

17. Salary schedules for members of the World Parliament and for members of the Presidium and of the Executive Cabinet shall be determined by the World Parliament.

Article 6. The World Executive

Sec. A Functions and Powers of the World Executive

1. To implement the basic system of world law as defined in the World Constitution and in the codified system of world law after approval by the World Parliament.

2. To implement legislation enacted by the World Parliament.

3. To propose and recommend legislation for enactment by the World Parliament.

4. To convene the World Parliament in special sessions when necessary.

5. To supervise the World Administration and the Integrative Complex and all of the departments, bureaus, offices, institutes and agencies thereof.

6. To nominate, select and remove the heads of various organs, branches, departments, bureaus, offices, commissions, institutes, agencies and other parts of the World Government, in accordance with the provisions of this World Constitution and as specified in measures enacted by the World Parliament.

7. To prepare and submit annually to the World Parliament a comprehensive budget for the operations of the World Government, and to prepare and submit

periodically budget projections over periods of several years.

8. To define and propose priorities for world legislation and budgetary allocations.

9. To be held accountable to the World Parliament for the expenditures of appropriations made by the World Parliament in accordance with approved and longer term budgets, subject to revisions approved by the World Parliament.

Sec. B. Composition of the World Executive

The World Executive shall consist of a Presidium of five members, and of an Executive Cabinet of from twenty to thirty members, all of whom shall be members of the World Parliament.

Sec. C. The Presidium

1. The Presidium shall be composed of five members, one to be designated as President and the other four to be designated as Vice Presidents. Each member of the Presidium shall be from a different Continental Division.

2. The Presidency of the Presidium shall rotate each year, with each member in turn to serve as President, while the other four serve as Vice Presidents. The order of rotation shall be decided by the Presidium.

3. The decisions of the Presidium shall be taken collectively, on the basis of majority decisions.

4. Each member of the Presidium shall be a member of the World Parliament, either elected to the House of Peoples or to the House of Counselors, or appointed or elected to the House of Nations.

5. Nominations for the Presidium shall be made by the House of Counselors. The number of nominees shall be from two to three times the number to be elected. No more than one-third of the nominees shall be from the House of Counselors or from the House of Nations, and nominees must be included from all Continental Divisions.

6. From among the nominees submitted by the House of Counselors, the Presidium shall be elected by vote of the combined membership of all three houses of the World Parliament in joint session. A plurality vote equal to at least 40 percent of the total membership of the World Parliament shall be required for the election of each member to the Presidium, with successive elimination votes taken as necessary until the required plurality is achieved.

7. Members of the Presidium may be removed for cause, either individually or collectively, by an absolute majority vote of the combined membership of the three houses of the World Parliament in joint session.

8. The term of office for the Presidium shall be five years and shall run concurrently with the terms of office for the members as Members of the World Parliament, except that at the end of each five year period, the Presidium members in office shall continue to serve until the new Presidium for the succeeding term is elected. Membership in the Presidium shall be limited to two consecutive terms.

Sec. D. The Executive Cabinet

1. The Executive Cabinet shall be composed of from twenty to thirty members, with at least one member from each of the ten World Electoral and Administrative Magna Regions of the world.

2. All members of the Executive Cabinet shall be Members of the World Parliament.

3. There shall be no more than two members of the Executive Cabinet from any single nation of the World Federation. There may be only one member of the Executive Cabinet from a nation from which a Member of the World Parliament is serving as a member of the Presidium.

4. Each member of the Executive Cabinet shall serve as the head of a department or agency of the World Administration or Integrative Complex, and in this capacity shall be designated as Minister of the particular department or agency.

5. Nominations for members of the Executive Cabinet shall be made by the Presidium, taking into consideration the various functions which Executive Cabinets members are to perform. The Presidium shall nominate no more than two times the number to be elected.

6. The Executive Cabinet shall be elected by simple majority vote of the combined membership of all three houses of the World Parliament in joint session.

7. Members of the Executive Cabinet either individually or collectively may be removed for cause by an absolute majority vote of the combined membership of all three houses of the World Parliament sitting in joint session.

8. The term of office in the Executive Cabinet shall be five years, and shall run concurrently with the terms of office for the members as Members of the World Parliament, except that at the end of each five year period, the Cabinet members in office s hall continue to serve until the new Executive Cabinet for the succeeding term is elected. Membership in the Executive Cabinet shall be limited to three consecutive terms, regardless of change in ministerial position.

Sec. E. Procedures of the World Executive

1. The Presidium shall assign the ministerial positions among the Cabinet members to head the several administrative departments and major agencies of the Administration and of the Integrative Complex. Each Vice President may also serve as a Minister to head an administrative department, but not the President. Ministerial positions may be changed at the discretion of the Presidium. A Cabinet member or Vice President may hold more than one ministerial post, but no more than three, providing that no Cabinet member is without a Ministerial post.

2. The Presidium, in consultation with the Executive Cabinet, shall prepare and present to the World Parliament near the beginning of each year a proposed program of world legislation. The Presidium may propose other legislation during the year.

3. The Presidium, in consultation with the Executive Cabinet, and in consultation with the World Financial Administration, (see Article VIII, Sec. G-1-i) shall be responsible for preparing and submitting to the World Parliament the proposed annual budget, and budgetary projections over periods of years.

4. Each Cabinet Member and Vice President as Minister of a particular department or agency shall prepare an annual report for the particular department or agency, to be submitted both to the Presidium and to the World Parliament.

5. The members of the Presidium and of the Executive Cabinet at all times shall be responsible both individually and collectively to the World Parliament.

6. Vacancies occurring at any time in the World Executive shall be filled within sixty days by nomination and election in the same manner as specified for filling the offices originally.

Sec. F.　Limitations on the World Executive

1. The World Executive shall not at any time alter, suspend, abridge, infringe or otherwise violate any provision of this World Constitution or any legislation or world law enacted or approved by the World Parliament in accordance with the provisions of this World Constitution.

2. The World Executive shall not have veto power over any legislation passed by the World Parliament.

3. The World Executive may not dissolve the World Parliament or any House of the World Parliament.

4. The World Executive may not act contrary to decisions of the World Courts.

5. The World Executive shall be bound to faithfully execute all legislation passed by the World Parliament in accordance with the provisions of this World Constitution, and may not impound or refuse to spend funds appropriated by the World Parliament, nor spend more funds than are appropriated by the World Parliament.

6. The World Executive may not transcend or contradict the decisions or controls of the World Parliament, the World Judiciary or the Provisions of this World Constitution by any device of executive order or executive privilege or emergency declaration or decree.

Article 7.　The World Administration

Sec. A.　Functions of the World Administration

1. The World Administration shall be organized to carry out the detailed and continuous administration and implementation of world legislation and world law.

2. The World Administration shall be under the direction of the World Executive, and shall at all times be responsible to the World Executive.

3. The World Administration shall be organized so as to give professional continuity to the work of administration and implementation.

Sec. B.　Structure and Procedures of the World Administration

1. The World Administration shall be composed of professionally organized departments and other agencies in all areas of activity requiring continuity of administration and implementation by the World Government.

2. Each Department or major agency of the World Administration shall be headed by a Minister who shall be either a member of the Executive Cabinet or a Vice President of the Presidium.

3. Each Department or major agency of the World Administration shall have as chief of staff a Senior Administrator, who shall assist the Minister and supervise the detailed work of the Department or agency.

4. Each Senior Administrator shall be nominated by the Minister of the particular Department or agency from among persons in the senior lists of the World Civil Service Administration, as soon as senior lists have been established by the World Civil Service Administration, and shall be confirmed by the Presidium. Temporary qualified appointments shall be made by the Ministers, with confirmation by the Presidium, pending establishment of the senior lists.

5. There shall be a Secretary General of the World Administration, who shall be nominated by the Presidium and confirmed by absolute majority vote of the entire Executive Cabinet.

6. The functions and responsibilities of the Secretary General of the World Administration shall be to assist in coordinating the work of the Senior Administrators of the several Departments and agencies of the World Administration. The Secretary General shall at all times be subject to the direction of the Presidium, and shall be directly responsible to the Presidium.

7. The employment of any Senior Administrator and of the Secretary General may be terminated for cause by absolute majority vote of both the Executive Cabinet and Presidium combined, but not contrary to civil service rules which protect tenure on grounds of competence.

8. Each Minister of a Department or agency of the World Administration, being also a Member of the World Parliament, shall provide continuous liaison between the particular Department or agency and the World Parliament, shall respond at any time to any questions or requests for information from the Parliament, including committees of any House of the World Parliament.

9. The Presidium, in cooperation with the particular Ministers in each case, shall be responsible for the original organization of each of the Departments and major agencies of the World Administration.

10. The assignment of legislative measures, constitutional provisions and areas of world law to particular Departments and agencies for administration and implementation shall be done by the Presidium in consultation with the Executive Cabinet and Secretary General, unless specifically provided in legislation passed by the World Parliament.

11. The Presidium, in consultation with the Executive Cabinet, may propose the creation of other departments and agencies to have ministerial status; and may propose the alteration, combination or termination of existing Departments and agencies of ministerial status as may seem necessary or desirable. Any such creation, alteration, combination or termination shall require a simple majority vote of approval of the three houses of the World Parliament in joint session.

12. The World Parliament by absolute majority vote of the three houses in joint session may specify the creation of new departments or agencies of ministerial status in the World Administration, or may direct the World Executive to alter, combine, or terminate existing departments or agencies of ministerial status.

13. The Presidium and the World Executive may not create, establish or maintain

any administrative or executive department or agency for the purpose of circumventing control by the World Parliament.

Sec. C. Departments of the World Administration

Among the Departments and agencies of the World Administration of ministerial status, but not limited thereto and subject to combinations and to changes in descriptive terminology, shall be those listed under this Section. Each major area of administration shall be headed by a Cabinet Minister and a Senior Administrator, or by a Vice President and a Senior Administrator.

1. Disarmament and War Prevention.
2. Population.
3. Food and Agriculture.
4. Water Supplies and Waterways.
5. Health and Nutrition.
6. Education.
7. Cultural Diversity and the Arts.
8. Habitat and Settlements.
9. Environment and Ecology.
10. World Resources.
11. Oceans and Seabeds.
12. Atmosphere and Space.
13. Energy.
14. Science and Technology.
15. Genetic Research and Engineering.
16. Labor and Income.
17. Economic and Social Development.
18. Commerce and Industry.
19. Transportation and Travel.
20. Multi-National Corporations.
21. Communications and Information.
22. Human Rights.
23. Distributive Justice.
24. World Service Corps.
25. World Territories, Capitals and Parks.
26. Exterior Relations.
27. Democratic Procedures.
28. Revenue.

Article 8. The Integrative Complex

Sec. A. Definition

1. Certain administrative, research, planning and facilitative agencies of the World Government which are particularly essential for the satisfactory functioning of all or most aspects of the World Government, shall be designated as the Integrative Complex. The Integrative Complex shall include the agencies listed

under this Section, with the proviso that other such agencies may be added upon recommendation of the Presidium followed by decision of the World Parliament.

   a. The World Civil Service Administration.

   b. The World Boundaries and Elections Administration.

   c. The Institute on Governmental Procedures and World Problems.

   d. The Agency for Research and Planning.

   e. The Agency for Technological and Environmental Assessment.

   f. The World Financial Administration.

   g. Commission for Legislative Review.

2. Each agency of the Integrative Complex shall be headed by a Cabinet Minister and a Senior Administrator, or by a Vice President and a Senior Administrator, together with a Commission as provided hereunder. The rules of procedure for each agency shall be decided by majority decision of the Commission members together with the Administrator and the Minister or Vice President.

3. The World Parliament may at any time define further the responsibilities, functioning and organization of the several agencies of the Integrative Complex, consistent with the provisions of Article VIII and other provisions of the World Constitution.

4. Each agency of the Integrative Complex shall make an annual report to the World Parliament and to the Presidium.

Sec. B. The World Civil Service Administration

1. The functions of the World Civil Service Administration shall be the following, but not limited thereto:

   a. To formulate and define standards, qualifications, tests, examinations and salary scales for the personnel of all organs, departments, bureaus, offices, commissions and agencies of the World Government, in conformity with the provisions of this World Constitution and requiring approval by the Presidium and Executive Cabinet, subject to review and approval by the World Parliament.

   b. To establish rosters or lists of competent personnel for all categories of personnel to be appointed or employed in the service of the World Government.

   c. To select and employ upon request by any government organ, department, bureau, office, institute, commission, agency or authorized official, such competent personnel as may be needed and authorized, except for those positions which are made elective or appointive under provisions of the World Constitution or by specific legislation of the World Parliament.

2. The World Civil Service Administration shall be headed by a ten member commission in addition to the Cabinet Minister or Vice President and Senior Administrator. The Commission shall be composed of one commissioner from each of ten World Electoral and Administrative Magna-Regions. The persons to serve as Commissioners shall be nominated by the House of Counselors and then appointed by the Presidium for five year terms. Commissioners may serve consecutive terms.

Sec. C. The World Boundaries and Elections Administration

1. The functions of the World Boundaries and Elections Administration shall include the following, but not limited thereto:

a. To define the boundaries for the basic World Electoral and Administrative Districts, the World Electoral and Administrative Regions and Magna-Regions, and the Continental Divisions, for submission to the World Parliament for approval by legislative action.

b. To make periodic adjustments every ten or five years, as needed, of the boundaries for the World Electoral and Administrative Districts, the World Electoral and Administrative Regions and Magna-Regions, and of the Continental Divisions, subject to approval by the World Parliament.

c. To define the detailed procedures for the nomination and election of Members of the World Parliament to the House of Peoples and to the House of Counselors, subject to approval by the World Parliament.

d. To conduct the elections for Members of the World Parliament to the House of Peoples and to the House of Counselors.

e. Before each World Parliamentary Election, to prepare Voters' Information Booklets which shall summarize major current public issues, and shall list each candidate for elective office together with standard information about each candidate, and give space for each candidate to state his or her views on the defined major issues as well as on any other major issue of choice; to include information on any initiatives or referendums which are to be voted upon; to distribute the Voter's Information Booklets for each World Electoral District, or suitable group of Districts; and to obtain the advice of the Institute on Governmental Procedures and World Problems, the Agency for Research and Planning, and the Agency for Technological and Environmental Assessment in preparing the booklets.

f. To define the rules for world political parties, subject to approval by the World Parliament, and subject to review and recommendations of the World Ombudsmus.

g. To define the detailed procedures for legislative initiative and referendum by the Citizens of Earth, and to conduct voting on supra- national or global initiatives and referendums in conjunction with world parliamentary elections.

h. To conduct plebiscites when requested by other Organs of the World Government, and to make recommendations for the settlement of boundary disputes.

i. To conduct a global census every five years, and to prepare and maintain complete demographic analyses for Earth.

2. The World Boundaries and Elections Administration shall be headed by a ten member commission in addition to the Senior Administrator and the Cabinet Minister or Vice President. The commission shall be composed of one commissioner each from ten World Electoral and Administrative Magna- Regions. The persons to serve as commissioners shall be nominated by the House of Counselors and then appointed by the World Presidium for five year terms. Commissioners may serve consecutive terms.

Sec. D. Institute on Governmental Procedures and World Problems

1. The functions of the Institute on Governmental Procedures and World Problems shall be as follows, but not limited thereto:

a. To prepare and conduct courses of information, education and training for all personnel in the service of the World Government, including Members of the World Parliament and of all other elective, appointive and civil service personnel, so that every person in the service of the World Government may have a better understanding of the functions, structure, procedures and inter-relationships of the various organs, departments, bureaus, offices, institutes, commissions, agencies and other parts of the World Government.

b. To prepare and conduct courses and seminars for information, education, discussion, updating and new ideas in all areas of world problems, particularly for Members of the World Parliament and of the World Executive, and for the chief personnel of all organs, departments and agencies of the World Government, but open to all in the service of the World Government.

c. To bring in qualified persons from private and public universities, colleges and research and action organizations of many countries, as well as other qualified persons, to lecture and to be resource persons for the courses and seminars organized by the Institute on Governmental Procedures and World Problems.

d. To contract with private or public universities and colleges or other agencies to conduct courses and seminars for the Institute.

2. The Institute on Governmental Procedures and World Problems shall be supervised by a ten member commission in addition to the Senior Administrator and Cabinet Minister or Vice President. The commission shall be composed of one commissioner each to be named by the House of Peoples, the House of Nations, the House of Counselors, the Presidium, the Collegium of World Judges, The World Ombudsmus, The World Attorneys General Office, the Agency for Research and Planning, the Agency for Technological and Environmental Assessment, and the World Financial Administration. Commissioners shall serve five year terms, and may serve consecutive terms.

Sec. E. The Agency for Research and Planning

1. The functions of the Agency for Research and Planning shall be as follows, but not limited thereto:

a. To serve the World Parliament, the World Executive, the World Administration, and other organs, departments and agencies of the World Government in any matter requiring research and planning within the competence of the agency.

b. To prepare and maintain a comprehensive inventory of world resources.

c. To prepare comprehensive long-range plans for the development, conservation, re-cycling and equitable sharing of the resources of Earth for the benefit of all people on Earth, subject to legislative action by the World Parliament.

d. To prepare and maintain a comprehensive list and description of all world problems, including their inter-relationships, impact time projections and proposed solutions, together with bibliographies.

e. To do research and help prepare legislative measures at the request of any Member of the World Parliament or of any committee of any House of the World Parliament.

f. To do research and help prepare proposed legislation or proposed legislative programs and schedules at the request of the Presidium or Executive Cabinet or of any Cabinet Minister.

g. To do research and prepare reports at the request of any other organ, department or agency of the World Government.

h. To enlist the help of public and private universities, colleges, research agencies, and other associations and organizations for various research and planning projects.

i. To contract with public and private universities, colleges, research agencies and other organizations for the preparation of specific reports, studies and proposals.

j. To maintain a comprehensive World Library for the use of all Members of the World Parliament, and for the use of all other officials and persons in the service of the World Government, as well as for public information.

2. The Agency for Research and Planning shall be supervised by a ten member commission in addition to the Senior Administrator and Cabinet Minister or Vice President. The commission shall be composed of one commissioner each to be named by the House of Peoples, the House of Nations, the House of Counselors, the Presidium, the Collegium of World Judges, the Office of World Attorneys General, World Ombudsmus, the Agency for Technological and Environmental Assessment, the Institute on Governmental Procedures and World Problems, and the World Financial Administration. Commissioners shall serve five year terms, and may serve consecutive terms.

Sec. F. The Agency for Technological and Environmental Assessment

1. The functions of the agency for Technological and Environmental Assessment shall include the following, but not limited thereto:

a. To establish and maintain a registration and description of all significant technological innovations, together with impact projections.

b. To examine, analyze and assess the impacts and consequences of technological innovations which may have either significant beneficial or significant harmful or dangerous consequences for human life or for the ecology of life on Earth, or which may require particular regulations or prohibitions to prevent or eliminate dangers or to assure benefits.

c. To examine, analyze and assess environmental and ecological problems, in particular the environmental and ecological problems which may result from any intrusions or changes of the environment or ecological relationships which may be caused by technological innovations, processes of resource development, patterns of human settlements, the production of energy, patterns of economic and industrial development, or other man-made intrusions and changes of the environment, or which may result from natural causes.

d. To maintain a global monitoring network to measure possible harmful effects of technological innovations and environmental disturbances so that corrective measures can be designed.

e. To prepare recommendations based on technological and environmental analyses and assessments, which can serve as guides to the World Parliament, the World Executive, the World Administration, the Agency for Research and Planning, and to the other organs, departments and agencies of the World Government, as well as to individuals in the service of the World Government and to national and local governments and legislative bodies.

f. To enlist the voluntary or contractual aid and participation of private and public universities, colleges, research institutions and other associations and organizations in the work of technological and environmental assessment.

g. To enlist the voluntary or contractual aid and participation of private and public universities and colleges, research institutions and other organizations in devising and developing alternatives to harmful or dangerous technologies and environmentally disruptive activities, and in devising controls to assure beneficial results from technological innovations or to prevent harmful results from either technological innovations or environmental changes, all subject to legislation for implementation by the World Parliament.

2. The Agency for Technological and Environmental Assessment shall be supervised by a ten member commission in addition to the Senior Administrator and Cabinet Minister or Vice President. The commission shall be composed of one commissioner from each of ten World Electoral and Administrative Magna-Regions. The persons to serve as commissioners shall be nominated by the House of Counselors, and then appointed by the World Presidium for five year terms. Commissioners may serve consecutive terms.

Sec. G. The World Financial Administration

1. The functions of the World Financial Administration shall include the following, but not limited thereto:

a. To establish and operate the procedures for the collection of revenues for the World Government, pursuant to legislation by the World Parliament, inclusive of taxes, globally accounted social and public costs, licenses, fees, revenue sharing arrangements, income derived from supra-national public enterprises or projects or resource developments, and all other sources.

b. To operate a Planetary Accounting Office, and thereunder to make cost/benefit studies and reports of the functioning and activities of the World Government and of its several organs, departments, branches, bureaus, offices, commissions, institutes, agencies and other parts or projects. In making such studies and reports, account shall be taken not only of direct financial costs and benefits, but also of human, social, environmental, indirect, long-term and other costs and benefits, and of actual or possible hazards and damages. Such studies and reports shall also be designed to uncover any wastes, inefficiencies, misapplications, corruptions, diversions, unnecessary costs, and other possible irregularities.

c. To make cost/benefit studies and reports at the request of any House or committee of the World Parliament, and of the Presidium, the Executive Cabinet, the World Ombudsmus, the Office of World Attorneys General, the World Supreme Court, or of any administrative department or any agency of the Integrative Complex, as well as upon its own initiative.

d. To operate a Planetary Comptrollers Office and thereunder to supervise the disbursement of the funds of the World Government for all purposes, projects and activities duly authorized by this World Constitution, the World Parliament, the World Executive, and other organs, departments and agencies of the World Government.

e. To establish and operate a Planetary Banking System, making the transition to a common global currency, under the terms of specific legislation passed by the World Parliament.

f. Pursuant to specific legislation enacted by the World Parliament, and in conjunction with the Planetary Banking System, to establish and implement the procedures of a Planetary Monetary and Credit System based upon useful productive capacity and performance, both in goods and services. Such a monetary and credit system shall be designed for use within the Planetary Banking System for the financing of the activities and projects of the World Government, and for all other financial purposes approved by the World Parliament, without requiring the payment of interest on bonds, investments or other claims of financial ownership or debt.

g. To establish criteria for the extension of financial credit based upon such considerations as people available to work, usefulness, cost/benefit accounting, human and social values, environmental health and esthetics, minimizing disparities, integrity , competent management, appropriate technology, potential production and performance.

h. To establish and operate a Planetary Insurance System in areas of world need which transcend national boundaries and in accordance with legislation passed by the World Parliament.

i. To assist the Presidium as may be requested in the technical preparation of budgets for the operation of the World Government.

2. The World Financial Administration shall be supervised by a commission of ten members, together with a Senior Administrator and a Cabinet Minister or Vice President. The commission shall be composed of one commissioner each to be named by the House of Peoples, the House of Nations, the House of Counselors, the Presidium, the Collegium of World Judges, the Office of Attorneys General, the World Ombudsmus, the Agency for Research and Planning, the Agency for Technological and Environmental Assessment, and the Institute on Governmental Procedures and World Problems. Commissioners shall serve terms of five years, and may serve consecutive terms.

Sec. H. Commission for Legislative Review

1. The functions of the Commission for Legislative Review shall be to examine World Legislation and World Laws which the World Parliament enacts or adopts

from the previous Body of International Law for the purpose of analyzing whether any particular legislation or law has become obsolete or obstructive or defective in serving the purposes intended; and to make recommendations to the World Parliament accordingly for repeal or amendment or replacement.

2. The Commission for Legislative Review shall be composed of twelve members, including two each to be elected by the House of Peoples, the House of Nations, the House of Counselors, the Collegium of World Judges, the World Ombudsmus and the Presidium. Members of the Commission shall serve terms of ten years, and may be re-elected to serve consecutive terms. One half of the Commission members after the Commission is first formed shall be elected every five years, with the first terms for one half of the members to be only five years.

Article 9. The World Judiciary

Sec. A. Jurisdiction of the World Supreme Court

1. A World Supreme Court shall be established, together with such regional and district World Courts as may subsequently be found necessary. The World Supreme Court shall comprise a number of benches.

2. The World Supreme Court, together with such regional and district World Courts as may be established, shall have mandatory jurisdiction in all cases, actions, disputes, conflicts, violations of law, civil suits, guarantees of civil and human rights, constitutional interpretations, and other litigations arising under the provisions of this World Constitution, world legislation, and the body of world law approved by the World Parliament.

3. Decisions of the World Supreme Court shall be binding on all parties involved in all cases, actions and litigations brought before any bench of the World Supreme Court for settlement. Each bench of the World Supreme Court shall constitute a court of highest appeal, except when matters of extra-ordinary public importance are assigned or transferred to the Superior Tribunal of the World Supreme Court, as provided in Section E of Article IX.

Sec. B. Benches of the World Supreme Court

The benches of the World Supreme Court and their respective jurisdictions shall be as follows:

1. Bench for Human Rights: To deal with issues of human rights arising under the guarantee of civil and human rights provided by Article XIII of this World Constitution, and arising in pursuance of the provisions of Article XIII of this World Constitution, and arising otherwise under world legislation and the body of world law approved by the World Parliament.

2. Bench for Criminal Cases: To deal with issues arising from the violation of world laws and world legislation by individuals, corporations, groups and associations, but not issues primarily concerned with human rights.

3. Bench for Civil Cases: To deal with issues involving civil law suits and disputes between individuals, corporations, groups and associations arising under world legislation and world law and the administration thereof.

4. Bench for Constitutional Cases: To deal with the interpretation of the World Constitution and with issues and actions arising in connection with the interpretation of the World Constitution.

5. Bench for International Conflicts: To deal with disputes, conflicts and legal contest arising between or among the nations which have joined in the Federation of Earth.

6. Bench for Public Cases: To deal with issues not under the jurisdiction of another bench arising from conflicts, disputes, civil suits or other legal contests between the World Government and corporations, groups or individuals, or between national governments and corporations, groups or individuals in cases involving world legislation and world law.

7. Appellate Bench: To deal with issues involving world legislation and world law which may be appealed from national courts; and to decide which bench to assign a case or action or litigation when a question or disagreement arises over the proper jurisdiction.

8. Advisory Bench: To give opinions upon request on any legal question arising under world law or world legislation, exclusive of contests or actions involving interpretation of the World Constitution. Advisory opinions may be requested by any House or committee of the World Parliament, by the Presidium, any Administrative Department, the Office of World Attorneys General, the World Ombudsmus, or by any agency of the Integrative Complex.

9. Other benches may be established, combined or terminated upon recommendation of the Collegium of World Judges with approval by the World Parliament; but benches number one through eight may not be combined nor terminated except by amendment of this World Constitution.

Sec. C. Seats of the World Supreme Court

1. The primary seat of the World Supreme Court and all benches shall be the same as for the location of the Primary World Capital and for the location of the World Parliament and the World Executive.

2. Continental seats of the World Supreme Court shall be established in the four secondary capitals of the World Government located in four different Continental Divisions of Earth, as provided in Article XV.

3. The following permanent benches of the World Supreme Court shall be established both at the primary seat and at each of the continental seats: Human Rights, Criminal Cases, Civil Cases, and Public Cases.

4. The following permanent benches of the World Supreme Court shall be located only at the primary seat of the World Supreme Court: Constitutional Cases, International Conflicts, Appellate Bench, and Advisory Bench.

5. Benches which are located permanently only at the primary seat of the World Supreme Court may hold special sessions at the other continental seats of the World Supreme Court when necessary, or may establish continental circuits if needed.

6. Benches of the World Supreme Court which have permanent continental locations may hold special sessions at other locations when needed, or may establish regional circuits if needed.

Sec. D. The Collegium of World Judges

1. A Collegium of World Judges shall be established by the World Parliament. The Collegium shall consist of a minimum of twenty member judges, and may be expanded as needed but not to exceed sixty members.

2. The World Judges to compose the Collegium of World Judges shall be nominated by the House of Counselors and shall be elected by plurality vote of the three Houses of the World Parliament in joint session. The House of Counselors shall nominate between two and three times the number of world judges to be elected at any one time. An equal number of World Judges shall be elected from each of ten World Electoral and Administrative Magna-Regions, if not immediately then by rotation.

3. The term of office for a World Judge shall be ten years. Successive terms may be served without limit.

4. The Collegium of World Judges shall elect a Presiding Council of World Judges, consisting of a Chief Justice and four Associate Chief Justices. One member of the Presiding Council of World Judges shall be elected from each of five Continental Divisions of Earth. Members of the Presiding Council of World Judges shall serve five year terms on the Presiding Council, and may serve two successive terms, but not two successive terms as Chief Justice.

5. The Presiding Council of World Judges shall assign all World Judges, including themselves, to the several benches of the World Supreme Court. Each bench for a sitting at each location shall have a minimum of three World Judges, except that the number of World Judges for benches on Continental Cases and International Conflicts, and the Appellate Bench, shall be no less than five.

6. The member judges of each bench at each location shall choose annually a Presiding Judge, who may serve two successive terms.

7. The members of the several benches may be reconstituted from time to time as may seem desirable or necessary upon the decision of the Presiding Council of World Judges. Any decision to re-constitute a bench shall be referred to a vote of the entire Collegium of World Judges by request of any World Judge.

8. Any World Judge may be removed from office for cause by an absolute two-thirds majority vote of the three Houses of the World Parliament in joint session.

9. Qualifications for Judges of the World Supreme Court shall be at least ten years of legal or juristic experience, minimum age of thirty years, and evident competence in world law and the humanities.

10. The salaries, expenses, remunerations and prerogatives of the World Judges shall be determined by the World Parliament, and shall be reviewed every five years, but shall not be changed to the disadvantage of any World Judge during a term of office. A ll members of the Collegium of World Judges shall receive the same salaries, except that additional compensation may be given to the Presiding Council of World Judges.

11. Upon recommendation by the Collegium of World Judges, the World Parliament shall have the authority to establish regional and district world courts below the World Supreme Court, and to establish the jurisdictions thereof, and the procedures for appeal to the World Supreme Court or to the several benches thereof.

12. The detailed rules of procedure for the functioning of the World Supreme Court, the Collegium of World Judges, and for each bench of the World Supreme Court, shall be decided and amended by absolute majority vote of the Collegium of World Judges.

Sec. E. The Superior Tribunal of the World Supreme Court

1. A Superior Tribunal of the World Supreme Court shall be established to take cases which are considered to be of extra-ordinary public importance. The Superior Tribunal for any calendar year shall consist of the Presiding Council of World Judges together with one World Judge named by the Presiding Judge of each bench of the World Court sitting at the primary seat of the World Supreme Court. The composition of the Superior Tribunal may be continued unchanged for a second year by decision of the Presiding Council of World Judges.

2. Any party to any dispute, issue, case or litigation coming under the jurisdiction of the World Supreme Court, may apply to any particular bench of the World Supreme Court or to the Presiding Council of World Judges for the assignment or transfer of the case to the Superior Tribunal on the grounds of extra-ordinary public importance. If the application is granted, the case shall be heard and disposed of by the Superior Tribunal. Also, any bench taking any particular case, if satisfied that the case is of extra-ordinary public importance, may of its own discretion transfer the case to the Superior Tribunal.

Article 10. The Enforcement System

Sec. A. Basic Principles

1. The enforcement of world law and world legislation shall apply directly to individuals, and individuals shall be held responsible for compliance with world law and world legislation regardless of whether the individuals are acting in their own capacity or as agents or officials of governments at any level or of the institutions of governments, or as agents or officials of corporations, organizations, associations or groups of any kind.

2. When world law or world legislation or decisions of the world courts are violated, the Enforcement System shall operate to identify and apprehend the individuals responsible for violations.

3. Any enforcement action shall not violate the civil and human rights guaranteed under this World Constitution.

4. The enforcement of world law and world legislation shall be carried out in the context of a non-military world federation wherein all member nations shall disarm as a condition for joining and benefitting from the world federation, subject to Article X VII, Sec. C-8 and D-6. The Federation of Earth and World Government under this World Constitution shall neither keep nor use weapons of mass destruction.

5. Those agents of the enforcement system whose function shall be to apprehend and bring to court violators of world law and world legislation shall be equipped only with such weapons as are appropriate for the apprehension of the individuals responsible for violations.

6. The enforcement of world law and world legislation under this World Constitution shall be conceived and developed primarily as the processes of effective design and administration of world law and world legislation to serve the welfare of all people on Earth, with equity and justice for all, in which the resources of Earth and the funds and the credits of the World Government are used only to serve peaceful human needs, and none used for weapons of mass destruction or for war making capabilities.

Sec. B. The Structure for Enforcement: World Attorneys General

1. The Enforcement System shall be headed by an Office of World Attorneys General and a Commission of Regional World Attorneys.
2. The Office of World Attorneys General shall be comprised of five members, one of whom shall be designated as the World Attorney General and the other four shall each be designated an Associate World Attorney General.
3. The Commission of Regional World Attorneys shall consist of twenty Regional World Attorneys.
4. The members to comprise the Office of World Attorneys General shall be nominated by the House of Counselors, with three nominees from each Continental Division of Earth. One member of the Office shall be elected from each of five Continental Divisions by plurality vote of the three houses of the World Parliament in joint session.
5. The term of office for a member of the Office of World Attorneys General shall be ten years. A member may serve two consecutive terms. The position of World Attorney General shall rotate every two years among the five members of the Office. The order of rotation shall be decided among the five members of the Office.
6. The Office of World Attorneys General shall nominate members for the Commission of twenty Regional World Attorneys from the twenty World Electoral and Administrative Regions, with between two and three nominees submitted for each Region. From these nominations, the three Houses of the World Parliament in joint session shall elect one Regional World Attorney from each of the twenty Regions. Regional World Attorneys shall serve terms of five years, and may serve three consecutive terms.
7. Each Regional World Attorney shall organize and be in charge of an Office of Regional World Attorney. Each Associate World Attorney General shall supervise five Offices of Regional World Attorneys.
8. The staff to carry out the work of enforcement, in addition to the five members of the Office of World Attorneys General and the twenty Regional World Attorneys, shall be selected from civil service lists, and shall be organized for the following functions:
   a. Investigation.
   b. Apprehension and arrest.
   c. Prosecution.
   d. Remedies and correction.
   e. Conflict resolution.

9. Qualifications for a member of the Office of World Attorneys General and for the Regional World Attorneys shall be at least thirty years of age, at least seven years legal experience, and education in law and the humanities.

10. The World Attorney General, the Associate World Attorneys General, and the Regional World Attorneys shall at all times be responsible to the World Parliament. Any member of the Office of World Attorneys General and any Regional World Attorney can be removed from office for cause by a simple majority vote of the three Houses of the World Parliament in joint session.

Sec. C. The World Police

1. That section of the staff of the Office of World Attorneys General and of the Offices of Regional World Attorneys responsible for the apprehension and arrest of violators of world law and world legislation, shall be designated as World Police.

2. Each regional staff of the World Police shall be headed by a Regional World Police Captain, who shall be appointed by the Regional World Attorney.

3. The Office of World Attorneys General shall appoint a World Police Supervisor, to be in charge of those activities which transcend regional boundaries. The World Police Supervisor shall direct the Regional World Police Captains in any actions which require coordinated or joint action transcending regional boundaries, and shall direct any action which requires initiation or direction from the Office of World Attorneys General.

4. Searches and arrests to be made by World Police shall be made only upon warrants issued by the Office of World Attorneys General or by a Regional World Attorney.

5. World Police shall be armed only with weapons appropriate for the apprehension of the individuals responsible for violation of world law.

6. Employment in the capacity of World Police Captain and World Police Supervisor shall be limited to ten years.

7. The World Police Supervisor and any Regional World Police Captain may be removed from office for cause by decision of the Office of World Attorneys General or by absolute majority vote of the three Houses of the World Parliament in joint session.

Sec. D.   The Means of Enforcement

1. Non-military means of enforcement of world law and world legislation shall be developed by the World Parliament and by the Office of World Attorneys General in consultation with the Commission of Regional World Attorneys, the Collegium of World Judges , the World Presidium, and the World Ombudsmus. The actual means of enforcement shall require legislation by the World Parliament.

2. Non-military means of enforcement which can be developed may include: Denial of financial credit; denial of material resources and personnel; revocation of licenses, charters, or corporate rights; impounding of equipment; fines and damage payments; performance of work to rectify damages; imprisonment or isolation; and other means appropriate to the specific situations.

3. To cope with situations of potential or actual riots, insurrection and resort to armed violence, particular strategies and methods shall be developed by the World Parliament and by the Office of World Attorneys General in consultation with the Commission of Regional World Attorneys, the collegium of World Judges, the Presidium and the World Ombudsmus. Such strategies and methods shall require enabling legislation by the World Parliament where required in addition to the specific provisions of this World Constitution.

4. A basic condition for preventing outbreaks of violence which the Enforcement System shall facilitate in every way possible, shall be to assure a fair hearing under non-violent circumstances for any person or group having a grievance, and likewise to assure a fair opportunity for a just settlement of any grievance with due regard for the rights and welfare of all concerned.

Article 11. The World Ombudsmus

Sec. A. Functions and Powers of the World Ombudsmus

The functions and powers of the World Ombudsmus, as public defender, shall include the following:

1. To protect the People of Earth and all individuals against violations or neglect of universal human and civil rights which are stipulated in Article 12 and other sections of this World Constitution.

2. To protect the People of Earth against violations of this World Constitution by any official or agency of the World Government, including both elected and appointed officials or public employees regardless of organ, department, office, agency or rank.

3. To press for the implementation of the Directive Principles for the World Government as defined in Article 13 of this World Constitution.

4. To promote the welfare of the people of Earth by seeking to assure that conditions of social justice and of minimizing disparities are achieved in the implementation and administration of world legislation and world law.

5. To keep on the alert for perils to humanity arising from technological innovations, environmental disruptions and other diverse sources, and to launch initiatives for correction or prevention of such perils.

6. To ascertain that the administration of otherwise proper laws, ordinances and procedures of the World Government do not result in unforeseen injustices or inequities, or become stultified in bureaucracy or the details of administration.

7. To receive and hear complaints, grievances or requests for aid from any person, group, organization, association, body politic or agency concerning any matter which comes within the purview of the World Ombudsmus.

8. To request the Office of World Attorneys General or any Regional World Attorney to initiate legal actions or court proceedings whenever and wherever considered necessary or desirable in the view of the World Ombudsmus.

9. To directly initiate legal actions and court proceedings whenever the World Ombudsmus deems necessary.

10. To review the functioning of the departments, bureaus, offices, commissions,

institutes, organs and agencies of the World Government to ascertain whether the procedures of the World government are adequately fulfilling their purposes and serving the welfare of humanity in optimum fashion, and to make recommendations for improvements.

11. To present an annual report to the World Parliament and to the Presidium on the activities of the World Ombudsmus, together with any recommendations for legislative measures to improve the functioning of the World Government for the purpose of better serving the welfare of the People of Earth.

Sec. B. Composition of the World Ombudsmus

1. The World Ombudsmus shall be headed by a Council of World Ombudsmen of five members, one of whom shall be designated as Principal World Ombudsman, while the other four shall each be designated as an Associate World Ombudsman.

2. Members to compose the Council of World Ombudsmen shall be nominated by the House of Counselors, with three nominees from each Continental Division of Earth. One member of the Council shall be elected from each of five Continental Divisions by plurality vote of the three Houses of the World Parliament in joint session.

3. The term of office for a World Ombudsman shall be ten years. A World Ombudsman may serve two successive terms. The position of Principal World Ombudsman shall be rotated every two years. The order of rotation shall be determined by the Council of World Ombudsmen.

4. The Council of World Ombudsmen shall be assisted by a Commission of World Advocates of twenty members. Members for the Commission of World Advocates shall be nominated by the Council of World Ombudsmen from twenty World Electoral and Administrative Regions, with between two and three nominees submitted for each Region. One World Advocate shall be elected from each of the twenty World Electoral and Administrative Regions by the three Houses of the World Parliament in joint session. World Advocates shall serve terms of five years, and may serve a maximum of four successive terms.

5. The Council of World Ombudsmen shall establish twenty regional offices, in addition to the principal world office at the primary seat of the World Government. The twenty regional offices of the World Ombudsmus shall parallel the organization of the twenty Offices of Regional World Attorney.

6. Each regional office of the World Ombudsmus shall be headed by a World Advocate. Each five regional offices of the World Ombudsmus shall be supervised by an Associate World Ombudsman.

7. Any World Ombudsman and any World Advocate may be removed from office for cause by an absolute majority vote of the three Houses of the World Parliament in joint session.

8. Staff members for the World Ombudsmus and for each regional office of the World Ombudsmus shall be selected and employed from civil service lists.

9. Qualifications for World Ombudsman and for World Advocate shall be at least thirty years of age, at least five years legal experience, and education in law and other relevant education.

Article 12. Bill of Rights for the Citizens of Earth

The inhabitants and citizens of Earth who are within the Federation of Earth shall have certain inalienable rights defined hereunder. It shall be mandatory for the World Parliament, the World Executive, and all organs and agencies of the World Government to honor, implement and enforce these rights, as well as for the national governments of all member nations in the Federation of Earth to do likewise. Individuals or groups suffering violation or neglect of such rights shall have full recourse through the World Ombudsmus, the Enforcement System and the World Courts for redress of grievances. The inalienable rights shall include the following:

1. Equal rights for all citizens of the Federation of Earth, with no discrimination on grounds of race, color, caste, nationality, sex, religion, political affiliation, property, or social status.

2. Equal protection and application of world legislation and world laws for all citizens of the Federation of Earth.

3. Freedom of thought and conscience, speech, press, writing, communication, expression, publication, broadcasting, telecasting, and cinema, except as an overt part of or incitement to violence, armed riot or insurrection.

4. Freedom of assembly, association, organization, petition and peaceful demonstration.

5. Freedom to vote without duress, and freedom for political organization and campaigning without censorship or recrimination.

6. Freedom to profess, practice and promote religious or religious beliefs or no religion or religious belief.

7. Freedom to profess and promote political beliefs or no political beliefs.

8. Freedom for investigation, research and reporting.

9. Freedom to travel without passport or visas or other forms of registration used to limit travel between, among or within nations.

10. Prohibition against slavery, peonage, involuntary servitude, and conscription of labor.

11. Prohibition against military conscription.

12. Safety of person from arbitrary or unreasonable arrest, detention, exile, search or seizure; requirement of warrants for searches and arrests.

13. Prohibition against physical or psychological duress or torture during any period of investigation, arrest, detention or imprisonment, and against cruel or unusual punishment.

14. Right of habeas corpus; no ex-post-facto laws; no double jeopardy; right to refuse self-incrimination or the incrimination of another.

15. Prohibition against private armies and paramilitary organizations as being threats to the common peace and safety.

16. Safety of property from arbitrary seizure; protection against exercise of the power of eminent domain without reasonable compensation.

17. Right to family planning and free public assistance to achieve family planning objectives.

18. Right of privacy of person, family and association; prohibition against surveillance as a means of political control.

Article 13. Directive Principles for the World Government

It shall be the aim of the World Government to secure certain other rights for all inhabitants within the Federation of Earth, but without immediate guarantee of universal achievement and enforcement. These rights are defined as Directive Principles, obligating the World Government to pursue every reasonable means for universal realization and implementation, and shall include the following:

1. Equal opportunity for useful employment for everyone, with wages or remuneration sufficient to assure human dignity.
2. Freedom of choice in work, occupation, employment or profession.
3. Full access to information and to the accumulated knowledge of the human race.
4. Free and adequate public education available to everyone, extending to the pre-university level; Equal opportunities for elementary and higher education for all persons; equal opportunity for continued education for all persons throughout life; the right of any person or parent to choose a private educational institution at any time.
5. Free and adequate public health services and medical care available to everyone throughout life under conditions of free choice.
6. Equal opportunity for leisure time for everyone; better distribution of the work load of society so that every person may have equitable leisure time opportunities.
7. Equal opportunity for everyone to enjoy the benefits of scientific and technological discoveries and developments.
8. Protection for everyone against the hazards and perils of technological innovations and developments.
9. Protection of the natural environment which is the common heritage of humanity against pollution, ecological disruption or damage which could imperil life or lower the quality of life.
10. Conservation of those natural resources of Earth which are limited so that present and future generations may continue to enjoy life on the planet Earth.
11. Assurance for everyone of adequate housing, of adequate and nutritious food supplies, of safe and adequate water supplies, of pure air with protection of oxygen supplies and the ozone layer, and in general for the continuance of an environment which can sustain healthy living for all.
12. Assure to each child the right to the full realization of his or her potential.
13. Social Security for everyone to relieve the hazards of unemployment, sickness, old age, family circumstances, disability, catastrophes of nature, and technological change, and to allow retirement with sufficient lifetime income for living under conditions of human dignity during older age.
14. Rapid elimination of and prohibitions against technological hazards and man-made environmental disturbances which are found to create dangers to life on Earth.
15. Implementation of intensive programs to discover, develop and institute safe alternatives and practical substitutions for technologies which must be eliminated and prohibited because of hazards and dangers to life.
16. Encouragement for cultural diversity; encouragement for decentralized administration.
17. Freedom for peaceful self-determination for minorities, refugees and dissenters.

18. Freedom for change of residence to anywhere on Earth conditioned by provisions for temporary sanctuaries in events of large numbers of refugees, stateless persons, or mass migrations.

19. Prohibition against the death penalty.

Article 14. Safeguards and Reservations

Sec. A. Certain Safeguards

The World Government shall operate to secure for all nations and peoples within the Federation of Earth the safeguards which are defined hereunder:

1. Guarantee that full faith and credit shall be given to the public acts, records, legislation and judicial proceedings of the member nations within the Federation of Earth, consistent with the several provisions of this World Constitution.

2. Assure freedom of choice within the member nations and countries of the Federation of Earth to determine their internal political, economic and social systems, consistent with the guarantees and protections given under this World Constitution to assure civil liberties and human rights and a safe environment for life, and otherwise consistent with the several provisions of this World Constitution.

3. Grant the right of asylum within the Federation of Earth for persons who may seek refuge from countries or nations which are not yet included within the Federation of Earth.

4. Grant the right of individuals and groups, after the Federation of Earth includes 90 percent of the territory of Earth, to peacefully leave the hegemony of the Federation of Earth and to live in suitable territory set aside by the Federation neither restricted nor protected by the World Government, provided that such territory does not extend beyond five percent of Earth's habitable territory, is kept completely disarmed and not used as a base for inciting violence or insurrection within or against the Federation of Earth or any member nation, and is kept free of acts of environmental or technological damage which seriously affect Earth outside such territory.

Sec. B. Reservation of Powers

The powers not delegated to the World Government by this World Constitution shall be reserved to the nations of the Federation of Earth and to the people of Earth.

Article 15. World Federal Zones and the World Capitals

Sec. A. World Federal Zones

1. Twenty World Federal Zones shall be established within the twenty World Electoral and Administrative Regions, for the purposes of the location of the several organs of the World Government and of the administrative departments, the world courts, the offices of the Regional World Attorneys, the offices of the World Advocates, and for the location of other branches, departments, institutes, offices, bureaus, commissions, agencies and parts of the World Government.

2. The World Federal Zones shall be established as the needs and resources of the World Government develop and expand. World Federal Zones shall be established first within each of five Continental Divisions.

3. The location and administration of the World Federal Zones, including the first five, shall be determined by the World Parliament.

Sec. B. The World Capitals

1. Five World Capitals shall be established in each of five Continental Divisions of Earth, to be located in each of the five World Federal Zones which are established first as provided in Article 15 of this World Constitution.

2. One of the World Capitals shall be designated by the World Parliament as the Primary World Capital, and the other four shall be designated as Secondary World Capitals.

3. The primary seats of all organs of the World Government shall be located in the Primary World Capital, and other major seats of the several organs of the World Government shall be located in the Secondary World Capitals.

Sec. C. Locational Procedures

1. Choices for location of the twenty World Federal Zones and for the five World Capitals shall be proposed by the Presidium, and then shall be decided by a simple majority vote of the three Houses of the World Parliament in joint session. The Presidium shall offer choices of two or three locations in each of the twenty World Electoral and Administrative Regions to be World Federal Zones, and shall offer two alternative choices for each of the five World Capitals.

2. The Presidium in consultation with the Executive Cabinet shall then propose which of the five World Capitals shall be the Primary World Capital, to be decided by a simply majority vote of the three Houses of the World Parliament in joint session.

3. Each organ of the World Government shall decide how best to apportion and organize its functions and activities among the five World Capitals, and among the twenty World Federal Zones, subject to specific directions from the World Parliament.

4. The World Parliament may decide to rotate its sessions among the five World Capitals, and if so, to decide the procedure for rotation.

5. For the first two operative stages of World Government as defined in Article 17, and for the Provisional World Government as defined in Article 19, a provisional location may be selected for the Primary World Capital. The provisional location need not be continued as a permanent location.

6. Any World Capital or World Federal Zone may be relocated by an absolute two-thirds majority vote of the three Houses of the World Parliament in joint session.

7. Additional World Federal Zones may be designated if found necessary by proposal of the Presidium and approval by an absolute majority vote of the three Houses of the World Parliament in joint session.

Article 16. World Territories and Exterior Relations

Sec. A. World Territory

1. Those areas of the Earth and Earth's moon which are not under the jurisdiction of existing nations at the time of forming the Federation of Earth, or which are not reasonably within the province of national ownership and administration, or which are declared to be World Territory subsequent to establishment of the Federation of Earth, shall be designated as World Territory and shall belong to all of the people of Earth.

2. The administration of World Territory shall be determined by the World Parliament and implemented by the World Executive, and shall apply to the following areas:

    a. All oceans and seas having an international or supra-national character, together with the seabeds and resources thereof, beginning at a distance of twenty kilometers offshore, excluding inland seas of traditional national ownership.

    b. Vital straits, channels, and canals.

    c. The atmosphere enveloping Earth, beginning at an elevation of one kilometer above the general surface of the land, excluding the depressions in areas of much variation in elevation.

    d. Man-made satellites and Earth's moon.

    e. Colonies which may choose the status of World Territory; non-independent territories under the trust administration of nations or of the United Nations; any islands or atolls which are unclaimed by any nation; independent lands or countries which choose the status of World Territory; and disputed lands which choose the status of World Territory.

3. The residents of any World Territory, except designated World Federal Zones, shall have the right within reason to decide by plebiscite to become a self-governing nation within the Federation of Earth, either singly or in combination with other World Territories, or to unite with an existing nation with the Federation of Earth.

Sec. B. Exterior Relations

1. The World Government shall maintain exterior relations with those nations of Earth which have not joined the Federation of Earth. Exterior relations shall be under the administration of the Presidium, subject at all times to specific instructions and approval by the World Parliament.

2. All treaties and agreements with nations remaining outside the Federation of Earth shall be negotiated by the Presidium and must be ratified by a simple majority vote of the three Houses of the World Parliament.

3. The World Government for the Federation of Earth shall establish and maintain peaceful relations with other planets and celestial bodies where and when it may become possible to establish communications with the possible inhabitants thereof.

4. All explorations into outer space, both within and beyond the solar system in which Planet Earth is located, shall be under the exclusive direction and control of the World

Government, and shall be conducted in such manner as shall be determined by the World Parliament.

Article 17. Ratification and Implementation

Sec. A. Ratification of the World Constitution

This World Constitution shall be submitted to the nations and people of Earth for ratification by the following procedures:

1. The World Constitution shall be transmitted to the General Assembly of the United Nations Organization and to each national government on Earth, with the request that the World Constitution be submitted to the national legislature of each nation for preliminary ratification and to the people of each nation for final ratification by popular referendum.

2. Preliminary ratification by a national legislature shall be accomplished by simple majority vote of the national legislature.

3. Final ratification by the people shall be accomplished by a simple majority of votes cast in a popular referendum, provided that a minimum of twenty-five percent of eligible voters of age eighteen years and over have cast ballots within the nation or country or within World Electoral and Administrative Districts.

4. In the case of a nation without a national legislature, the head of the national government shall be requested to give preliminary ratification and to submit the World Constitution for final ratification by popular referendum.

5. In the event that a national government, after six months, fails to submit the World Constitution for ratification as requested, then the global agency assuming responsibility for the worldwide ratification campaign may proceed to conduct a direct referendum for ratification of the World Constitution by the people. Direct referendums may be organized on the basis of entire nations or countries, or on the basis of existing defined communities within nations.

6. In the event of a direct ratification referendum, final ratification shall be accomplished by a majority of the votes cast whether for an entire nation or for a World Electoral and Administrative District, provided that ballots are cast by a minimum o f twenty-five percent of eligible voters of the area who are over eighteen years of age.

7. For ratification by existing communities within a nation, the procedure shall be to request local communities, cities, counties, states, provinces, cantons, prefectures, tribal jurisdictions, or other defined political units within a nation to ratify the World Constitution, and to submit the World Constitution for a referendum vote by the citizens of the community or political unit. Ratification may be accomplished by proceeding in this way until all eligible voters of age eighteen and above within the nation or World Electoral and Administrative District have had the opportunity to vote, provided that ballots are cast by a minimum of twenty-five percent of those eligible to vote.

8. Prior to the Full Operative Stage of World Government, as defined under Section E of Article XVII, the universities, colleges and scientific academies and institutes in any country may ratify the World Constitution, thus qualifying them

for participation in the nomination of Members of the World Parliament to the House of Counselors.

9. In the case of those nations currently involved in serious international disputes or where traditional enmities and chronic disputes may exist among two or more nations, a procedure for concurrent paired ratification shall be instituted whereby the nations which are parties to a current or chronic international dispute or conflict may simultaneously ratify the World Constitution. In such cases, the paired nations shall be admitted into the Federation of Earth simultaneously, with the obligation for each such nation to immediately turn over all weapons of mass destruction to the World Government, and to turn over the conflict or dispute for mandatory peaceful settlement by the World Government.

10. Each nation or political unit which ratifies this World Constitution, either by preliminary ratification or final ratification, shall be bound never to use any armed forces or weapons of mass destruction against another member or unit of the Federation of Earth, regardless of how long it may take to achieve full disarmament of all the nations and political units which ratify this World Constitution.

11. When ratified, the Constitution for the Federation of Earth becomes the supreme law of Earth. By the act of ratifying this Earth Constitution, any provision in the Constitution or Legislation of any country so ratifying, which is contrary to this Earth Constitution, is either repealed or amended to conform with the Constitution for the Federation of Earth, effective as soon as 25 countries have so ratified. The amendment of National or State Constitutions to allow entry into World Federation is not necessary prior to ratification of the Constitution for the Federation of Earth.

Sec. B. Stages of Implementation

1. Implementation of this World Constitution and the establishment of World Government pursuant to the terms of this World Constitution, may be accomplished in three stages, as follows, in addition to the stage of a Provisional World Government as provided under Article 19:

    a. First Operative Stage of World Government.

    b. Second Operative Stage of World Government.

    c. Full Operative Stage of World Government.

2. At the beginning and during each stage, the World Parliament and the World Executive together shall establish goals and develop means for the progressive implementation of the World Constitution, and for the implementation of legislation enacted by the World Parliament.

Sec. C. First Operative Stage of World Government

1. The first operative stage of World Government under this World Constitution shall be implemented when the World Constitution is ratified by a sufficient number of nations and/or people to meet one or the other of the following conditions or equivalent :

    a. Preliminary or final ratification by a minimum of twenty-five nations, each having a population of more than 100,000.

b. Preliminary or final ratification by a minimum of ten nations above 100,000 population, together with ratification by direct referendum within a minimum of fifty additional World Electoral and Administrative Districts.

c. Ratification by direct referendum within a minimum of 100 World Electoral and Administrative Districts, even though no nation as such has ratified.

2. The election of Members of the World Parliament to the House of Peoples shall be conducted in all World Electoral and Administrative Districts where ratification has been accomplished by popular referendum.

3. The Election of Members of the World Parliament to the House of Peoples may proceed concurrently with direct popular referendums both prior to and after the First Operative Stage of World Government is reached.

4. The appointment or election of Members of the World Parliament to the House of Nations shall proceed in all nations where preliminary ratification has been accomplished.

5. One-fourth of the Members of the World Parliament to the House of Counselors may be elected from nominees submitted by universities and colleges which have ratified the World Constitution.

6. The World Presidium and the Executive Cabinet shall be elected according to the provisions in article VI, except that in the absence of a House of Counselors, the nominations shall be made by the members of the House of Peoples and of the House of Nations in joint session. Until this is accomplished, the Presidium and Executive Cabinet of the Provisional World Government as provided in Article 19, shall continue to serve.

7. When composed, the Presidium for the first operative stage of World Government shall assign or re-assign Ministerial posts among Cabinet and Presidium members, and shall immediately establish or confirm a World Disarmament Agency and a World Economic and Development Organization.

8. Those nations which ratify this World Constitution and thereby join the Federation of Earth, shall immediately transfer all weapons of mass destruction as defined and designated by the World Disarmament Agency to that Agency. (See Article 19, Sections A-2-d, B-6 and E-5). The World Disarmament Agency shall immediately immobilize all such weapons and shall proceed with dispatch to dismantle, convert to peacetime use, re-cycle the materials thereof or otherwise destroy all such weapons. During the first operative stage of World Government, the ratifying nations may retain armed forces equipped with weapons other than weapons of mass destruction as defined and designated by the World Disarmament Agency.

9. Concurrently with the reduction or elimination of such weapons of mass destruction and other military expenditures as can be accomplished during the first operative stage of World Government, the member nations of the Federation of Earth shall pay annually to the Treasury of the World Government amounts equal to one-half the amounts saved from their respective national military budgets during the last year before joining the Federation, and shall continue such payments until the full operative stage of World Government is reached. The World Gov-

ernment shall use fifty percent of the funds thus received to finance the work and projects of the World Economic Development Organization.

10. The World Parliament and the World Executive shall continue to develop the organs, departments, agencies and activities originated under the Provisional World Government, with such amendments as deemed necessary; and shall proceed to establish and beg in the following organs, departments and agencies of the World Government, if not already underway, together with such other departments, and agencies as are considered desirable and feasible during the first operative stage of World Government:

a. The World Supreme Court;

b. The Enforcement System;

c. The World Ombudsmus;

d. The World Civil Service Administration;

e. The World Financial Administration;

f. The Agency for Research and Planning;

g. The Agency for Technological and Environmental Assessment;

h. An Emergency Earth Rescue Administration, concerned with all aspects of climate change and related factors;

i. An Integrated Global Energy System, based on environmentally safe sources;

j. A World University System, under the Department of Education;

k. A World Corporations Office, under the Department of Commerce and Industry;

l. The World Service Corps;

m. A World Oceans and Seabeds Administration.

11. At the beginning of the first operative stage, the Presidium in consultation with the Executive Cabinet shall formulate and put forward a proposed program for solving the most urgent world problems currently confronting humanity.

12. The World Parliament shall proceed to work upon solutions to world problems. The World Parliament and the World Executive working together shall institute through the several organs, departments and agencies of the World Government whatever means shall seem appropriate and feasible to accomplish the implementation and enforcement of world legislation, world law and the World Constitution; and in particular shall take certain decisive actions for the welfare of all people on Earth, applicable throughout the world, including but not limited to the following:

a. Expedite the organization and work of an Emergency Earth Rescue Administration, concerned with all aspects of climate change and climate crises;

b. Expedite the new finance, credit and monetary system, to serve human needs;

c. Expedite an integrated global energy system, utilizing solar energy, hydrogen energy, and other safe and sustainable sources of energy;

d. Push forward a global program for agricultural production to achieve maximum sustained yield under conditions which are ecologically sound;

e. Establish conditions for free trade within the Federation of Earth;

f. Call for and find ways to implement a moratorium on nuclear energy projects until all problems are solved concerning safety, disposal of toxic wastes and the dangers of use or diversion of materials for the production of nuclear weapons;

g. Outlaw and find ways to completely terminate the production of nuclear weapons and all weapons of mass destruction;

h. Push forward programs to assure adequate and non-polluted water supplies and clean air supplies for everybody on Earth;

i. Push forward a global program to conserve and re-cycle the resources of Earth.

j. Develop an acceptable program to bring population growth under control, especially by raising standards of living.

Sec. D. Second Operative Stage of World Government

1. The second operative stage of World Government shall be implemented when fifty percent or more of the nations of Earth have given either preliminary or final ratification to this World Constitution, provided that fifty percent of the total population of Earth is included either within the ratifying nations or within the ratifying nations together with additional World Electoral and Administrative Districts where people have ratified the World Constitution by direct referendum.

2. The election and appointment of Members of the World Parliament to the several Houses of the World Parliament shall proceed in the same manner as specified for the first operative stage in Section C-2,3,4 and 5 of Article 17.

3. The terms of office of the Members of the World Parliament elected or appointed for the first operative stage of World Government, shall be extended into the second operative stage unless they have already served five year terms, in which case new elections or appointments shall be arranged. The terms of hold-over Members of the World Parliament into the second operative stage shall be adjusted to run concurrently with the terms of those who are newly elected at the beginning of the second operative stage.

4. The World Presidium and the Executive Cabinet shall be re-constituted or reconfirmed, as needed, at the beginning of the second operative stage of World Government.

5. The World Parliament and the World Executive shall continue to develop the organs, departments, agencies and activities which are already underway from the first operative stage of World Government, with such amendments as deemed necessary; and shall proceed to establish and develop all other organs and major departments and agencies of the World Government to the extent deemed feasible during the second operative stage.

6. All nations joining the Federation of Earth to compose the second operative stage of World Government, shall immediately transfer all weapons of mass destruction and all other military weapons and equipment to the World Disarmament Agency, which shall immediately immobilize such weapons and equipment and shall proceed forthwith to dismantle, convert to peacetime uses, recycle the materials thereof, or otherwise destroy such weapons and equipment. During the

second operative stage, all armed forces and para-military forces of the nations which have joined the Federation of Earth shall be completely disarmed and either disbanded or converted on a voluntary basis into elements of the non-military World Service Corps.

7. Concurrently with the reduction or elimination of such weapons, equipment and other military expenditures as can be accomplished during the second operative stage of World Government, the member nations of the Federation of Earth shall pay annually to the Treasury of the World Government amounts equal to one-half of the amounts saved from their national military budgets during the last year before joining the Federation and shall continue such payments until the full operative stage of World Government is reached. The World Government shall use fifty percent of the funds thus received to finance the work and projects of the World Economic Development Organization.

8. Upon formation of the Executive Cabinet for the second operative stage, the Presidium shall issue an invitation to the General Assembly of the United Nations Organization and to each of the specialized agencies of the United Nations, as well as to other useful international agencies, to transfer personnel, facilities, equipment, resources and allegiance to the Federation of Earth and to the World Government thereof. The agencies and functions of the United Nations Organization and of its specialized agencies and of other international agencies which may be thus transferred, shall be reconstituted as needed and integrated into the several organs, departments, offices and agencies of the World Government.

9. Near the beginning of the second operative stage, the Presidium in consultation with the Executive cabinet, shall formulate and put forward a proposed program for solving the most urgent world problems currently confronting the people of Earth.

10. The World Parliament shall proceed with legislation necessary for implementing a complete program for solving the current urgent world problems.

11. The World Parliament and the World Executive working together shall develop through the several organs, departments and agencies of the World Government whatever means shall seem appropriate and feasible to implement legislation for solving world problems; and in particular shall take certain decisive actions for the welfare of all people on Earth, including but not limited to the following:

a. Declaring all oceans, seas and canals having supra-national character (but not including inland seas traditionally belonging to particular nations) from twenty kilometers offshore, and all the seabeds thereof, to be under the ownership of the Federation of Earth as the common heritage of humanity, and subject to the control and management of the World Government.

b. Declare the polar caps and surrounding polar areas, including the continent of Antarctica but not areas which are traditionally a part of particular nations, to be world territory owned by the Federation of Earth as the common heritage of humanity, and subject to control and management by the World Government.

c. Outlaw the possession, stockpiling, sale and use of all nuclear weapons, all weapons of mass destruction, and all other military weapons and equipment.

    d. Establish an ever-normal granary and food supply system for the people of Earth.

    e. Develop and carry forward insofar as feasible all actions defined under Sec. C-10 and C-12 of the First Operative Stage.

Sec. E. Full Operative Stage of World Government

1. The full operative stage of World Government shall be implemented when this World Constitution is given either preliminary or final ratification by meeting either condition (a) or (b).

    a. Ratification by eighty percent or more of the nations of Earth comprising at least ninety percent of the population of Earth; or

    b. Ratification which includes ninety percent of Earth's total population, either within ratifying nations or within ratifying nations together with additional World Electoral and Administrative Districts where ratification by direct referendum has been accomplished, as provided in Article 17, Section A.

2. When the full operative stage of World Government is reached, the following conditions shall be implemented:

    a. Elections for Members of the House of Peoples shall be conducted in all World Electoral and Administrative Districts where elections have not already taken place; and Members of the House of Nations shall be elected or appointed by the national legislatures or national governments in all nations where this has not already been accomplished.

    b. The terms of office for Members of the House of Peoples and of the House of Nations serving during the second operative stage, shall be continued into the full operative stage, except for those who have already served five years, in which case elections shall be held or appointments made as required.

    c. The terms of office for all holdover Members of the House of Peoples and of the House of Nations who have served less than five years, shall be adjusted to run concurrently with those Members of the World Parliament whose terms are beginning with the full operative stage.

    d. The second 100 Members of the House of Counselors shall be elected according to the procedure specified in Section E of Article 5. The terms of office for holdover Members of the House of Counselors shall run five more years after the beginning of the full operative stage, while those beginning their terms with the full operative stage shall serve ten years.

    e. The Presidium and the Executive Cabinet shall be reconstituted in accordance with the provisions of Article VI.   f. All organs of the World Government shall be made fully operative, and shall be fully developed for the effective administration and implementation of world legislation, world law and the provisions of this World Constitution.

    g. All nations which have not already done so shall immediately transfer all military weapons and equipment to the World Disarmament Agency, which shall immediately immobilize all such weapons and shall proceed forthwith to dismantle, convert to peaceful usage, recycle the materials thereof, or otherwise to destroy such weapons and equipment.

h. All armies and military forces of every kind shall be completely disarmed, and either disbanded or converted and integrated on a voluntary basis into the non-military World Service Corps.

i. All viable agencies of the United Nations Organization and other viable international agencies established among national governments, together with their personnel, facilities and resources, shall be transferred to the World Government and reconstituted and integrated as may be useful into the organs, departments, offices, institutes, commissions, bureaus and agencies of the World Government.

j. The World Parliament and the World Executive shall continue to develop the activities and projects which are already underway from the second operative stage of World Government, with such amendments as deemed necessary; and shall proceed with a complete and full scale program to solve world problems and serve the welfare of all people on Earth, in accordance with the provisions of this World Constitution.

Sec. F. Costs of Ratification

The work and costs of private Citizens of Earth for the achievement of a ratified Constitution for the Federation of Earth, are recognized as legitimate costs for the establishment of constitutional world government by which present and future generations will benefit, and shall be repaid double the original amount by the World Financial Administration of the World Government when it becomes operational after 25 countries have ratified this Constitution for the Federation of Earth. Repayment specifically includes contributions to the World Government Funding Corporation and other costs and expenses recognized by standards and procedures to be established by the World Financial Administration.

Article 18. Amendments

1. Following completion of the first operative stage of World Government, amendments to this World Constitution may be proposed for consideration in two ways:

a. By a simple majority vote of any House of the World Parliament.

b. By petitions signed by a total of 200,000 persons eligible to vote in world elections from a total of at least twenty World Electoral and Administrative Districts where the World Constitution has received final ratification.

2. Passage of any amendment proposed by a House of the World Parliament shall require an absolute two-thirds majority vote of each of the three Houses of the World Parliament voting separately.

3. An amendment proposed by popular petition shall first require a simple majority vote of the House of Peoples, which shall be obliged to take a vote upon the proposed amendment. Passage of the amendment shall then require an absolute two-thirds majority vote of each of the three Houses of the World Parliament voting separately.

4. Periodically, but no later than ten years after first convening the World Parliament for the First Operative Stage of World Government, and every 20 years

thereafter, the Members of the World Parliament shall meet in special session comprising a Constitutional Convention to conduct a review of this World Constitution to consider and propose possible amendments, which shall then require action as specified in Clause 2 of Article XVIII for passage.

5. If the First Operative Stage of World Government is not reached by the year 1995, then the Provisional World Parliament, as provided under Article XIX, may convene another session of the World Constituent Assembly to review the Constitution for the Federation of Earth and consider possible amendments according to procedure established by the Provisional World Parliament.

6. Except by following the amendment procedures specified herein, no part of this World Constitution may be set aside, suspended or subverted, neither for emergencies nor caprice nor convenience.

Article 19. Provisional World Government

Sec. A. Actions to be Taken by the World Constituent Assembly

Upon adoption of the World Constitution by the World Constituent Assembly, the Assembly and such continuing agency or agencies as it shall designate shall do the following, without being limited thereto:

1. Issue a Call to all Nations, communities and people of Earth to ratify this World Constitution for World Government.

2. Establish the following preparatory commissions:
    a. Ratification Commission.
    b. World Elections Commission.
    c. World Development Commission.
    d. World Disarmament Commission.
    e. World Problems Commission.
    f. Nominating Commission.
    g. Finance Commission.
    h. Peace Research and Education Commission.
    i. Special commissions on each of several of the most urgent world problems.
    j. Such other commissions as may be deemed desirable in order to proceed with the Provisional World Government.

3. Convene Sessions of a Provisional World Parliament when feasible under the following conditions:
    a. Seek the commitment of 500 or more delegates to attend, representing people in 20 countries from five continents, and having credentials defined by Article 19, Section C;
    b. The minimum funds necessary to organize the sessions of the Provisional World Parliament are either on hand or firmly pledged.
    c. Suitable locations are confirmed at least nine months in advance, unless emergency conditions justify shorter advance notice.

Sec. B. Work of the Preparatory Commissions

1. The Ratification Commission shall carry out a worldwide campaign for the ratification of the World Constitution, both to obtain preliminary ratification by national governments, including national legislatures, and to obtain final ratification by people, including communities. The ratification commission shall continue its work until the full operative stage of World Government is reached.

2. The World Elections Commission shall prepare a provisional global map of World Electoral and Administrative Districts and Regions which may be revised during the first or second operative stage of World Government, and shall prepare and proceed with plans to obtain the election of Members of the World Parliament to the House of Peoples and to the House of Counselors. The World Elections Commission shall in due course be converted into the World Boundaries and Elections Administration.

3. After six months, in those countries where national governments have not responded favorable to the ratification call, the Ratification Commission and the World Elections Commission may proceed jointly to accomplish both the ratification of the World Constitution by direct popular referendum and concurrently the election of Members of the World Parliament.

4. The Ratification Commission may also submit the World Constitution for ratification by universities and colleges throughout the world.

5. The World Development Commission shall prepare plans for the creation of a World Economic Development Organization to serve all nations and people ratifying the World Constitution, and in particular less developed countries, to begin functioning when the Provisional World Government is established.

6. The World Disarmament Commission shall prepare plans for the organization of a World Disarmament Agency, to begin functioning when the Provisional World Government is established.

7. The World Problems Commission shall prepare an agenda of urgent world problems, with documentation, for possible action by the Provisional World Parliament and Provisional World Government.

8. The Nominating Commission shall prepare, in advance of convening the Provisional World Parliament, a list of nominees to compose the Presidium and the Executive Cabinet for the Provisional World Government.

9. The Finance Commission shall work on ways and means for financing the Provisional World Government.

10. The several commissions on particular world problems shall work on the preparation of proposed world legislation and action on each problem, to present to the Provisional World Parliament when it convenes.

Sec. C. Composition of the Provisional World Parliament

1. The Provisional World Parliament shall be composed of the following members:

   a. All those who were accredited as delegates to the 1977 and 1991 Sessions of the World Constituent Assembly, as well as to any previous Session of the Provisional World Parliament, and who re-confirm their support for the Constitution for the Federation of Earth, as amended.

  b. Persons who obtain the required number of signatures on election petitions, or who are designated by Non-Governmental Organizations which adopt approved resolutions for this purpose, or who are otherwise accredited according to terms specified in Calls which may be issued to convene particular sessions of the Provisional World Parliament.

  c. Members of the World Parliament to the House of Peoples who are elected from World Electoral and Administrative Districts up to the time of convening the Provisional World Parliament. Members of the World Parliament elected to the House of Peoples may continue to be added to the Provisional World Parliament until the first operative stage of World Government is reached.

  d. Members of the World Parliament to the House of Nations who are elected by national legislatures or appointed by national governments up to the time of convening the Provisional World Parliament. Members of the World Parliament to the House of Nations may continue to be added to the Provisional World Parliament until the first operative stage of World Government is reached.

  e. Those universities and colleges which have ratified the World Constitution may nominate persons to serve as Members of the World Parliament to the House of Counselors. The House of Peoples and House of Nations together may then elect from such nominees up to fifty Members of the World Parliament to serve in the House of Counselors of the Provisional World Government.

2. Members of the Provisional World Parliament in categories (a) and (b) as defined above, shall serve only until the first operative stage of World Government is declared, but may be duly elected to continue as Members of the World Parliament during the first operative stage.

Sec. D. Formation of the Provisional World Executive

1. As soon as the Provisional World Parliament next convenes, it will elect a new Presidium for the Provisional World Parliament and Provisional World Government from among the nominees submitted by the Nominating Commission.

2. Members of the Provisional World Presidium shall serve terms of three years, and may be re-elected by the Provisional World Parliament, but in any case shall serve only until the Presidium is elected under the First Operative Stage of World Government.

3. The Presidium may make additional nominations for the Executive Cabinet.

4. The Provisional World Parliament shall then elect the members of the Executive Cabinet.

5. The Presidium shall then assign ministerial posts among the members of the Executive Cabinet and of the Presidium.

6. When steps (1) through (4) of section D are completed, the Provisional World Government shall be declared in operation to serve the welfare of humanity.

Sec. E. First Actions of the Provisional World Government

1. The Presidium, in consultation with the Executive Cabinet, the commissions on particular world problems and the World Parliament, shall define a program for

action on urgent world problems.

2. The Provisional World Parliament shall go to work on the agenda of world problems, and shall take any and all actions it considers appropriate and feasible, in accordance with the provisions of this World Constitution.

3. Implementation of and compliance with the legislation enacted by the Provisional World Parliament shall be sought on a voluntary basis in return for the benefits to be realized, while strength of the Provisional World Government is being increased by the progressive ratification of the World Constitution.

4. Insofar as considered appropriate and feasible, the Provisional World Parliament and Provisional World Executive may undertake some of the actions specified under Section C-12 of Article 17 for the first operative stage of World Government.

5. The World Economic Development Organization and the World Disarmament Agency shall be established, for correlated actions.

6. The World Parliament and the Executive Cabinet of the Provisional World Government shall proceed with the organization of other organs and agencies of the World Government on a provisional basis, insofar as considered desirable and feasible, in particular those specified under Section C-10 of Article 17.

7. The several preparatory commissions on urgent world problems may be reconstituted as Administrative Departments of the Provisional World Government.

8. In all of its work and activities, the Provisional World Government shall function in accordance with the provisions of this Constitution for the Federation of Earth.

*   *   *   *   *

Campaign for Ratification and Signatures

The *Constitution for the Federation of Earth* was originally ratified at the second session of the World Constituent Assembly held in Innsbruck, Austria in June 1977, and was amended and ratified at the fourth session of the World Constituent Assembly held at Troia, Portugal in May 1991. The amended Constitution is being personally ratified by outstanding personalities throughout the world as the campaign for ratification by the people and governments of the world gets underway. The following sixteen pages contain the signatures from both sessions.

After the final changes were made at the Fourth Constituent Assembly, the Global Ratification and Elections Network (GREN) was formed to work with the World Constitution and Parliament Association (WCPA) to obtain ratification of the Constitution by the people and nations of Earth under the provisions set forth in Article 17. In 2004, GREN was transformed into the Earth Federation Movement (EFM) that works both for ratification and continues to build the institutions of the Earth Federation within the shell of the old, decaying world order.

Participants in the World Constituent Assembly, 16 to 29 of June, 1977, have affixed their
signatures to the draft of the CONSTITUTION FOR THE FEDERATION OF EARTH herewith:

[signatures]   India

     MEXICO

Philip Isely   EARTH, USA

Lucile W. Green   Earth, USA

[signature]   Hon. Legal Advisor

[signature]   Canada

T.P. Amerasinghe   Sri Lanka.

[signature]   [Nepal]

Archie Casely Hayford   Ghana.

K. Koma   Botswana

Helen Tucker (Canada)   Women's Universal Movement

[signature]   Fed. Rep. of Germany.

Thane Read   U.S.A.

[signature] Spencer   India.

Rachoommuk A. Ammugy   Thailand.

Rose J. Chesney   Australia.

[signature]   [Germany]

[signature]   Netherlands

Toshio Miyake   JAPAN

Name	Country
ANDREA von SCHNOY	GERMANY
Edith Barvich	Germany
Gisela Gärtnel	Germany
Klaus Frahur-Schlichtmann	Germany
Ann Miscle	World, U.S.A
Gerald Mische	U.S.A.
Dr. Ludwig C. beau	W. Germany
Dr. Fred Karl Scheele	U.S.A.
Maasauer	Germany
Odja Jäger	Germany
Beatrice Meyers	U.S.A.
Elisabeth Klauenbaeur	INNSBRUCK
Theo Fenelia	Switzerland
Dr. Helen K. Billings	USA
Magister Kirsti Baltthaspi.	Finland live in Mexico.
Robert Rosamond	United Peoples Federation of Earth
Valerie Hagenhuber	Austria
Herbert Grodler	

Name	Country
R. Gamby	U. S. A
Malhotra India	
nd Heuer	Schweiz
SINGH AZAD.	(INDIA)
.. Geeta Shah	INDIA.
Treli	Schweiz
Krenty	Innsbruz
ne Allen	U. S. A
M. Bharucha	India.
.Bryant	USA
C. Burrus	UsiA. World
Murray se (Per Christ USA)	
m R Lad	Botswana
Renée Dangoor	United Kingdor
. Lelaka	Botswana
lohman	
elt LLelman	Australia
	Australie
us Galks	AUSTRIA

Name	Country
Dr. Hildegard Durfee	U.S.A.
Hera Lynne Allen	
Samar Basu	India.
Robert W. Kaminski	Earth USA, Wilm Del
Hobe Thya	Holland
Yogi Shantiswaroop.	India - for one world
Carmel Kussman	U.S.A.
Mortimer Lifely	U.S.A.
Hermann Ways	Austria
Kim Harolde	Canada
Ann Marin	P.R
Naim Dangoor	U.K.
	(Sri Lanka)
	Bangalore - India
Bernadette F. Trattner.	
Craig Orr White, Ph.D.	Ohio. U.S.A.
Everett Reffni	Wis., U.S.A.
Mildred E. Parmelee.	U.S.A.
Dr (Mrs) Kamon Patel	Pondichery (India)
Margaret Gadge	United Kingdom.

Name	Country
Bandula Sri Gunawardhana	Sri Lanka
Margaret Isely	U.S.A.
Matfenbenja Misibett	Austria
(signature)	Puerto Rico
Gregory Alexander	U.S.A.
Edward R. Leader	Puerto Rico
(signature)	India
Dorothy L. Mann Baker	U.S.A.
Carl F. Cottam	Earth !
(signature)	Denmark
Heather Isely	U. S. A.
Foster Parmelee	U.S.A.
Ogelo Justus	Kenya
J. A. Hartwig	W. Germany
Kemper Isely	U.S.A.
Bernard Shaw Maji	Nigeria
Mitsuo Miyake	Japan
Johanna Materbell	Netherlands
(signature)	Botswana

Name	Address
Eggert, Charlotte Luise	Deutschland
Josephine Baker	N.Y. e. WPPC
Martha Fillebrown	USA
Pistenolli Kurt	Innsbruck Austria
Suzanne Gomberg	San Francisco USA
+ Fokapfel Heiner	Innsbruck
+usapfel smille	Innsbruck
Leora Herold	Mexico City
Hazel Ingeborg	Germany
Ghroeding, Hans-Friedrich	Germany
Nay, Ludwig	Germany
B. Molcar	World Citizen
Leland P. Stewart	Los Angeles
John Stockwell	San Francisco
Guido Graziani	Rome, Italy
Dorothea Saccari	Hannover, WOMAN

Name　　　　　　　　　　Country

[Signatures]

Holla

Gren

U.S.A.

U S A

USA

stateless

Pakistan

Italy　México

Por el mundo espiritual
Dr. José M. Gálvez

Por la unión en el arte en el espíritu (México)
Sra. Elsa Green

Rev. GAGPA　Maria Carlota Ade Estrada (México)
"Por el mundo Espiritual"
Rev. Gagpa (México)
"Por el mundo Espiritual"
Adolfo Olivera (México)

Name   Country

Trakoga Ruge   Mexico

Jufani Wollager   Austria

[signature]   Austria

Herbert Jhin   Deutschland (BRD)

Siddharta Patel   Kenya.

Kalaben Patet   Indian

Umesh A Patel   Great Britain.

Kumud I. Patel   Great Britain.

Ahmad Subardjo g   Indonesia

Asetyobudianti   Indonesia

Sybil Stridt   New Zealand + USA

Alice Stephens   England.

Elizabeth E. Stewart   United States

[signature]   *[signature]* Bangladesh

HARSHAJAN SIKH Khalsa
yogiji   USA
Sikh Dharma   Western Hemp.

Note: This list of initial signers of the CONSTITUTION FOR THE FEDERATION OF EARTH would include several hundred more persons from fifty countries, prevented only by the cost of travel to attend the Assembly at Innsbruck, Austria.

PERSONAL RATIFIERS OF THE CONSTITUTION FOR THE FEDERATION OF EARTH
AS AMENDED AT THE 4th SESSION OF THE WORLD CONSTITUENT ASSEMBLY
HELD AT TROIA, PORTUGAL, 29th APRIL, to 9th MAY, 1991

Prof. Dr. Kalman Abraham, Hungary

Atiku Abubakar, Nigeria

Dr. Ebenezer Ade. Adenekan, Nigeria

Malcolm S. Adiseshiah, India

Abdur Rahim Ahamed, Bangladesh

Shahzada Kabir Ahmed

Mohsin A. Alaini, Yemen

MD. Nural Alam, U.S.A.

MD. Maser Ali, Bangladesh

Dr. Terence P. Amerasinghe, Sri Lanka

Samir Amin, Senegal

Benjamin K. Amonoo, Ghana

George Anca, Romania

Mauricio Andres-Ribeiro, Brazil

Dr. Munawar A. Anees, U.S.A.

Rev. Ebenezer Annan, Ivory Coast

Jose Ayala-Lasso, Ecuador

Ir. Hasan Basri, Indonesia

Samar Basu, India

Tony Benn, United Kingdom

PERSONAL RATIFIERS - page 2

Prof. Mrs. Edvige Bestazzi, Italy

Petter Jakob Bjerve, Norway

Goran von Bonsdorff, Finland

Selma Brackman, U.S.A.

Jean-Marie BRETON

Jean-Marie Breton, Int. Regis. World Citizens

Tomas Bruckman, Germany (East)

Dennis Brutus, South Africa (U.S.A.)

Dr. Mihai Titus Carapancea, Romania

Prof. Henri Cartan, France

Amb. Khub Chand, India

Dr. Sripati Chandrasekhar, India

Most Rev. French Chang-Him, Seychelles

Munyaradzi Chiwashira, Zimbabwe

Dr. Pratap Chandra Chunder, India

Prof. Dr. Rodney Daniel, France

Daniel G. De Culla, Spain

Dr. Dimitrios J. Delivanis, Greece

Prof. Dr. Francis Dessart, Belgium

Raymond F. Douw, Germany

Prof. Hans-Peter Duerr, Germany

Kennedy Emekan, Nigeria

M. Necati Munir Ertekun, Cyprus

Douglas Nixon Everingham, Australia

John R. Ewbank, U.S.A.

PERSONAL RATIFIERS – page 3

Marjorie Ewbank, U.S.A.

Miss Lianmangi Fanai, India

Dr. Mark Farber, U.S.A.

Feng Ping-Chung, China

Prof. Dr. Mihnea Georghiu, Romania

Lucile W. Green, U.S.A.

Dr. Dauji Gupta, India

Kisholoy Gupta, India

Takeshi Haruki, Japan

Dr. Gerhard Herzberg, Canada

Jozsef Holp, Hungary

A. K. Fazlul Hoque, Bangladesh

Chowdhury Anwar Husain, Bangladesh

Margaret Isely, U.S.A. (Earth)

Philip Isely, U.S.A. (Earth)

Ram K. Jiwanmitra, Nepal

Roy E. Johnstone, Jamaica

Mohammed Kamaluddin, Bangladesh

Mohammad Rezaul Karim, Bangladesh

Rev. George Karunakeran, India

Dr. Inamullah Khan, Pakistan

Johnson S. Khan, Pakistan

Roger Kotila, Ph.D., U.S.A.

PERSONAL RATIFIERS - page 6

Prof. Sir A. M. Sadek, South Africa

Abdus Salam, Italy

Akbar Ali Saleh, Comoros Islands

Blagovest Sendov, Bulgaria

Indira Shrestha, Nepal

Rabi Charan Shrestha, Nepal

Jon Silkin, United Kingdom

Jozef Simuth, Slovak Republic

Dr. Kewal Singh, India

Blaine Sloan, U.S.A.

Ross Smyth, Canada

Lord Donald Soper, United Kingdom

Scott Jefferson Starquester, U.S.A.

Homi J. H. Taleyarkhan, India

Rev. Yoshiaki Toeda, Japan

Dr. Duja K. Torki, Tunisia

Helen Tucker, Canada

Evelyn Utulu, Nigeria

Mrs. Justina N. Uwechue, Nigeria

Ogieva O. Uwuigbe, Nigeria

Ann Valentin, U.S.A.

Mohamed Ezzedine Mili, Switzerland

Rev. Toshic Miyake, Japan

Shettima Ali Monguno, Nigeria

Swapan Mukherjee, India

Hanna Newcombe, Canada

Brij P. Nigam, India

Josephine Okafor, Nigeria

Johnson Olatunde, Sierre Leone

Rev. Nelson Onono-Onweng, Uganda

Umit Ozturk, Turkey

Yasar Ozturk, Turkey

Linus Pauling, U.S.A.

Fernando Perez Tella, Spain

Emil Otto Peter, Austria

Dr. Alex Quaison-Sackey, Ghana

Soili Raikkonen, Finland

Sudhir Kumar Rangh, India

Thane Read, U.S.A.

Dr. Sayed Qassem Reshtia, Switzerland

Erzebet Rethy, Hungary

Miguel B. Ricardo, Portugal

G. Rivas Mijares, Venezuela

Reinhart Ruge, Mexico

PERSONAL RATIFIERS - page 4

David M. Krieger, U.S.A.

Diemuth Kuebart, Germany

Jul Lag, Norway

Ben M. Leito, Netherlands Antilles

Thomas Lim, East Malaysia

Adam Lopatka, Poland

Anwarul Majid, Bangladesh

Dr. M. Sadiq Malik, Pakistan

Guy Marchand, France

Alvin M. Marks, U.S.A.

Bernardshaw Mazi, Nigeria

Dr. Zhores A. Medvedev, U. K. (USSR)

Anna Medvegey, Hungary

R. C. Mehrotra, India

Charles Mercieca, U.S.A.

Lt. Col. Pedro B. Merida, Philippines

Yerucham Meshel, Israel

Sheta Mikayele, Zaire

PERSONAL RATIFIERS - page 7

T. Nejat Veziroglu, U.S.A.

Jorgen Laursen Vig, Denmark

George Wald, U.S.A.

Prof. D. A. Walker, United Kingdom

Richard W. Wilbur, U.S.A.

Dr. Sylwester Zawadzki, Poland

Additional Original Ratifiers:

Kenneth B. Clark, U.S.A.

David Daube, U.S.A.

Nzo Ekangaki, Cameroon

ADDITIONAL PERSONAL RATIFIERS -- Signatures on file at the World Office of the W.C.P.A.

PROF. CHIEF J. O. AGBOYE, Nigeria

DR. FRANCIS ALEXIS, Grenada

SIR ABDUL W. M. AMEER, Sri Lanka

HANAN AWWAD, Palestine

HON. LUKASZ BALCER, Poland

CHIEF DR. KOLAWOLE BALOGUN, Nigeria

DR. SABURI O. BIOBAKU, Nigeria

DR. JUR. JAN CARNOGURSKY, Slovakia

DR. GOUIN CEDIEU, Cote D'Ivoire

AMARSINH CHAUDHARY, India

MDM. JUSTICE L. P. CHIBESAKUNDA, Zambia

ASHIS KUMAR DE, India

DR. MOSTAFA EL DESOUKY, Kuwait

DR. ROLF EDBERG, Sweden

DR. BENJAMIN B. FERENCZ, U.S.A.

PROF. VITALII I. GOLDANSKII, Russia

PROF. DR. ZBIGNIEW GERTYCH, Poland

PROF. ERROL E. HARRIS, U.S.A./U.K.

LIC. JUAN HORACIO S., Argentina

SIR DR. AKANU IBIAM, Nigeria

49.

ADDITIONAL PERSONAL RATIFIERS --

K. JEEVAGATHAS, Sri Lanka

R. B. JUNOO, India

DR. JAN KLEINERT, Slovakia

DR. YURI A. KOSYGIN, Russia

ADV. RANJAN LAKHANPAL, India

ADV. AQIL LODHI, Pakistan

DR. NIKOLAI A. LOGATCHEV, Russia

MOCHTAR LUBIS, Indonesia

PERRY MAISON, Ghana

KAPASA MAKASA, Zambia

DR. IGNACY MALECKI, Poland

PROF. IVAN MALEK, Czechoslovakia

DR. MRS. ALLA G. MASSEVITCH, Russia

MHLAGANO S. MATSEBULA, Switzerland

DR. MIHAJLO MIHAJLOV, Yugoslavia

HON. RAM NIWAS MIRDHA, India

DR. ROBERT MULLER, Costa Rica

JUSTICE M. A. MUTTALIB, Bangladesh

DR. SITEKE G. MWALE, Zambia

DR. RASHMI MAYUR, India

DR. JAYANT V. NARLIKAR, India

PAUL NKADI, Nigeria

OSMAN N. OREK, Turkish Rep. N. Cyprus

PROF. LENARD PAL, Poland

PROF. JEAN-CLAUDE PECKER, France

PROF. GAMINI L. PEIRIS, Sri Lanka

GERARD PIEL, U.S.A.

REV. DANIEL O. PEPRAH, Cote D'Ivoire

PROF. M. S. RAJAN, India

PROF. C. N. R. RAO, India

SRI N. S. RAO, India

MICHAL RUSINEK, Poland

DR. FREDERICK SANGER, U.K.

SIR AINSWORTH D. SCOTT, Jamaica

DAVID SHAHAR, Israel

TOMA SIK, Israel

CHANDAN SOM, India

HON. ROBERT D. G. STANBURY, Canada

DR. BOGDAN SUCHODOLSKI, Poland

ABDUL HATHY SULAIMAN, Sri Lanka

DR. SOL TAX, U.S.A.

MILLICENT OBENEWAA TERRY, Ghana

DR. WALTER E. THIRRING, Austria

MOST REV. DESMOND M. TUTU, South Africa

KENJI URATA, Japan

DR. PIETER VAN DIJK, Netherlands

CARLOS WARTER, M.D., U.S.A.

ROD WELFORD, M.L.A., Australia

Since 1991, thousands of additional people from many countries
have placed their signatures on file with the
World Constitution and Parliament Association.

Chapter Five

Summary and Analysis of the Earth Constitution

Glen T. Martin

This chapter examines the main features of the *Constitution for the Federation of Earth* and the democratic world governmental system that it creates. The *Constitution* itself deserves careful study as one of the great documents of the Twentieth Century, going far beyond such documents as the U.N. Universal Declaration of Human Rights. In this small chapter, it is not possible to encompass all the richness of the *Constitution*. An entire volume needs to be written to bring out the wealth and wisdom of this great document. Here I have only attempted to point out its most fundamental and unique features. For clarity, I have placed all quotations from the *Constitution* in italics.

1. The Preamble

The Preamble to the *Earth Constitution* is an important statement in itself. In a mere 246 words, this Preamble crystallizes our situation in the modern world and lays out the justification for world revolution through world law. The Preamble lays out the "ideals" that are embodied in the *Earth Constitution* in a practical and entirely realizable way. It is a summary statement of why a new era is absolutely necessary and why the *Constitution* must be immediately ratified. Let us examine it clause by clause.

"Realizing that Humanity today has come to a turning point in history and that we are on the threshold of an new world order which promises to usher in an era of peace, prosperity, justice and harmony...." The Preamble embodies the clear awareness that a new world order is entirely possible simply by eliminating the impediments to civilization that are today creating a nightmare for the peoples of Earth – the so-called system of "sovereign" nation-states and the system of global monopoly capitalism.

There are many signs that ours is a "threshold" age in poetry, literature, philosophy, and science. The first photos of the Earth from space began to beam back to Earth from the early spaceships of the 1960s. From these recent beginnings, the consciousness has spread rapidly throughout the planet that we are one species living on this tiny, beautiful spaceship of a planet. Today, those photos of the planet from space are everywhere. We are truly on the threshold of an age when the entire planet will unite to solve our common problems and global crises.

"Aware of the interdependence of people, nations and all life...." This is the very principle denied by the nation-state system and the fragmented institutions of the modern world that has dominated the Earth from the Renaissance to the twenty-first century. The system of autonomous nation-states, recognizing no enforceable law above themselves and recognizing only voluntary "treaties" as their guide for international conduct, is the antithesis of this principle of interdependence. Yet this principle has been demonstrated by every modern science, from biology to physics to ecology to sociology (Harris 2000).

The photos of the Earth from space help make this interdependence clear. No artificial political boundaries appear, only a tiny blue-green home to millions of species and seven billion human beings who are only one of these species. Economic and cultural "globalization" has transformed the world in a very short time. Yet our antiquated system of "sovereign" nation-states fractures our world into autonomous units and defeats the globalization of that which is the greatest legacy of modernity: democracy itself. Without global democracy and the worldwide rule of enforceable law, our interdependence and the other aspects of globalization become destructive and dangerous.

"Aware that man's abuse of science and technology has brought Humanity to the brink of disaster through the production of horrendous weaponry of mass destruction and to the brink of ecological and social catastrophe...." The largest scientific effort in history and throughout the twentieth century has been directed toward the creation of ever more hideous means of destroying people and property. Not only "weapons of mass destruction," but automated, computerized, and mechanized weapons systems of every sort have created a nightmare for the people of Earth.

These same vast resources, close to a trillion U.S. dollars per year throughout the last decades of the twentieth century, could have been used to prevent the ecological catastrophe of global warming now engulfing the Earth, a catastrophe that includes vast extinctions of species, desertification of much of the Earth's agricultural land, the flooding of the coastlines of the planet, and ever more devastating super-storms and weather disruptions. Those ratifying the *Earth Constitution* are directly aware of this insanity and the need to end it now.

Weapons of mass destruction on intercontinental missiles can circle the globe in twenty minutes, bringing holocaust to entire nations in seconds. The United States is now working on placing such weapons in space. Science and technology, which could be our greatest benefit for creating a decent world order for everyone, including a healthy environment, instead are used to bring us ever closer to the brink of destruction.

"Aware that the traditional concept of security through military defense is a total illusion both for the present and for the future...." This truth is only now beginning to sink into the peoples of Earth even though it has been self-evident to thoughtful persons since the development of nuclear weapons at the close of World War Two. The intellectual and moral leaders who expressed this at that time, and called for the creation of democratic world government, were ignored.

This group included such eminent scientists and intellectuals as Mortimer Adler, Albert Camus, Norman Cousins, Walter Cronkite, Garry Davis, William O. Douglas, Albert Einstein, Robert Muller, and U-Thant (see Tetalman and Belitsos, 2005). Today we reap the whirlwind, the consequences of our arrogant ignorance and refusal to listen as terrorist attacks occur daily worldwide, as superpowers invade and destroy other nations at will, and as global poverty and environmental destruction grow out of control.

"Aware of the misery and conflicts caused by ever increasing disparity between rich and poor...." The world-system of global monopoly capitalism controlled by the imperial nation-states inevitably leads to this result. The promise of "development" through World Bank and IMF loans is now more and more seen for the lie that it truly is (Martin 2005, ch. 13). It only makes sense that if the vast scientific research and resources of humanity are focused on war and destruction there cannot be the kind of sustainable, equitable development required to end poverty and protect the environment.

Yet the vast propaganda resources of the dominant media and the imperial governments have managed to successfully perpetuate this lie throughout the twentieth century. It is time we based our world order on gigantic truth, not lies. Those who ratify the *Constitution* know that poverty is not a requirement of the human condition but a social and moral blight that can be readily eliminated if there is a world government really concerned for the common good.

"Conscious of our obligation to posterity to save Humanity from imminent and total annihilation...." The ease with which chemical and biological weapons of mass destruction can be created, the growing collapse of the planetary environment, the growing despair of the twenty percent of humanity engulfed in lethal "absolute" poverty, the exploding world population, the continuing militarism and deployment of nuclear weapons is something of which all thoughtful persons cannot help be conscious. To face the impending disasters of the twenty-first century is not alarmism or extremism. It is plain, practical common sense. Unless we act now, there can be no decent future for the Earth or for our children.

"Conscious that Humanity is One despite the existence of diverse nations, races, creeds, ideologies and cultures and that the principle of unity in diversity is the basis for a new age when war shall be outlawed and peace prevail; when the earth's total resources shall be equitably used for human welfare; and when basic human rights and responsibilities shall be shared by all without discrimination...." Once again the Preamble expresses the principle of unity-in-diversity that is at the heart of all viable democracy and is the basic truth of nature, the universe, and society expressed by every modern science. Absolute nation-states and monopoly capitalism are both systems of fragmentation and division that deny the truth of this principle.

The only viable unity on Earth is that of all the world's people, for sovereignty resides with the people of Earth and nowhere else. By embracing this unity, we make possible the real commitment to diversity, for only the collective democratic force of the whole can protect the freedom and individuality of all the diverse parts. We will see this principle embodied over and over in the *Earth Constitution* as we examine it below.

"Conscious of the inescapable reality that the greatest hope for the survival of life on earth is the establishment of a democratic world government; We, citizens of the world, hereby resolve to establish a world federation to be governed in accordance with this constitution for the Federation of Earth." The Preamble ends with the affirmation of the most fundamental truth of our epoch: there is no future for the Earth, even for survival on Earth, without democratic world government. The *Constitution for the Federation of Earth* is a concrete, practical key to our survival and future. It establishes a truly new world order, yet one based on the most obvious common sense, as we will see in this chapter.

2. Article 1: Broad Functions of the Earth Federation

Article I of the *Constitution for the Federation of Earth* lists the six most basic primary functions of the Federation. Let us examine them in turn. (This section is drawn from Martin, 2005, pp. 330-332.)

(1) *"To prevent war, secure disarmament, and resolve territorial and other disputes which endanger peace and human rights."* No longer could the "cycle of violence" exist where rebellions because of the structural violence of extreme poverty meet with repression from third-world governments financed and supported by first-world governments or with "interventions" by first world military to prevent progressive social change from occurring. Nation-states, like the federal government, would be disarmed by law, and the process of changing the structural violence of poverty would be open to non-violent methods of conflict resolution such as the courts, demonstrations, social organizing, creative and just economic policies, and so on.

(2) The second primary function of the federation will be *"To protect universal human rights, including life, liberty, security, democracy, and equal opportunities in life."* Again, the very foundations of the world federal government would allow the progressive transformation of institutionalized violence and exploitation, protecting the security of those who militate for change, and allowing them to legally base their claim for just economic and social institutions on the right to *equal opportunities in life* (an idea that is a bold-faced lie under the capitalist monopoly system).

(3) *"To obtain for all people on Earth the conditions required for equitable economic and social development and for diminishing social differences."* The *Constitution* specifies its affirmation of cultural diversity and local autonomy in other places (for example, Article XIII-16), but here we see concern to diminish the *"social differences"* of the present system of wealth and power versus the poor and exploited. The mandate of the world government, stated repeatedly in the *Constitution*, is *"equal opportunity for useful employment for everyone, with wages or remuneration sufficient to assure human dignity"* (Article XIII-1), in other words, to end the extremes of poverty and wealth worldwide as we know them.

The remaining three "broad functions" of the Federation would again work in favor of the socialist struggle for a fully realized human community:

(4) *To regulate world trade,* (5) *To protect the environment and the ecological fabric of life from all damage,* (6) *To devise and implement solutions to all problems which are beyond the capability of national governments, or which are now or may become of global or international concern or consequence.*

World trade would no longer easily interfere with the rights of every person to a life of dignity with a home, security, health care, and opportunity (Article XIII, numbers 4-7 and 11-13). The exploitation of the poor by multinational corporations would be brought to a rapid end with the regulation of world trade, and the destruction of the global environment though multinational exploitation of resources would be quickly ended (and can only be quickly ended) through the power of the Earth Federation.

For the first time, a consistent set of worldwide laws regarding the environment, enforced by the world police armed only with weapons sufficient to apprehend individuals, could be enacted. (*"World Police shall be armed only with weapons appropriate for the apprehension of individuals responsible for the violation of world law"* (Article 10-C-5).) No longer would the poor nations have to sacrifice their environmental standards to attract rapacious corporations to their resources. International debt will be assumed by the Federation and rapidly paid off in Earth Currency and under terms determined by the Federation. A government concerned with global prosperity within the framework of environmental sustainability would be initiated for the first time in history.

These articles also give the world government the means to raise capital to be used for the global common good through taxes, fees, and other ways of generating federal income. The present system of capitalism unregulated by enforceable world laws cannot with any effectiveness create investment capital capable of promoting the common good, whether within nations or globally. For competition (which is directed to private advantage) will always force private investment capital in the direction of a high enough rate of return to (1) stay in business and (2) make a profit for the private benefit of the wealthy investors. The pressure of the market also mandates (3) continual growth, for as technology and competitors evolve and the rate of return drops, without a continual eye to growth businesses will tend to fail.

Sustainable development is not likely under this system, for the incentive is to neglect, for example, the impact of production on the environment or communities in order to maximize growth and protect the rate of profit (Daly, 1996). World government, on the other hand, will be free of this irrational and destructive pressure now compromising corporations and territorial nation-states. It will be able to invest directly in the common good (the good that makes possible the survival and flourishing of all the parts of the whole) (Martin, 2003).

On the planetary level, the *common good* has taken on a deeper meaning than within nation-states where it rarely has the seriousness of survival itself. Many global problems, including global wealth and poverty, global militarism and lawlessness, and global environmental preservation, are *"beyond the capacity of national governments"* to address. The *World Constitution* provides the only viable hope for humanity to move in the direction of non-military democratic world of justice and peace.

3. The World Parliament

The Sovereignty and democratic authority of the people of Earth is invested in the World Parliament that has the responsibility for protecting the *Constitution* and governing the Earth Federation. Under the *Constitution*, the Parliament consists of three houses: the House of Nations, the House of Peoples, and the House of Counselors.

The House of Nations represents all the nations of the Earth. Every nation will have one, two, or three representatives in the House of Nations, depending on population. The largest nations, therefore, will have three representatives, while even the smallest will have one. This concession to the size of nations in terms of population is, of course, appropriate if this house of Parliament is to be truly representative of the nations of Earth. As is often pointed out, this feature of the *Earth Constitution* makes the House of Nations similar in function to the Senate in the system of the United States, where each state in the U.S. federal structure has its own direct representatives in the legislature.

Because of the size of the House of Nations (perhaps three hundred representatives) whether or not new nations are formed that have a vote and a voice in Parliament will not be a major issue. The tendency will be to want to have a many voices represented as possible, since it is precisely a voice and mechanism for having one's needs and interests represented that undercuts the perceived need for violent or subversive attitudes towards other nations.

The Parliament may well welcome new nations into the community of nations: the Palestinians, for example, and the Kurds. Protecting national "sovereign" territory, and oppressing dissenting groups within nation-states, will no longer be considered necessary for the preservation of the "motherland." Nation-state-hood will no longer be raised to the level of a mythical god-like idol, to be worshiped and preserved at all costs, as it often is under the current world system.

The second house in the tricameral World Parliament is the House of Peoples. One representative will be directly elected by the people from each of 1000 electoral districts worldwide. The electoral districts will be apportioned by population and will conform as far as feasible to existing national boundaries. The people of the Earth in their vast diversity will be directly represented in the World Parliament through 1000 representatives in the House of Peoples.

Like the other houses of Parliament, this house may meet separately or in joint session with the other houses. The *Constitution* defines the parameters and responsibilities of each of the Houses as separate houses and as part of the combined World Parliament. This system of direct representation of the people in districts apportioned by population is often compared with the House of Representatives within the U.S. internal governance system.

As the population of the Earth continues to explode uncontrollably, the number of persons represented by each of the 1000 representatives in the House of Peoples increases. As the population of the Earth approaches seven billion in this year of 2005, there is, of course, great cause for concern among thoughtful people. Economists and thinkers concerning ecological sustainability such as Herman E. Daly (1996) estimate a sustainable population for the Earth at perhaps 2-3 billion persons.

The *Constitution* was written to prevent such uncontrollable disasters. However, as time passes and the Earth sinks ever farther into environmental disaster, military disaster, population disaster, and the disaster of poverty, disease, and misery, the task before the initial World Parliament and government of the Earth Federation becomes ever-more immense and untenable.

The same is true of population in relation to the 1000 representatives in the House of Peoples. At a seven billion population for the Earth this calculates to one representative for every seven million people. Even though the offices of each representative will be very well staffed and designed to interact with the people in his or her constituency, this remains an untenable number of people for each representative. The initial world government could, of course, amend the *Constitution* according to the procedures set forth in Article 18. It could modify the House of Peoples to, for example, 2000 persons and electoral districts.

But the early world government will likely be working through the Earth Emergency Rescue Administration created by the Provisional World Parliament to deal with all the above named global crises, including voluntary, non-coercive population reduction programs. It may be before long the population of the Earth will return to a sustainable size and the 1000 electoral districts and representatives will function very efficiently.

Even though the legislative acts passed by the Provisional World Parliament are not binding on the final World Parliament once the Constitution has been ratified, we delegates of the Provisional World Parliament are making every effort to facilitate the work of the World Parliament through legislative measures addressing the multiple, growing global crises faced by the Earth.

Anticipating these growing crises that the initial World Parliament will face, the Provisional World Parliament passed an Education Act at its Eighth Session in which every public school in the Earth Federation will integrate into its curriculum discussion of sustainability, the population crisis, and quality of life issues. This program will be part of a massive education effort on internet, radio, and television that may alone rapidly influence the people of Earth to reduce family sizes.

The Eighth Session of the Provisional World Parliament also passed an act creating a Global People's Assembly to complement and activate democratic participation and representation within the framework of the present structure of the House of Peoples. The Global People's Assembly sets up mechanisms to draw in grass roots participation from the local neighborhood or village level up through regional levels and integrates this participation into the system of representatives to the House of Peoples.

In this way democracy becomes a real and effective force worldwide and the House of Peoples is strengthened in its role as the direct voice of the people within the Earth Federation. The Global Peoples' Assembly feature of the Earth Federation will greatly enhance the democratic responsiveness of the House of Peoples even at an Earth population of seven billion persons.

The third house is the House of Counselors. This feature of the *Earth Constitution* is a brilliant and unique innovation to the concept of parliamentary democracy. For the House of Counselors is intended to represent the good of the whole, the public interest of the entire planet, the common good. World democracy requires not simply representatives who serve particular interests (whether the people of an electoral district or the interests of a nation-state), but wise, highly educated persons who are concerned with the common good of the Earth, its environmental integrity, its suitability as a home for all the Earth's inhabitants, and the well-being of future generations.

The candidates for the House of Counselors are nominated by the students and faculty from all universities worldwide and elected by the other two houses of Parliament, ten persons each from twenty administrative districts worldwide. The Counselors do not have to reside in the districts that elect them. They are to represent the whole, the common good, the public interest. This feature of the *Earth Constitution* brings democracy itself to an entirely new level, beyond anything that has gone before.

These 200 Counselors will act as part of the combined World Parliament, which will consist of about 1500 representatives altogether.

Their separate function will be largely for nominating candidates for office of the world government within the World Judiciary, World Executive, World Attorneys General and Police and World Ombudsmus, to be elected by a plurality vote of the three houses of Parliament in joint session.

Counselors may also introduce world legislation to Parliament to be debated and voted upon, as will all world legislation, by the three houses in joint session. They may also introduce advisory or scientific documents into the World Parliament as needed by the Parliament to conduct the business of the Earth Federation with the appropriate knowledge and wisdom.

As the above summary makes clear, the *Constitution for the Federation of Earth* establishes a parliamentary system for democratic, federal world government. This is particularly significant for ensuring democracy at the mundial level. A parliamentary system is one in which the supreme authority of government is invested in the World Parliament, itself organized to represent the diverse voices of the people and nations of Earth.

The system does not try to "balance" power between an executive branch, a judicial branch, and a legislative branch of government. For the three houses of the World Parliament are already balanced to democratically represent all possible constituencies of the Earth. The legislative branch (institutionalized so that no group or constituency can assume inordinate power) is directly involved in a number of ways in the running of the four main branches of government that report to it: the World Judiciary, the World Executive, the World Attorneys General and Police, and the World Ombudsmus.

The framers of the *Constitution* understood that a parliamentary system is the best expression of democracy in a world that has eliminated the nation-state-war system. Indeed, ratification of the *Constitution* will initiate a new world order that eliminates the present war system at the heart of today's world disorder. The *Constitution* not only creates a demilitarized world and prohibits any military for the Earth Federation itself, but it institutionalizes a new economic, administrative, and legal order that removes all economic, political, and national incentives for militarism and war.

Just as the system of sovereign nation-states, with its institutionalized insecurity as well as inherent imperial systems of economic domination and exploitation, is the root cause of war, so a new economic and political order under a federation of nations will eliminate the root causes of war. A parliamentary democracy for the world reflects this new order in a direct, democratic way.

We have seen that the present world system is a war system in which nations find their very existence threatened by the possibility of invasion from non-democratic neighboring states, subversion and destabilization by terrorist forces, a never-ending arms race to keep up with other nations in destructive (military) power, or imperial domination by the large and powerful nations of the world. The history of nation-states over the past five centuries shows that nations tend to fall into the trap of the present world system that creates political, economic, and practical incentives for military readiness and organization.

In practice this means that nation-states tend to rely on an executive branch that has authority over the military and administrative branches of government. In a dangerous world, where external and internal subversion or attack many happen at any time, nations feel that power must be invested in a branch of government that has the authority to deal with these dangers.

In today's world, therefore, the legislative branch of government (that in democracy is the most direct voice of the people) is subordinate to the executive. It should be clear that no genuine democracy can or does exist in a dangerous, militarized world characterized by the threats of terrorism, subversion, invasion, domination, or war.

Repeatedly, under the nation-state-war system, we have seen the executive branch become dictatorial, bring the nations into wars, perpetuate secrets and deceits even from its own people, produce corrupt and self-serving leaders, or sacrifice internal freedoms to the need for security. Even the United States, which once seemed a beacon of democracy and freedom to oppressed peoples worldwide, is today seen as a dictatorial center of empire run by an imperial executive branch and a bloated military-security apparatus that are the very antitheses of democracy.

Under the *Earth Constitution* there is no need for a powerful executive branch with command over a ready military and security apparatus. Not only are the economic and political incentives for such a system removed, but the parliamentary system is set up so that the executive branch of government has need of very little power of this kind. The World Executive has no military power (for all military is illegal under the *Constitution*), no police power (for the police are a separate organ of government accountable, like the executive, to the Parliament), no power to suspend the *Constitution* in a state of emergency, and no power to refuse to administer and spend the budget allocated to it by Parliament.

Under this system, the World Parliament is truly the democratic voice the people and nations of the world and institutionalizes a system in which world problems can be dealt with effectively without danger to the democratic structures of government itself. Since the greatest internal danger in any democracy comes from investing executive powers in a few persons (such as Prime Ministers or Presidents), or from a standing military that may take action into its own hands or inordinately influence the policies of the executive branch, the *Earth Constitution* sees to it that this danger is permanently removed from government. The war system of autonomous nation-states is abolished with the advent of the Federation, and the government of the Federation itself is designed to forever prevent inordinate power from accruing in the hands of any few persons.

4. The World Courts

A World Supreme Court is established by the *Constitution* and the Parliament may also establish district and regional World Courts as necessary for a properly functioning, efficient, and just world courts system. No democracy can function without an impartial, non-politicized, efficient judicial system. Democracy is precisely that governmental mechanism through which orderly change can continually occur without people having to find recourse through violence or revolution.

To be effective, people's needs and interests must really be represented through the legislative process. That is, they must have their voices heard and their interests really represented. This is the function of the World Parliament (as well as several other organs created by the *Earth Constitution*). Nations and groups will not resort to violence if they have a real voice in the affairs of the world and a real power of self-determination that is protected by the Earth Federation.

Secondly, their disputes, conflicts, and misunderstandings must be resolved nonviolently through an impartial, fair, and efficient judicial system. Such a system of courts on the world level is one of the keys to world peace. This becomes clear if we consider the eight benches of the World Supreme Court set up by the *Constitution*.

(1) The Bench for Human Rights will deal with claims that human rights have been violated as these are guaranteed under Articles 12 and 13 of the *Constitution*. It is the function of the World Supreme Court to uphold the *Constitution for the Federation of Earth* and therefore ensure the protection of human rights globally as specified in Articles 12 and 13.

(2) The Bench for Criminal Cases will deal with *"issues arising from the violation of world laws and world legislation by individuals, corporations, groups and associations, but not issues primarily concerned with human rights."* Corporate polluters of the environment will be jailed; terrorists will be prosecuted and jailed; anyone dealing in weapons of war (design, transport, buying, selling, or deploying) will be prosecuted and

jailed. Currently there is no enforceable world law and such persons act with impunity. The World Court system will bring the rule of law to the world for the first time.

(3) The Bench for Civil Cases will *"deal with issues involving civil law suits and disputes between individuals, corporations, groups and associations arising under world legislation and world law and the administration thereof."* Again and again disputes arise within any society. We do not live in a perfect world and the *Earth Constitution* is not a proposed utopia. What is important is that there is an impartial Collegium of World Judges who can make binding, just decisions and therefore undercut both the drive toward violence and the drive toward criminal disdain for the law.

(4) The Bench for Constitutional Cases will *"deal with the interpretation of the World Constitution and with issues and actions arising in connection with the interpretation of the World Constitution."* All thoughtful people understand that no document, whether this be a sacred text like the Bible, or an *Earth Constitution*, can be written without ambiguity, without being open to various interpretations in some passages, and without the need for a procedure to deal with ambiguities. The Bench for Constitutional cases will play an absolutely crucial role in the protection of the *Constitution* and the integrity of the Earth Federation.

(5) The Bench for International Conflicts will *"deal with disputes, conflicts and legal contest arising between or among the nations which have joined in the Federation of Earth."* A forerunner of this bench already exists in the form of the International Court of Justice in the Hague that is mandated to deal with disputes between nations. The differences, however, are also immense.

For a court to be effective in preserving the peace and good will among the community of nations its jurisdiction must be mandatory, it must have the power of subpoena, the power of ordering hearings concerning evidence, and the power of making binding, enforceable decisions. The International Court of Justice in the Hague, attempting to operate as it does under the unworkable system of nation-states, has none of these powers and is therefore impotent to keep the peace and good will among nations.

(6) The Bench for Public Cases must *"deal with issues not under the jurisdiction of another bench arising from conflicts, disputes, civil suits or other legal contests between the World Government and corporations, groups or individuals, or between national governments and corporations, groups or individuals in cases involving world legislation and world law."* In other words, whenever there is conflict in the world, there must be a court in existence that can justly deal with this conflict and thereby inhibit

both violence and criminality. The Bench for Public Cases is meant to cover all cases not specific to the other benches of the World Supreme Court system.

(7) The Appellate Bench is designed to *"deal with issues involving world legislation and world law which may be appealed from national courts; and to decide which bench to assign a case or action or litigation when a question or disagreement arises over the proper jurisdiction."* In other words, it is an appeal bench that may operate when litigants are not satisfied with the decisions of lower courts.

(8) The Advisory Bench must *"give opinions upon request on any legal question arising under world law or world legislation, exclusive of contests or actions involving interpretation of the World Constitution. Advisory opinions may be requested by any House or committee of the World Parliament, by the Presidium, any Administrative Department, the Office of World Attorneys General, the World Ombudsmus, or by any agency of the Integrative Complex."* Judges within the Collegium of World Judges will be highly trained experts on the *Earth Constitution* and the functioning of the Earth Federation. The final bench will make their expertise available to the organs of the Earth Federation, including the World Parliament, as an aid in making intelligent decisions or passing good world legislation.

It should be clear that all these eight benches of the World Supreme Court serve functions vital to the maintenance of a decent, law abiding world society. The amazing thing is that none of them exists today. Under the system of so-called "sovereign" nation-states, these is only anarchy, the use of violence or threat of violence, deceptive political maneuvering for position or bargaining power, unenforceable treaty agreements that may or may not be honored, or the arbitrary veto by one of the five big powers on the Security Council of the United Nations. A world without a World Court System such as the above is a world of terror, war, violence, and anarchy, exactly the world we see before us today.

5. The World Attorneys General and Police

Every society employs public prosecutors who work with the police in gathering evidence against those suspected of violating the law, serving arrests, and prosecuting the alleged offenders. Under the *Earth Constitution* this dual function (of police and prosecutors) serves as one of the four main branches of government responsible to the World Parliament. The World Attorney General, the four Associate World Attorneys General, and the twenty Regional Attorneys General are all nominated by the House of Counselors and elected by a simple majority vote of the World Parliament in combined session.

They in turn appoint the World Regional Police Captains. However, this system of enforcement for the Earth Federation has an additional function not often found in national enforcement systems. In addition to the functions of investigation, apprehension and arrest, prosecution, and remedies and correction, the world enforcement system specifies "conflict resolution." The enforcement system of the Earth Federation will have as its goal the minimization of conflict not only through formal systems of conflict resolution, a just system of federal world courts, and a truly representative world parliament, but through an "enforcement system" that is designed to promote nonviolent means of conflict resolution and to enforce world law with an absolute minimum of violence.

By constitutional law, there will be no military or military police in the Earth Federation. There will only be civilian police trained to serve the public and perform their duties with a minimum of violence and careful protection from harm of innocent bystanders. This distinction is crucial. Military and military police do not serve the public but rather an absolute command structure in which some "enemy" is designated to whom they are allowed to do lethal harm. This is the old war system in which harm to a designated "enemy" through lethal means is acceptable, as is "collateral" damage to innocent bystanders, in the course of achieving this military objective.

Civilian police, on the other hand, are accountable to civilian authorities precisely for protection of the innocent and the use of the minimum necessary force to apprehend lawbreakers. The two systems are entirely different. Secondly, the military system targets collective enemies – some other nation-state or some collectively defined groups who are designated the "enemy" to be militarily destroyed or dominated. However, the first "basic principle" of the enforcement system under the *Earth Constitution* is the following:

> *The enforcement of world law and world legislation shall apply directly to individuals, and individuals shall be held responsible for compliance with world law and world legislation regardless of whether the individuals are acting in their own capacity or as agents or officials of governments at any level or of the institutions of governments, or as agents or officials of corporations, organizations, associations or groups of any kind.*

The world system of war and militarism of today is predicated on the destruction of entire groups as designated "enemies." A civilized world order under the rule of law bases enforcement on individuals alone.

As one of the main organs of government reporting to the World Parliament, the world enforcement system will be qualitatively different from most national enforcement systems and all militarized enforcement systems. For as we have seen, the entire apparatus of the world government is designed to end war and promote the living together on Earth of individuals, nations, cultures, religions, and ethnic groupings. The enforcement system is no different.

The *Constitution* puts this as follows:

> *A basic condition for preventing outbreaks of violence which the Enforce-ment System shall facilitate in every way possible, shall be to assure a fair hearing under non-violent circumstances for any person or group having a grievance, and likewise to assure a fair opportunity for a just settlement of any grievance with due regard for the rights and welfare of all concerned.*

In a just and nonviolent world order, the attorneys general and police will function to promote peace, freedom, and democratic law. They will not be seen as oppressors or enemies as is often the case with police and militaries within today's nation-states.

6. The World Ombudsmus

We have seen that one unique feature of the *Earth Constitution* is the House of Counselors as one house of the World Parliament concerned with the common good of humanity and the Earth. Another unique feature is the World Ombudsmus as one of the four principle organs of government under the World Parliament. The World Ombudsmus is yet another aspect of the *Earth Constitution* that will create a new just, prosperous, and peaceful world order for the Earth.

The first two functions of the World Ombudsmus are the following:

> *(1) To protect the People of Earth and all individuals against violations or neglect of universal human and civil rights which are stipulated in Article 12 and other sections of this World Constitution. (2) To protect the People of Earth against violations of this World Constitution by any official or agency of the World Government, including both elected and appointed officials or public employees regardless of organ, department, office, agency or rank.*

An entire branch of government, with the power of investigation, subpoena, and initiating court actions, is directed toward the protection of human rights, not only from national or group forces that might violate these rights but from the world government itself.

As with the World Attorneys General, the Council of five World Ombudsmen is nominated by the House of Counselors and elected by the three houses of the World Parliament in joint session. These functions of the World Ombudsmus harmonize with the functions of the Parliament, the Courts, and the Enforcement System in their emphasis on human rights, the responsibility of individuals (not groups or nations) before the law, the creation of institutions of mediation and conflict resolution, and the construction of a just and peaceful world order.

The World Ombudsmus is also directly concerned with the second bill of rights in the *Constitution* (Article 13). Article 13 is entitled "Directive Principles" for world government because it deals with economic, social, and environmental rights that will not be immediately enforceable when the *Earth Constitution* is first ratified and the newly created Earth Federation must deal with the mess of poverty, violence, injustice, and environmental destruction left behind by the old system of "sovereign" nation-states.

The third and fourth principles of the World Ombudsmus are the following:

> *(3) To press for the implementation of the Directive Principles for the World Government as defined in Article 13 of this World Constitution. (4) To promote the welfare of the people of Earth by seeking to assure that conditions of social justice and of minimizing disparities are achieved in the implementation and administration of world legislation and world law.*

The World Ombudsmus is one of the four main branches of the world government directly responsible to the World Parliament. Its function is to activate the highest potential embodied within the *Constitution* for a world of peace, prosperity, freedom, and justice. The *Constitution* does not represent a set of ideals that are unrealizable. It is internally designed to realize the very ideals that are embodied in the noble words of the Preamble.

7. The World Executive

The World Executive consists of a Presidium of five persons, one from each continental division, nominated by the House of Counselors and elected by a simple majority vote of the World Parliament in joint session. The World Executive Cabinet of an additional twenty to thirty persons, two or three from each of the ten world magna-regions, are nominated by the Presidium and elected by the Parliament in joint session. All twenty-five persons must be members of one of the three houses of the World Parliament. The twenty members of the Executive Cabinet are appointed as Ministers to head the agencies of the world government in the Integrative Complex or the World Administration.

We have seen that the World Presidium (as head of the World Executive) has no police or military powers, no court or judicial powers, no legislative powers, no power to declare a state of emergency suspending the *Constitution*, and no power to refuse to implement the budget. Limitations on the World Executive are explicitly formulated in the *Constitution*:

The World Executive shall not at any time alter, suspend, abridge, infringe or otherwise violate any provision of this World Constitution or any legislation or world law enacted or approved by the World Parliament in accordance with the provisions of this World Constitution. The World Executive shall not have veto power over any legislation passed by the World Parliament,.... may not dissolve the World Parliament,...may not act contrary to decisions of the World Courts. The World Executive shall be bound to faithfully execute all legislation passed by the World Parliament in accordance with the provisions of this World Constitution, and may not impound or refuse to spend funds appropriated by the World Parliament, nor spend more funds than are appropriated by the World Parliament. The World Executive may not transcend or contradict the decisions or controls of the World Parliament, the World Judiciary or the Provisions of this World Constitution by any device of executive order or executive privilege or emergency declaration or decree.

These series of explicit limitations show a deep awareness in the framers of the *Constitution* of the dangers inherent in any executive function. The World Executive does have the power to appoint heads of the agencies and departments of the Integrative Complex and World Administration. The Executive is responsible to make up a budget for the operations of the Earth Federation and submit it to Parliament. The Executive may frame and submit legislation to the World Parliament and is responsible for annual reporting to Parliament. Such authority needs this sort of careful and explicit limitations placed upon it.

However, it is important to note that there is no world president or individual head of the world government. The Presidium of five acts by consensus or by vote, occasionally in conjunction with a vote of the entire Executive Cabinet. This feature of the *Constitution* serves to promote the sense of a collective effort by a professional ministerial and civil service to efficiently maintain the operations of the world government and democratically implement the legislative decisions of the World Parliament. This insight is also behind the Constitutional descriptions of the functions of the various agencies of the Integrative Complex and World Administration. This intent for the functioning of the executive branch of the Earth Federation is made explicit in the following way:

The World Administration shall be composed of professionally organized departments and other agencies in all areas of activity requiring continuity of administration and implementation by the World Government....Each Senior Administrator shall be nominated by the Minister of the particular Department or agency from among persons in the senior lists of the World Civil Service Administration, as soon as senior lists have been established by the World Civil Service Administration, and shall be confirmed by the

Presidium. Temporary qualified appointments shall be made by the Ministers, with confirmation by the Presidium, pending establishment of the senior lists.

The Earth Federation is to be run efficiently and competently by qualified professionals accountable to the World Executive who in turn is responsible to the World Parliament. The World Civil Service Administration shall

formulate and define standards, qualifications, tests, examinations and salary scales for the personnel of all organs, departments, bureaus, offices, commissions and agencies of the World Government, in conformity with the provisions of this World Constitution and requiring approval by the Presidium and Executive Cabinet, subject to review and approval by the World Parliament.

Since heads of governmental agencies are also members of the World Parliament, the *Constitution* sets up the requirement that there be continuous communication between each agency (staffed by qualified professionals) and Parliament. No longer will there be, as in the United States and many other countries, political appointments of unqualified persons to important posts, fomenting inefficiency and waste. No longer will there be the corruption that attends unaccountable power. Every person can be removed for cause according to constitutionally defined due process procedures. The stage is set for government that is really democratic, really directed toward service to the people of Earth, and really able to serve the common good of everyone as well as future generations.

8. Article 12: The First Bill of Rights

The Bill of Rights of the *Earth Constitution* specifies as "inalienable" a list of eighteen rights, the first of which is *"equal rights for all citizens of the Federation of Earth, with no discrimination on grounds of race, color, caste, nationality, sex, religion, political affiliation, property, or social status."* A major achievement of the Earth Federation, as well as genuine democracy, will be the effective realization of equality before the law for all the citizens of the Earth.

This seemingly self-evident requirement of any bill of rights is violated by every nation-state, since they all legislate rights only for their own citizens, effectively denying the rights of all other peoples on Earth. Either rights are inalienably held by all persons equally or they are a lie and a sham. To claim that "inalienable human rights" are only valid on a territorial basis is false. The nation-state system, like the United Nations that represents it, makes a mockery of the concept of inalienable rights.

The persons of the Earth Federation are not only guaranteed the usual democratic political rights of freedom of speech, press, assembly, association, habeas corpus, and due process of law, they are also guaranteed rights that are now routinely violated by all nations under the barbaric system of nation-states. Article 12 also guarantees

Freedom to travel without passport or visas or other forms of registration.... Prohibition against military conscription.... Prohibition against physical or psychological duress or torture during any period of investigation, arrest, detention or imprisonment, and against cruel or unusual punishment.... Prohibition against private armies and paramilitary organizations as being threats to the common peace and safety.... and the right to family planning and free public assistance to achieve family planning objectives.

The violation of the right of citizens of this Earth to travel is a disgrace of the modern system of nation-states. The visa system is a criminal attack on our dignity and freedom as human beings. The right to travel is at the very heart of democracy and the restriction of this right is one reason why under the nation-state system no democracy exists anywhere in the world.

The supposed right of national governments to conscript young people into their criminal war-making system is another disgrace of the nation-state system. To require of young people public work for the nation as a civic duty is a wonderful idea. To make of them trained killers and destroyers of other peoples on Earth is the most corrupt of criminal acts.

In democratic countries people supposedly have a vote, but their vote is meaningless to deal with the most pressing problems of humanity that are beyond the scope of any nation. People vote on secondary domestic issues while they are forced to fight in foreign wars that are beyond their democratic decision-making power. Individual persons are disenfranchised under this system. Their vote cannot give them freedom from war, nor the freedom to travel. Democracy is a sham unless it is world democracy.

The same is true of family planning knowledge and assistance. The current policies of many nations and the U.N. is the violation of people's right to family planning knowledge and resources. Given the population crisis that is rapidly diminishing the life-prospects of everyone on Earth, of the ecosystem of the Earth, and of future generations, these policies constitute a criminal attack on the future of our planet, its people, and future generations. The Bill of Rights in the *Earth Constitution* institutes a compete set of political rights for the first time in history. Many of these rights, such as the right to travel, are impossible under the nation-state system.

We have seen that the entire structure of the *Earth Constitution* is designed to protect and enforce these rights from every angle possible. The first paragraph of Article 12 reviews and repeats this fact:

> *It shall be mandatory for the World Parliament, the World Executive, and all organs and agencies of the World Government to honor, implement and enforce these rights, as well as for the national governments of all member nations in the Federation of Earth to do likewise. Individuals or groups suffering violation or neglect of such rights shall have full recourse through the World Ombudsmus, the Enforcement System and the World Courts for redress of grievances.*

9. Article 13: The Second Bill of Rights

Given the ravages to the world left by the system of nation-states and global monopoly capitalism, the *Constitution for the Federation of Earth* wisely separates people's rights into those political rights of freedom and democracy that are immediately enforceable (Article 12) and those rights (equally important and vital to human life) that the newly formed Earth Federation will be unable to fully guarantee until the global crises have been brought under control (Article 13).

The rights guaranteed in Article 13 show the immense promise and potential for a decent world order under the Earth Federation. We have seen that it is the explicit mandate of the World Ombudsmus and other organs of the Earth Federation to realize the rights named in Article 13 as rapidly as possible. The first paragraph of Article 13 reads:

> *It shall be the aim of the World Government to secure certain other rights for all inhabitants within the Federation of Earth, but without immediate guarantee of universal achievement and enforcement. These rights are defined as Directive Principles, obligating the World Government to pursue every reasonable means for universal realization and implementation.*

This list of 19 additional rights largely includes economic, social, and environmental rights that must be actualized if human beings are going to create a decent civilization for the Earth. People have the right to work with wages sufficient to ensure human dignity (abolishing forever the horrors of economic exploitation, sweatshop work, and starvation wages). They have the right to free and adequate public education for everyone on the planet, the right to social security for their old age, the right to free and adequate health care for all citizens of the Earth Federation, and the right of every child to develop his or her potential.

Among the rights guaranteed by Article 13 and the immediate goals mandated by the *Constitution* are rights to a decent, safe, and healthy environment. These rights are of course fundamental and self-evident to any thoughtful person. However under the present world system of nation-states and global monopoly capitalism, they are impossible of realization. Rather, the present world system prevents their realization.

Not only can nation-states do nothing about the planetary environment, since they have authority only over their internal territories, they are active contributors to the destruction of the environment as the rich nations protect a system of corporate rapacity that externalizes pollution, toxic wastes, and environmentally destructive practices onto the planet and future generations. Multinational corporations use the nation state system to avoid their environmental responsibilities, shifting from one poor country to another with their toxic practices, and the imperial nation-states protect this very system. They fool themselves into believing that the destruction of the environment in poor countries will not impact them or their children in the wealthy fortress countries that they have built for themselves at the expense of the entire world and its future.

Among the 19 rights listed in Article 13 we find the following four:

(8) Protection for everyone against the hazards and perils of technological innovations and developments. (9) Protection of the natural environment which is the common heritage of humanity against pollution, ecological disruption or damage which could imperil life or lower the quality of life. (10) Conservation of those natural resources of Earth which are limited so that present and future generations may continue to enjoy life on the planet Earth. (11) Assurance for everyone of adequate housing, of adequate and nutritious food supplies, of safe and adequate water supplies, of pure air with protection of oxygen supplies and the ozone layer, and in general for the continuance of an environment which can sustain healthy living for all.

Two of the most fundamental rights that people have, rights that provide a framework for everything else, are the right to peace and the right to a clean, healthy environment. The right to peace is so fundamental that the Earth *Constitution* makes it the very framework of world government: abolishing all military activities from the Earth forever. It recognizes that all military activities are criminal in nature, since war is the attempt to destroy other peoples and their life-support systems outside the rule of civilized law, due process, justice, or respect for human dignity.

As we have seen, the right to a clean and healthy environment is violated by both the nation-states and their system of global monopoly capitalism. The *Constitution* is also designed to ensure the restoration of health to our damaged planet and restore the environment for future generations. We recall that the fifth "broad function" of the Earth

Federation as given in Article 1 is *"To protect the environment and the ecological fabric of life from all damage."*

In the second bill of rights (Article 13), this principle is spelled out further in the form of rights guaranteed to all the Earth's citizens. These rights are summed up by number eleven which recognizes that food supplies, safe and adequate water, pure air, an integral ozone layer, and the global environment are all interconnected and interdependent. This is the principle of interdependence of all life recognized in the Preamble that serves as the fundamental insight of the science of ecology.

The entire planet is an integrated and interdependent ecosystem and every environmentally destructive activity under the present unsustainable world system interacts with others to degrade the entire planetary ecosystem. Every activity from throw away plastic packaging to gasoline engines to the dumping of toxic wastes to the emission of ozone destroying chemicals to the production of cancer causing compounds contributes to the general degradation of the planet and violates the rights of everyone to a clean and healthy environment.

Just as the right to peace is institutionalized throughout the Earth *Constitution*, so is the right to a clean and healthy environment. The *Constitution* sets up the Agency for Technology and Environmental Assessment within the Integrative Complex and the department of Environment and Ecology within the World Administration to monitor the global environment and report to the World Parliament on progress toward actualizing the right to a clean and healthy environment for the people of Earth.

Among the "specific powers" granted to the world government in Article 4 of the *Constitution* is number 18 that reads: *"Plan for and regulate the development, use, conservation and re-cycling of the natural resources of Earth as the common heritage of Humanity; protect the environment in every way for the benefit of both present and future generations."* The words "environment" or "environmental" appear thirty-five times in the *Constitution* reflecting a network of provisions such as this one directed to ensuring the people of Earth their right to a clean and healthy environment. Article 13 puts this in the form of rights, but the *Constitution* itself builds these rights into the very structure of the Earth Federation.

10. Article 14: Safeguards and Reservations for People and Nations

Article 14 guarantees the nations the rights to determine their own economic and political systems within the framework of the human rights guaranteed to everyone by Articles 12 and 13 of the *Constitution*. It also guarantees that governments within the Earth Federation will be recognized as authoritative within their respective territories and "full faith and credit" is to be given to their decisions, records, legislation, etc.:

> *The World Government shall operate to secure for all nations and peoples within the Federation of Earth the safeguards which are defined hereunder: (1) Guarantee that full faith and credit shall be given to the public acts, records, legislation and judicial proceedings of the member nations within the Federation of Earth, consistent with the several provisions of this World Constitution. (2) Assure freedom of choice within the member nations and countries of the Federation of Earth to determine their internal political, economic and social systems, consistent with the guarantees and protections given under this World Constitution to assure civil liberties and human rights and a safe environment for life, and otherwise consistent with the several provisions of this World Constitution.... The powers not delegated to the World Government by this World Constitution shall be reserved to the nations of the Federation of Earth and to the people of Earth.*

All nations must be "democratic" for this is the only system that recognizes these inalienable rights in people. But major variations can and do occur in how democracy is organized and implemented. In addition, there are major disagreements as to what constitutes authentic democracy that must be allowed for within the framework of the Earth Federation.

For example, the Revolutionary Committees Movement of Libya has powerful and legitimate criticisms of the failings of the systems of "representative democracy" that operate in many nations. They argue that the Libyan system of "direct democracy" is more democratic and more legitimate as an expression of the will of the people than the elitist, often corrupt systems of representative democracy. They certainly have the right, under Article 14, to be part of the Earth Federation and to determine their own political system.

Something similar is the case with economic systems. There is wide debate about what economic system is "more democratic," more an expression of human freedom, more efficient, etc. As long as the internal systems of nations within the Earth Federation do not interfere with the political, social, and economic rights guaranteed in Articles 12 and 13 of the *Constitution*, a wide variety of economic and political systems must be welcome within the Earth Federation.

Article 14 asserts the integrity and autonomy of the nation-states within the Earth Federation. Nation-states are only illegitimate when they claim for themselves a spurious "sovereignty" that in effect denies the sovereignty of the people of Earth and claims an arrogant independence from the rest of humanity. Within the Federation of Earth, as territorial units of government, they are not only legitimate but important and necessary.

On each of my six visits to Cuba, the people of Cuba have repeatedly told me that they are a "sovereign nation." The United States, they said, has no right to sponsor terrorism against Cuba or to economically blockade their country as it has done for more than forty years. What they do not realize is that under the nation-state system there is only the law of power, the law of the jungle. The system of so-called "sovereign nations" is precisely this law of the jungle.

When there is no rule of enforceable law in the world, the powerful presume the "right" to do whatever they please. No one can stop them so why shouldn't they crush weaker countries? The integrity and autonomy of Cuba can only be ensured under an Earth Federation in which the barbaric rule of power and force in the world is replaced by the civilized rule of law.

The entire *Earth Constitution* (as well as Article 14) is the way out of victimization for smaller and weaker countries in a world of domination. Article 14 is consonant with other features of the *Constitution* that emphasize the right of diversity and individuality for nations and peoples of the world. The Preamble, we have seen, places the Earth Federation on the bedrock principle of unity-in-diversity, and Article 13, number 16, sets before world government the goal of "*encouragement for cultural diversity*" and "*decentralized administration.*"

Article 14 ends with recognition of the sovereignty of the people of Earth. The powers given to the Earth Federation by the *Constitution* are delegated by the people of Earth, who retain all power to themselves, and all inalienable rights, and delegate only such authority to governments from the local to the mundial level as shall protect their peace, environmental integrity, security, and freedoms. The right of nation-states to determine their own cultural, political, and economic systems also ultimately comes from their people.

11. Article 17: The Process of Ratification

The people of Earth must ratify the *Constitution* through direct referendum. National governments, or their governmental authorities, may give preliminary ratification, for example, by the head of state or by a simple majority vote of the national legislature. Preliminary ratification must be followed by submitting the *Constitution* to the people in a direct referendum. Ratification will be confirmed by a simple majority vote in which at least twenty-five percent of all eligible voters over the age of eighteen have voted.

Provision number one of Article 17 says that the *Constitution* will be submitted to each member of the U.N. General Assembly and each national government (this has already been done several times). But it is important to realize that ratification of the *Constitution* is *not dependent* on approval by either the U.N. or national governments. Neither of these is a legitimate representative of the sovereignty of the people of Earth.

Neither of these has any authority regarding the *Constitution*. Only the people of Earth in direct referendum may ratify the *Constitution*. Only the people of Earth have sovereignty. Governments of limited national territories make only illegitimate claims to sovereignty. The *Constitution* represents all the people who live upon the Earth. It is they who have inalienable rights and sovereignty, not national governments and certainly not the U.N.

Article 17 allows for preliminary ratification by national governments and then direct referendum by the people of these respective nations. This is for convenience, since many nations have procedures for referendums already set up. But again this is not necessary. If national governments are uncooperative, world electoral districts may be defined and the people may ratify the *Constitution* directly, irrespective of the national territories in which they happen to live.

Article 17 defines three operative stages in the implementation of world government under the *Constitution*. It recognizes three possible combinations of events that constitute ratification of the *Constitution* and initiation of the each stage of the Earth Federation. For each stage there may be preliminary or final ratification by so many nation-states. Or there may be a combination of preliminary or final ratification by nation-states along with direct ratification by so many electoral districts. Or there may be direct referendum by so many districts irrespective of whether any nation-states ratify the *Constitution*.

The powers, organization, and rights of the Earth Federation at each operative stage are defined by Article 17. Full implementation of the Earth Federation is achieved after there is

> *Ratification by eighty percent or more of the nations of Earth comprising at least ninety percent of the population of Earth; or ratification which includes ninety percent of Earth's total population, either within ratifying nations or within ratifying nations together with additional World Electoral and Administrative Districts where ratification by direct referendum has been accomplished....*

At this point, when ninety percent of the Earth's population have ratified the *Constitution* in direct referendum, the *World Constitution* achieves full force as the official government of the Federation of Earth.

12. Article 19: Provisional World Government

Until preliminary ratification of the *Constitution* occurs, the people of Earth are empowered by Article 19 to begin elaborating Provisional World Government. They are so empowered by the *Constitution* but ultimately also by their sovereignty. The governments and economic institutions of today's world, we have seen, are illegitimate.

As we saw in the Declaration of the Rights of Peoples above (Chapter Two), the people of Earth have both the right and the duty to live under the legitimate rule of democratically legislated laws. Since most nation-states serve as an impediment to this right and duty, the people must take upon themselves the task of elaborating democratic world government. Article 19 serves as a guideline for proceeding with this endeavor.

It defines various working commissions that people may set up to facilitate dealing with the global crises beyond the scope of nation-states and with ratification of the *Constitution*. It defines the manner in which the Provisional World Executive can be created and the responsibilities and duties of this office. It deals with financing for the Provisional World Government, and with the possibility of elaborating a world court system.

Perhaps most importantly, it defines criteria by which a Provisional World Parliament can be created and maintained. This has been the aspect of Provisional World Government that has been elaborated the most. As we have seen, the Parliament has met eight times in eight different locations worldwide from 1982 until 2004. A significant body of provisional world legislation has emerged that should be of great help to the actualized World Parliament when the *Constitution* is finally ratified. The world will need all the help it can get to pull itself out of military chaos, population crisis, environmental collapse, and global poverty, disease, and misery.

The Provisional World Government and the *Constitution for the Federation of Earth* exist today in a unique and interesting legal status. They have more moral and philosophical legitimacy than any government on Earth, for we have seen that territorial governments cannot themselves be legitimate outside of an Earth Federation representing the sovereignty of the people of Earth. In addition, they have been democratically constructed through a thirty-three year process involving four Constituent Assemblies. On the other hand, the morally and politically legitimate *Constitution* does not yet have enforceability, nor is it yet ratified by the people of Earth.

Many national governments have effective enforceability for their internal laws. There is no democratic enforceability for anything on a world scale, however, since the only mechanism for such is generalized economic sanctions affecting entire populations or military action against entire countries. Both these U.N. mechanisms for "enforcement" are illegitimate and illegal according to the *Earth Constitution*. According to any decent human standards, they are also both immoral.

Hence, on the world scale, the only forms of "enforceability" are criminal in nature (violating peoples due process rights, rights to be treated as individuals, rights to be presumed innocent until proven guilty in a court of law, rights to life, liberty, peace, freedom, and a decent environment). Just ask the good people of Iraq (poisoned by depleted uranium) or the good people of Vietnam (poisoned by dioxin infected Agent Orange) how their right to a healthy environment has faired under the nation-state system. The world system as we experience it today is not only illegitimate but criminal in nature. All nations and their leaders who participate in or support this system are complicit in this criminal activity.

On all these grounds, the *Constitution for the Federation of Earth* and its Provisional World Government activated under Article 19 are more legitimate than any existing laws or governments. We are all morally and politically obligated to live under democratic world government. The *Constitution* deserves and demands our *civil obedience* to its higher, legitimate authority.

Chapter Six

Essays on the Promise and Necessity of World Law

The Philosophy of Anarchism versus the Philosophy of Democratic World Government

Glen T. Martin

During my college years at the University of Buffalo in the late 1960s, I studied the philosophy of anarchism and thought of myself as an anarchist. The background for my interest included the tumultuous events of that era – riots in the urban ghettos, mass protests against the Vietnam War, police repression of dissidents, and my understanding of the corruption of democracy and government within the U.S.

I studied the classical anarchist writings of William Godwin, Prince Peter Kropotkin, Michael Bakunin, and Pierre Joseph Prudhon and did an independent study in my senior year in which I attempted to systematically compare the philosophies of Anarchism and Marxism. Anarchism spoke to my socialist and communitarian sympathies and to my insight into the need for rebellion against the repressive and authoritarian nation-state.

I understood that the state in the United States was a class-based state, not a true democracy, with a government that protected vast accumulations of private wealth. It was a system that repressed the people and human freedom in the name of the legal right of corporations to exploit people and nature to steal ever greater wealth for themselves.

I adopted the main principle of Anarchism – the belief that the seemingly "corrupt" human nature that we see all around us is due to the authoritarian and illegitimate coercive structures of government. I embraced the basic anarchist view that the removal of these structures would result in our innate goodness and communitarian human nature emerging.

Without the coercive apparatus of government and its protection of unjust property relations, I assumed that people would begin living on the Earth in peace with one another, in voluntary communities, controlling their own productive facilities and reaping the full benefit of their own labor. There would no longer be war, racial or religious hatred, greed, or the desire of some people to interfere with the liberty of others. Government itself distorted the goodness of our human nature.

Over many subsequent years I continued to study socialist theory, democratic theory, theories of government, theories of imperialism (such as those of Vladimir Lenin and Immanuel Wallerstein), psychoanalytic social theories (such as those of Herbert Marcuse and Eric Fromm), and philosophies of liberation (such as those of Che Guevara and Enrique Dussel). I also began to travel widely outside of the U.S. and experience different cultures, religions, ethnic groupings, and governmental systems. From this process emerged several conclusions incompatible with anarchism.

1) My most basic conclusion from these years of study and experience is that there is no such thing as an "innate human nature" waiting to emerge if all forms of governmental organization are eliminated. Neither is human nature "innately bad" as advocates of strong, coercive government assume.

Human nature is extremely malleable – we become one kind of creature in one social-cultural-governmental setting and another in another setting. Eliminating government will leave people victim to the chaos of social prejudices, bigotries, fears, angers, stupidities, and unjust cultural practices (like female circumcision) that sweep through any social community. How do we promote human freedom, democracy, intelligence, mutual tolerance, and understanding? Both attempts to eliminate government, and structures of coercive government, tend to destroy these qualities.

2) I reflected long and hard on the concepts of human "equality" and "freedom." Regarding the concept of equality, it is patently obvious that people are all individuals – with different physical and mental strengths and weaknesses and unique characteristics that defy any concept of general equality. Even though there are theoretical perspectives that posit equality (all are "children of God," have the same "species-being," have "inalienable rights"), these have very little force in actual human interactions where the strong (mentally or physically) will nearly always take advantage of the weak if they are not constrained from doing so.

I began to realize that human equality and freedom are political concepts that must be legislated. We are all free and equal if we have an enforceable bill of rights that ensures equal protection before the law. We are all free and equal if we have real, functioning democracy that enforces freedom, equal treatment before the law, equal due process, and equal rights for all citizens. The U.N. Declaration of human rights, which is unenforceable, is practically meaningless in today's world where rights are violated with impunity by any group with unaccountable power over others. There can be no universal human equality without universal, enforceable law legislating and mandating that equality.

For example, if men and women are to be equal, they must be equal before the law and because of the law. Universal suffrage that women struggled so hard to obtain would not exist today if it were left up to the "innate goodness" of men. Women, like everyone else, are made equal by law. This is not to deny natural rights, but to institutionalize them. Human freedom and equality are the goals. And these will come about as the result of high quality, well-written enforceable laws – laws that will create a framework of freedom and equality within which our uniqueness and individuality can flourish – laws that still need to be written.

In the thought of Karl Marx, the legislating of political equality in the newly formed political democracies of the 18th century was a "great advance" in human freedom and equality. But it did not achieve real freedom and equality because it left the system of economic domination and exploitation in place. Human freedom and real equality can only be created through legislation that protects a basic economic freedom and equality in addition to political freedom and equality. Good democratically formed laws, in which people have really participated in the making and enforcing of these laws, are the only effective basis of human freedom and equality.

In the U.S. today, we do not have true freedom, nor equality, because the U.S. is not a democracy. It is an oligarchy of the rich (mostly Caucasian males), a propaganda system run by the rich, and a system of injustice and coercion enforced against the poor at home and abroad. However, we are morally obligated to demand and live by principles of freedom and equality as the great 18th century philosopher Immanuel Kant argued. For these are the fundamental principles of all morality.

Hence, in the U.S. today, we are in a condition of what I call "structural immorality." We are morally obligated to live under free, truly democratic government, for that is the only possible basis for actual, functioning freedom and equality. To live without good government, is to live in what Kant called a "state of nature," which is really a state of *defacto* war. For without good government the stronger can always attack, dominate, exploit, or coerce the weaker. We must oppose both the destruction of all governmental authority (anarchism) and the imposition of unequal, unjust coercive government (our present system in the U.S.). Freedom and equality must be legislated by truly democratic, participatory government. There is no other way to achieve these goals, goals that are inherent in our human moral and spiritual lives.

3) Third, I began to understand the hundreds of everyday functions of government from which we all benefit that have little to do the highly visible repressive features of the undemocratic aspects of government. When I go to the doctor or dentist, I am very happy that the government certifies

their competencies. Imagine people "free" to set themselves up as doctors or dentists without government regulation? When I buy drugs or foods, I benefit from enforceable standards of drug and food quality. Imagine what corporations would do to us if there were no such standards? When someone is hired for a job on the basis of their college degree, imagine what it would be like, if no such awarded certificates were coordinated or sanctioned by law?

When I draw water from the tap, I benefit from uniform, enforceable standards of water quality. The same is true with air quality, automobile safety, and every other aspect of life. Fire codes and building codes evolved from very real experiences of gigantic fire tragedies or building disasters during a period when government left people "free" from standards with respect to these things.

The very real failures with regard to good doctors, food, fire or building disasters of which we are all aware are due to lack of good, democratic government. They are not the result of government itself, but of bad government as the rich or unscrupulous distort good government for their own purposes. What we need is good, citizen run, democracy that serves the interests of everyone by promoting true freedom and equality.

Government is a designed social institution that can be substantially improved through building in checks and balances, citizen oversight, true freedom of information, and democratic participation. It must be "federated" in a series of levels from the smallest community units, to the largest planetary units in order to preserve citizens' control over their local affairs. The point is not to get rid of government but to create good government.

For the last 40 years, the propaganda coming from the big corporations has been anti-government (quasi-anarchist) propaganda. They tell us that the source of our problems is "big government" that takes our taxes and inhibits business enterprise, creativity, etc. But the truth of the matter is that good government is the only thing that can prevent the domination, exploitation, and injustice flowing out of corporate greed and all other forms of unaccountable power.

4) But why are there so many "bad" governments in the world? Why is it so difficult to create good government? A fundamental reason for this difficulty emerges if we study the world system that developed from the Renaissance of 16th and 17th century Europe and soon became the dominant world system. The governments of the world system, which have always been largely controlled by the wealthy classes of their respective countries, understood that control of the wealth-producing process internationally was essential to the power and wealth of nations. Governments and their capitalist ruling classes have worked hand in hand.

Spain, Portugal, Britain, Holland, France, Germany, Italy, Russia, China, Japan, the United States, and other nations began the race for domination of the wealth and resources worldwide with the horrid history (continuing to this day) of wars, conquests, colonialism, slavery, mercantilism, and other forms of exploitation of the world's cheap labor and resources by the imperial centers of capital. Thus emerged the modern system of territorial nation-states – all in competition with one another for wealth, military power, and spheres of hegemony.

Under this system, authentic democracy is impossible. Under this system, nations are impelled to militarize, to operate through a secret foreign policy, using "intelligence" gathering, diplomatic deception, treaty alliances, and economic, political, or military coercion to secure their control over the wealth-producing process and their spheres of trade, domination, and exploitation. Democracy cannot flourish within this system, since governmental secrecy, militarism, and lack of civilian oversight are entirely incompatible with democracy.

Similarly, the modern world system has generated vast concentrations of private, corporate wealth that operates in secret from the public (since corporations are considered to have the same "right to privacy" as persons) in an undemocratic and unaccountable fashion. Corporations under this system operate not out of a concern for the environment, democracy, or the public good but to maximize profits for investors regardless of the consequences. They also operate in cooperation with imperial nation-states to dominate and control cheap labor, resources, and the wealth-producing process worldwide.

Study of this world system shows that two fundamental presuppositions of bad government are monopoly capitalism and the sovereign nation-state. These are the two anti-democratic pillars of the world system since the Renaissance. Therefore, we can only create true democracy and true good government on the planetary level.

Democratic world government under the *Constitution for the Federation of Earth* demilitarizes the world entirely (and the world government itself by law has no military). Hence, it makes possible for the first time the elimination of governmental secrecy and true citizen oversight of all government functions (the necessary basis for any functioning democracy). Only complete governmental transparency can give authentic democracy.

Without military or international competition for unjust wealth both national governments and the world government will be completely transparent for the first time. Citizen privacy must be respected but there is no legitimate reason for government or its officials to claim the need for secrecy. Hence, only a demilitarized world under world government can give us real democracy.

Secondly, democratic world government under the *Constitution* gives the people of Earth through the World Parliament the power and duty to make corporations accountable to the common good (of freedom, equality, and environmental integrity). Just as democracy cannot function while there is governmental secrecy, so corporations must be publicly accountable and not be allowed to exploit, price fix, bean count, buy political favors, bust unions, suppress unfavorable research, funnel funds into off-shore accounts, manipulate the market, etc., etc., in secrecy.

Under today's world system, where corporations dominate nations in their own interest and some corporations have more assets (and more power) than many nations, democracy cannot flourish. Only the authority of world government can control multi-national corporations, since these are beyond the legal reach of any particular national government. Here also, democratic world government makes possible real democracy on Earth for the first time, from the local to the planetary level.

5) Finally, the global crises that our planet faces today can only be dealt with by democratic world government. Anarchism, like theories of political democracy focusing on nation-states (such has those of Jean Jacques Rousseau or John Locke), arose in the 17th and 18th centuries when people did not dream that there could be such a thing as "global crises." With the dawn of awareness (beginning in the 20th century) of our planetary crises that are beyond the scope of any nation-state to deal with, some have realized that we need to have a new political philosophy, and an entirely new understanding of our human situation, if we are to survive much longer on this planet. To put it bluntly, we must unite under nonmilitary, democratic world government or we will not survive the twenty-first century.

The global population explosion is threatening our existence on this planet. Eighty million new persons are added to the population of the Earth each year. Some scientists predict nine to eleven billion people by the year 2025. In 1900, the Earth had only one billion people, today: over six billion. Every person alive impacts the world's resources and environment. Sustainable economists such as Herman E. Daly assert that the Earth can only sustainably support two to three billion people. The impending consequences of overpopulation, already beginning today, will be massive migrations, starvations, wars, refugees, environmental damage, and economic chaos.

The global environmental crisis is also happening here and now and includes multiple forms of destruction leading to a possible collapse of the planetary ecosystem that supports life through global warming, ozone layer depletion, or other massive disruptions. Globally, soil erosion is devastating the farming lands of the planet which are disappearing at an astonishing rate. Fresh water aquifers are disappearing as is the total supply of fresh water from the Earth. Global deforestation occurs on the scale of an area half the size of California each year. Grazing lands are rapidly disappearing on which much of the planet's population raise animals for food. Ocean fisheries, which supply a large portion of the Earth's food, are collapsing everywhere. These are all well documented facts for anyone who cares to find out for themselves.

Global militarism and wars continue unabated. These are extremely destructive of the environment, of human rights, cause massive refugee problems, and cause the destruction of cultures, livelihoods, and civilized living for hundreds of millions. Nearly are one trillion U.S. dollars per year and immense human resources wasted world wide. Less than half this amount could supply clean water and sanitation for every person on Earth. Who is to stop this madness? The imperial nations themselves lead with world wide sales of "conventional weapons" on the scale of many billions of dollars per year – breeding conflicts, terrorism, dictatorships, genocides, and wars.

Global poverty and misery continue to increase. Current U.N. figures estimate 1.5 billion persons or 20% of the Earth's population are living in "absolute poverty," with hunger, malnutrition, and no hope. Three fifths or 60% of the Earth's population live in a condition of relative poverty that gives them little hope for education, freedom from disease, or a fulfilled life. There is massive international debt of the poor countries to first world lending institutions and hence massive undemocratic control over their destinies. The result is dictatorships, as well as social and economic chaos in "third world" countries that give them little hope under the current world system of ever seeing anything resembling freedom, equality, or democracy. I have personally seen some of these nightmare conditions.

Worldwide, there is little or no global regulation or planning regarding the future. Instead, there is global competition between nations and huge corporations for resources, military advantage, cheap labor, and avoiding environmental regulation. The United Nations, premised on the present world economic system, on the system of territorial nation-states, and on the war system, is totally helpless to address these crises as its record of failure on all these issues demonstrates. The U.N. is based on the failed assumptions of the modern world system: the sovereign nation-state and monopoly capitalism. Our only option, if we are to have a future at all, is nonmilitary, democratic world government.

All of these global crises destroy democracy, and the possibility of democracy, within the nations and localities of the world. They all portend the destruction of a future for humanity unless we unite as human beings, politically, economically, and democratically. The *Constitution for the Federation of Earth*, written with these global crises in mind, is directed explicitly to their solution. It is designed to rapidly control the world population explosion through non-coercive incentives, to restore and protect the global environment, to demilitarize the world and prevent remilitarization, and to eliminate global poverty rapidly and sustainably.

It is designed to ensure global democracy from the local to the planetary levels, and I have argued that real democracy even at the local level is impossible unless we also have it at the planetary level. There is no other force on Earth that can accomplish these immense and immediately necessary tasks. Without the planetary cooperation and coordination that would be an essential feature of democratic world government, there is simply no future for our planet.

That is why anarchism as well as political liberalism under the system of sovereign nation-states are outmoded political and economic philosophies. At the beginning of the 21st century, we must develop a planetary economic and political philosophy involving nonmilitary democratic world government or we will have failed our children and future generations – who will perish from the Earth.

The Earth Constitution
and the Question of Sovereignty

Dr. Terence P. Amerasinghe
International Lawyer, Colombo, Sri Lanka
President, World Constitution and Parliament Association

Grenville Clarke in his now celebrated book "A Plan for Peace" as far back as 1950 remarked: "No mater how urgent the need for world law, no matter how limited the delegation of power to a world authority, it is easy to raise the spectre of domination by 'foreigners'." Today, more than ever, militarists the world over use the bogey of "loss of sovereignty" to frighten national governments from joining the movement for a democratic federal world government.

Workers for Permanent Peace need to combat and dissolve this myth. It is imperative to do this if Planet Earth is to be saved from the holocaust of nuclear catastrophe or collapse of its planetary ecosystem. As Clarke argues, once this bogey is dissolved, "many suspicions and doubts" harbored by national governments about democratic federal world government "will be dissipated." Gradualists, realists, and defeatists will find the ground cut from under their feet and imagined or deliberately conjured up fears will vanish.

It is surprising that this bogey of sovereignty has not been laid to rest these many years. As early as 1943, the Hon. John J. Parker, then Senior Judge of the United States Circuit Court, in his treatise, "World Organization," cited the legal dictum "Sovereignty is the right to govern." He went on to state: "This right is not arbitrary, but arises out of the nature of the relationship to which it applies....If a matter concerns me and nobody else, I am the one to decide and nobody else. If it concerns the people of North Carolina and nobody else, then the people of North Carolina should decide. If, however, it concerns the international society of the world, that society, properly organized, should make the decision." Justice Parker went on to state that "there has been much nonsense talked about sovereignty."

To get the right answer to the question, "does establishing a Democratic Federal World Government involve any surrender of national sovereignty, we must examine the meaning given to the term 'sovereignty.'

Greed of powerful nations controlling the most sophisticated armaments has converted the term 'sovereignty' to 'anarchy.' Some national governments have elevated themselves to a status that makes them a law unto themselves, judging their own causes and enforcing their judgments by their own force and that of their allies.

'Sovereignty' really means that a nation is absolutely self-governing in its own affairs. This is not disputed and under a *Constitution for the Federation of Earth,* this conception of 'sovereignty' is left untouched. No surrender of 'sovereignty' is required by a national government that accepts impartial justice in its relations to other nations. In this sense, the rule of law increases national independence, for it makes it no longer necessary for any nation to become dependent on another nation, as a protector or ally.

A glance at the working of the United Nations Organization these last nearly 60 years will provide the best answer to those who pretend that a Democratic Federal Government is a threat to the sovereignty of national governments. As recently as January 20th, 1982, Ambassador Oleg A. Troyanousky of the U.S.S.R. told the Associated Press that the Veto is one of the pillars on which the United Nations rests, and added "we are strong on the veto."

The U.S. had just used the veto for the 33rd time to block Arab recommendations for sanctions against Israel because of its annexation of the Syrian Golan Heights. This led to an emergency special session of the 157 member General Assembly to debate and pass by a nearly 2/3 majority a condemnatory resolution against Israel. To what end? Where, one might ask, is the "Sovereign Equality of All Nations?" The threat to the 'sovereignty' of national governments comes from the United Nations itself.

It stems from the Charter of the United Nations. It is flagrantly displayed time and against when the former U.S.S.R. and the U.S. have used the veto. The cynicism with which the Superpowers (or today Superpower) view the 'sovereignty' of their so-called colleagues in the U.N. was exemplified best when Soviet Foreign Minister Gromyko once lectured the American delegates about the value of the veto. "Don't spit in the well. You may want to drink the water yourself one day."

'Sovereignty,' today, to national governments that cannot command the sophisticated weapons in the hands of the big powers, is an illusion. To make this illusive sovereignty real, national governments strive to get control of sophisticated weapons. Most national governments use up colossal sums from their gross national incomes and impoverish their people in this never-ending quest. The more they exert themselves to come abreast of the big powers, the further the big powers have advanced the arms race. The drive to war is unrelenting.

The world armament industry waxes fat and the yawning gap between rich and poor, North and South, becomes unbridgeable. It pays interested parties to talk nonsense about 'sovereignty' and spread the big lie that if nations come under the rule of World Law, their 'sovereignty' will be threatened. Because the more this bogey is held aloft and nations prevented from coming into a Democratic Federal World Government, the greater the possibilities for the big powers to sell their obsolete weapons at fantastic prices to small nations and keep their nuclear arsenals up to date.

It is time the canard of 'sovereignty' in the strict sense is nailed and the bogey of 'loss of sovereignty' is laid to rest. No one with any sense of responsibility will argue that nations have the right to be a law unto themselves in dealing with other nations, judging of its own cause and enforcing its judgments by its own force and that of its allies. The recent U.S. invasions of Iraq and Afghanistan, outside of even the U.N. Organization and against the opinion of the entire world, could not drive this point home any more clearly.

The 'sovereignty' of a nation only means autonomy in all domestic and economic affairs combined with acceptance of impartial justice in its relations to other nations. Any other interpretation is to condemn the world into an endless War-Peace-War-Peace-War cycle. There is and can be only one interpretation of 'sovereignty,' regardless of what the war-mongers and fascists may say, and that is what was stated in the Moscow Declaration of 1943. Sobered by the endless carnage and the fact that the Second World War had still to be won, the Allied Leaders promised a new international organization "based on the sovereign equality of all peace-loving states" and that this organization will maintain "peace and security with the least diversion of the world's human and economic resources for armaments."

There was then no talk by the signatories (Molotov of the U.S.S.R, Eden of Great Britain, Hull of the U.S., and Foo Ping-Sheung of China) about an entrenched veto for the nations they represented. The "sovereign equality" they spoke of must be considered in relation to "peace-loving nations" and what is more important that these nations were to join in an organization to "maintain peace and security with the least diversion of the world's human and economic resources for armaments." Who dare argue the nonsense that Molotov, Eden, Hull, and Foo Ping-Sheung meant a 'sovereignty' that would allow every state or any state to act as though it were independent and absolute in determining its relation to other states, because on that interpretation "sovereign equality" will be a contradiction in terms.

The United States statement on Foreign Policy coming six months later in March 1944 made the Moscow Declaration more pointed when it spoke of "in law and under the law" that each sovereign nation large or small, can be equal to every other nation. It stressed that 'sovereignty' must not mean license to behave at all times exactly as one pleases but the right to manage one's own affairs "in such a way as not to menace the peace and security of other nations." The recent U.S. statements to the world that it reserves the right to itself to initiate war against any nation that it feels might threaten its security gives the ultimate proof of the absurdity of the notion that the "sovereign equality of nations" can be maintained apart from enforceable World Law.

As the late Lord William Beveridge concluded in his treatise on "The Price of Peace": "Just as freedom of citizens is made greater and not less by the rule of law, so is the independence of nations. Freed from the fear of war, from endlessly growing burden of armaments, from the pressure of entangling alliances, every nation under the rule of law will have greater secure independence than any could achieve in the international anarchy of the past."

It is hard to believe that the 190 or more nations comprising Planet Earth can any longer be frightened and duped by the bogey of 'loss of sovereignty.' The very rebellion in the U.N. over the Israeli issue (and many subsequent issues) with the refusal of 86 nations to bow to the veto is a clear indication that the nations may be girding themselves to enter a democratic federation which will be truly "in Law and under the Law" in order to have greater secure independence. El Fattal said after the Israeli debate, the "veto does not count. The majority of world public opinion is with us."

Srimati Indira Gandhi, the Prime Minister of India, in her message to the New Delhi Conference of the World Constitution and Parliament Association in February 1981 anticipated the growing realization of national governments that, if their independence in world affairs is to be real, nations must be liberated from the bondage of the big powers: "A just international order is an inescapable necessity for man's survival. Such an order must rest on equal respect for all nations as well as equal opportunity for each people to develop to its fullest potential." Nations are sovereign at the appropriate level: as they become members of the Earth Federation. The time is long past due for the nations of the world to realize that real national autonomy and independence can only come through nonmilitary, democratic world government under the *Constitution for the Federation of Earth.*

The Roots of Terrorism in "Sovereign" Nation-states and the Path to a Secure World Order

(First published in *Culture and Quest: Issue on Violence, Nonviolence, and World Peace,* Kolkata, India: ISISAR, 5 January 05, pp. 53-58)

Glen T. Martin

The deeper assumptions behind our institutions and world order remain unquestioned and unthought by even highly educated people. If humankind is to survive much longer we must examine these unquestioned assumptions. The basic presuppositions guiding our institutions thwart the best intentioned actions and efforts to achieve a peaceful and just world order. People commit their life-energies to peace and the result is violence, war, and terror. People work to eradicate poverty, misery, and disease and the result is ever deepening poverty, misery and disease.

Nearly all people wish to eradicate terrorism, yet terrorism continues to grow and flourish within and between nations and groups. Without a deeper level of thought, without deep insight and understanding into what one thinker called "the perversity of what is perverted," we continue to rush headlong toward ever greater planetary disaster. What are the deeper assumptions behind our present world order that foment the terrorist mentality and terrorist forms of organization?

Today books and articles pour forth about terrorism, its causes and consequences. Conferences are held, governmental agencies formulate definitions, systems of monitoring and investigation are formed. Yet terrorism continues to increase. People in general lack a sense of security, peace, and well-being. They live in terror, in fear, regardless of whether they have had any direct experience of terrorism. Yet we will see that the foundations of a peaceful and secure world order are entirely within our grasp if we correctly diagnose the causes and remedies for world terrorism.

The 1999 FBI definition of terrorism can serve as a working definition for understanding this phenomenon. Terrorism, according to the FBI, is "the unlawful use of force or violence committed by a group or individual, who has some connection to a foreign power or whose activities transcend national boundaries, against persons or property to intimidate or coerce a government, the civilian population or any segment thereof, in furtherance or political or social objectives." The essential points of this definition are that terrorism is (1) connected with violence or the threat of violence that transcends national boundaries and (2) it is the "unlawful" use of violence to achieve political or social objectives.

One important principle that astute thinkers have pointed out repeatedly in our time is the distinction between non-governmental forms or terrorism and state-sponsored terrorism. We have come to understand that nation-states also engage in terrorism. It becomes more and more difficult to distinguish between private terrorism and terrorism routinely engaged in by nation-states. Military violence or the threat of violence by nation-states fits this FBI definition perfectly. The use of military power to achieve international political objectives in a world of isolated "sovereign" nation-states is inevitable in a world where there is no true, enforceable world law.

As the issue of terrorism continues to be discussed, the history of interventions by the imperialist powers has come to light. One discovers a history of interventions, surprise bombings, assassinations, support for death squads, overthrowing of small nations, subversion of democracy, mining of harbors, blowing up of facilities, covert actions, drug smuggling, torture, arbitrary execution of political enemies, and outright warfare.

Under the world system of the past five centuries, all imperial nations have engaged in such terrorism. Author William Blum describes this process with respect to the United States: "From 1945 to the end of the century, the United States attempted to overthrow more than 40 foreign governments, and to crush more than 30 populist-nationalist movements struggling against intolerable regimes. In the process the U.S. caused the end to life for several million people, and condemned many millions more to a life of agony and despair" (2000, p. 2). The selling of weapons to foreign regimes, the training and equipping of foreign military machines, and outright military interventions in foreign countries, all of which have been major policies of the U.S. throughout this period in order to politically manipulate or control the world order in its own interests, fit perfectly this FBI definition of terrorism.

Indeed, since the advent of the United Nations there have been some 150 wars resulting in some 25 million deaths. Most of these deaths were civilians. Compared to this, the number of people killed by non-governmental terrorists through car bombings, suicide bombings, assassinations, etc., is minuscule. Why is it that the vast preponderance of the terror of our world throughout the past fifty years has come from state terrorism, not private terrorism?

The majority of countries in the U.N. have called for study of the basic causes of terrorism, convene conferences on terrorism to define it and differentiate it from the [legitimate] struggles of people for national liberation. The U.S. has vetoed such actions by the U.N. for the obvious reason that its own unlawful and violent foreign policy to achieve global political objectives would be exposed and condemned by such conferences. Nevertheless, much excellent work has been done on the causes and conditions that foster terrorism.

The causes of private terrorism are often identified as extreme poverty, exploitation, imperial domination, and the humiliation that nations, groups, or religions impose on others. The terrorists think of themselves as being in a war against such forces. State terrorism is often understood in the literature as being the mirror of private terrorism, since it is the use of state military power to enforce a system resulting in extreme poverty for the majority, exploitation, domination, and humiliation. However, despite the important insights presented here, the real sources of terrorism lie deeper than this.

The real source of terrorism is the nation-state system itself, structured, as it is, to be inseparable from global monopoly capitalism. The modern system of nation-states first developed during the Renaissance at the same time the capitalist economic system developed in 15th century Italy. Some scholars define the "sovereign" nation-state as a political entity that has complete control over its internal affairs and complete independence with regard to other nation-states in its external affairs. The world today has about 190 of these territorial entities, all claiming to be "sovereign" and independent of all the others. A moment's reflection reveals this system as not only extremely irrational but morally perverse as well.

None of these "sovereign" entities lives under the rule of law. None of them lives under democracy. None of them in effect recognizes the equality, rights, and sovereignty of peoples outside their borders, since any such principles can only be enforced within nations. So-called "international law" is not law but a misnomer, since it is not democratically legislated, it is not enforceable, and compliance with it is merely voluntary. Relations between "sovereign" nation-states are mere treaties, that is, voluntary, unenforceable agreements that can be renounced or subverted at any time the nations party to these treaties feel it is in their self-interest to do so.

Hence, even though some nations claim to be "democracies" within their borders, and to believe in "democracy" as the only legitimate form of government, their defense of this bizarre concept of "national sovereignty" shows this to be false. They do not want to live under the rule of democratically legislated law but want to be entirely "independent" in a lawless, chaotic world of "international relations." If we redefine "Sovereignty" to mean integrity and independence with respect to the internal affairs of a particular national territory under the rule of world law, then the concept becomes harmless. But "sovereignty" as external independence from any world law is the main root of our present terroristic world order.

With modern weapons systems the absurdity of this system has been underlined over and over again as intercontinental ballistic missiles have been developed capable of bringing nuclear weapons to any city on earth in the space of twenty minutes. Today, U.S. Trident nuclear submarines patrol the bottom of the oceans of the world, each submarine capable of launching nuclear warheads sufficient to destroy 123 cities worldwide, upon being given the order to do so. The criminal nature of this system, the consequence of the absurd system of sovereign nation-states, is surely apparent to anyone who cares to think objectively.

Under this system every nation is thought to have the right to militarize itself for "self-defense" purposes. Nearly all of these 190 entities, living in a lawless world, arm themselves to the utmost, costing their citizens a large portion of the wealth they produce and causing other nations to perpetually renew their armaments to keep up with the possible threat from other sovereign nations, all independent and claiming the right to operate as they please in their foreign affairs and internal affairs.

Under this system a nation can violate human rights within its borders with impunity. Indeed, the imperial nations, led by the U.S., have supported brutal, repressive regimes around the world in the interest of both international political struggles (e.g. against Communism) and creating, as they put it, "a stable investment climate." World private arms dealing and official government "military aid" to regimes perceived to be "friendly" amounts to many billions of dollars per year. All told, the world spends close to a trillion U.S. dollars per year on militarism and weapons, while less than half of this amount could provide clean water and sanitation for every person on the planet. This entire system of militarization amounts to violence or the threat of violence.

On the rare occasion that the nations of the world claim they perceive massive human rights violations within some sovereign nation, the only option in a world of sovereign nations is to attack the entire nation by sanctions, military, or both. Individuals within these nations who may be responsible cannot be arrested because so called "international law" is a collection of treaties among "sovereign" nations, not law enforceable over individuals. Hence, economic sanctions causing starvation and misery or outright war are integral to the system of sovereign nations defined as independence from all external world law.

For example, when the claim was made in 1998 that Yugoslavia was committing massive human rights violations (a claim never made against the official client states of the imperial powers whose human rights records were equally as bad or worse), the supposed suffering of the Yugoslav people from their government had to be compounded by militarily attacking them with cruise missiles and cluster bombs, destroying their factories, homes, and hospitals. In the FBI definition of terrorism, this was clearly the "unlawful" (between nations there is no genuine law) use of violence to achieve political or social objectives. Whether these objectives are thought to be noble is irrelevant, since all terrorists believe their objectives are noble. The nation-state system is nothing if not terrorist in its very foundations.

The international system of militarized violence is based on a false analogy that the propaganda machines of the imperial powers do not wish us to examine too closely. It is an analogy with the individual's right of self-defense under the rule of law. Under democratically legislated law within nations, individuals and groups are prohibited from using violence against one another to achieve political or social objectives. Mechanisms such as arbitration, courts, the right of political participation, and freedom of expression are created by law to allow for the nonviolent adjudication of differences and the achieving of political or social goals.

If one is threatened or attacked, the law requires that citizens call the police or otherwise handle the provocation nonviolently. On the rare occasion that one's bodily integrity, property, or life is threatened and it is impossible to call the police, then the law provides for "the right of self-defense." Under these narrowly defined circumstances, it is legal to use violence or the threat of violence to protect oneself, one's property, or family.

But to project this "right of self-defense" to the system of nation-states is entirely fallacious. For under the world system of "sovereign" nations, there is no rule of law, no democracy, and no police protection of nations, groups, or individuals. Without the rule of enforceable law in the world, we have nothing left but what the philosopher Immanuel Kant (1957) called the "savage" and "barbaric" condition of the world without the rule of law. Under the system of "sovereign" nations, the big nations do what they please and the weaker nations suffer. For under this system, each nation may decide for itself what constitutes legitimate self-defense and act accordingly.

Under the rule of law within nations, I may not machine-gun all the people in the next neighborhood, claiming self-defense, because I surmise they might some day attack or threaten me. The courts and enforceable laws decide what is legitimate self-defense and what is not. However, in international affairs, there is no superior force (government and law) that can decide the legitimacy of any particular nation's claim to self-defense. The powerful do what they please and use the "self-defense" argument to justify whatever they perceive to be in their self-interest. That is why Kant called this an immoral system of "barbarism" and "savagery."

Even the very existence of a military organization within nations is a terrorist consequence of the present world system as the FBI definition quoted above makes clear. Nations create a military for self-defense. The very existence of these military organizations constitutes a "threat of violence" to other nations, saying that if you attack us we will use violence to defend ourselves. In a world without genuine law (which is inevitable under the system of "sovereign" nation-states) the existence of such militaries constitutes the threat of the use of violence to achieve political or social objectives, namely, the protection and preservation of this government vis-a-vis all other "sovereign" governments.

A world order without democratically legislated, enforceable law over everyone is inherently terrorist, that is, the use of violence or threat of violence to achieve political or social objectives is built into the system itself. As long as nations claim there that there can be no world law above themselves (because they are "sovereign") and as long as they claim the "right of self-defense" in a world without law, then the use of violence or the threat of violence to achieve political or social objectives is inevitable. It is built into the very system of lawlessness itself.

For several decades the World Constitution and Parliament Association has offered the world a practical alternative – the creation of nonmilitary, democratic world government under the *Constitution for the Federation of Earth*. The ascent to democratically legislated world law under this *Constitution* is not just another arbitrary possibility among the many peace proposals offered today by the U.N. and NGOs. For only democratic world government can move us beyond the "barbaric" and "savage" condition of international lawlessness and terrorism to a morally legitimate world of peace and security. There is no other option. Without the rule of democratically legislated enforceable law over all nations and individuals, we continue in the immoral mode of the rule of violence and the threat of violence to achieve political or social objectives.

Sentimental appeals to peace and respect for human rights like the Hague Appeal to Peace will not make a substantial difference. Neither will attempts to reform the U.N. achieve peace or put an end to terrorism. The U.N. charter is explicitly premised on the preservation of the system of sovereign nation-states. Treaties among sovereign nations controlling weapons of mass destruction or other militarized systems will not be successful. For none of these addresses the root cause of terrorism which is the system of "sovereign" nations itself. Only nonmilitary world government under the *Constitution for the Federation of Earth* can give us a world of peace.

For only democratic world government creates enforceable rights for all people and nations under the rule of law. We move out of the barbaric world system of the past four centuries which was predicated on the use of violence or the threat of violence in international affairs. We move forward to a new world order that is the only morally legitimate order. For the use of violence for reasons of self-defense is only justifiable in extreme circumstances under the rule of democratically legislated laws with guaranteed due process, freedom of expression, and equal rights for all peoples and nations. No longer will there be the rule of power in world affairs but the rule of right, law, and due process.

There is no other way beyond terrorism, since terrorism is predicated on the lawlessness of a world order that abjures democracy, law, and universal human rights in favor of the rule of violence and the threat of violence. The present system of so-called "sovereign" nation-states is inherently terroristic. Terrorism can only be overcome through democracy and a democratic world order. Terrorism can only be overcome through ratification of the *Constitution for the Federation of Earth.*

ARE WE UNTEACHABLE ?

Dr. Errol E. Harris

John Evans Professor of Moral Philosophy, Emeritus,
Northwestern University
Vice-President, World Constitution and
Parliament Association

(A version of this article was first published in *United World - CDWG
News and Views,* Carbondale, IL:
Coalition for Democratic World Government,
Vol. 18, No. 1, Jan.-Feb. 2005, pp. 7-13)

*In 1939, just as the second World War was beginning, W.B.Curry,
in his book The Case for Federal Union, wrote:*

*"The argument for international government can surely only be strength-
ened by this war, which is the plainest demonstration (if after 1914-39
further demonstration were needed) of the tragic and futile idiocy of international anarchy. If we fail to learn the lesson this time, then we are
indeed unteachable, and the sooner the human experiment comes to an
end the better." (p. 151).*

Immediately after these words were written the world suffered six
years of the most costly, devastatingly destructive conflict ever experi-
enced, involving all the major powers. It was a desperate struggle for
survival by the democracies and Soviet Russia (a totalitarian regime later
to pose a further menace to world freedom) against a tripartite alliance of
the worst forms of tyranny, the outcome of which hung in the balance until
almost the last moment. It was finally decided by the use of the most powerful weapon of mass destruction ever developed against which no reliable
defense has yet been discovered.

Two distinguished International Law theorists, Professors George
Keeton, and Georg Schwarzenberger, at much the same time as Curry,
wrote persuasive books demonstrating that international relations were al-

ways power-politics which the League of Nations was powerless to over-come for the sole reason that its members claimed and exercised sovereign independence (see Keaton, 1939, Curry makes no reference to this source). E.H. Carr, a prominent Cambridge historian produced a book (*The Twenty Years Crisis*) illustrating this thesis with convincing evidence. The sovereign independence of states was and has always (since the sixteenth century) been the root cause of what Curry calls "the tragic and futile idiocy of international anarchy."

This is inevitable if states are sovereign, because sovereignty recognizes no superior legislation to its own, so that the Rule of Law among sovereign states can never be maintained. The lesson that Curry said was to be learned was what George Keeton had taught: that national sovereignty is the evil genius of inter-national relations (see Keeton, 1939) and fail to learn it we certainly did. Now, after another sixty-four years, we face a world situation that does indeed threaten the end of the "human experiment": a world threatened by recurrent international conflicts, by worldwide terrorism, and as much or more by global warming.

That the root of the problem is the persistent claim of the nations to sovereign independence is demonstrable from the very nature of sovereignty. An independent state has a primary interest in defending itself from aggression by foreign powers which overrides all other considerations. So it builds up its military strength to the limits of its capacity and seeks alliances with other countries whose national interests are compatible with its own. If this condition is not met, other states are viewed potentially at least as enemies.

Consequently, the tendency is for nations to form opposing blocs between which they strive to maintain a balance of power. It is, however, an extremely unstable balance, which can be upset by as little as a technical advance in weaponry on either side. The result is a perpetual and unstoppable arms-race, involving repeated tensions and intermittent crises, breaking out from time to time into violent hostilities that constantly threaten to escalate, and finally to issues in a major conflagration.

This has been the persistent pattern of world history, especially after the Napoleonic wars during the nineteenth and twentieth centuries, and is unavoidable as long as the nations are sovereign and mutually independent. Napoleon's aggressive exploits engulfed the whole of Europe in warfare, which the battle of Waterloo brought to an end for the time-being. But the peace did not endure. Intermittent crises arose and minor wars broke out all over the world (e.g., the 1812 war between Britain and the newly constituted United States, the Crimean War, the Opium War in the far east, the Franco-Prussian war, the Zulu and Boer wars in South Africa), until in 1914 world peace was shattered by the First Great World War. This was followed by another twenty years of crises and minor conflicts leading to the Second World War.

The legacy of these two devastating world wars has been the development of nuclear and other weapons of mass destruction capable of wiping out whole populations. Since then there have been more than 150 minor wars, and with the growing power of China, we have the seeds of another major confrontation between east and west. Today, do what we can, we do not know how to prohibit nuclear proliferation or to prevent nuclear material of weapons grade falling into the hands of terrorists; international and civil wars continue to multiply, with the ever-present possibility of escalation and the premonition of thermo-nuclear holocaust and nuclear winter that would decimate, if not extinguish, all life on the planet.

As a further result of the continuing power politics in international affairs and the hegemony of the United States a new style of conflict has arisen between east (or rather, Middle East) and west: terrorism, committed anywhere in the world where American influence is apparent, a terrorism on which President George W. Bush has declared war – a new kind of war that is not against any one specific nation, but against any who are held to harbour terrorists, be they Taliban in Afghanistan or Saddam Hussain in Iraq. Such terrorism, however, is not defeated but is only exacerbated by violent and draconian measures taken to counteract it by those threatened, measures that at the same time undermine the democratic practices the terrorists seek to disrupt.

The United Nations, for more than half a century, has proved incapable of preventing war; on the contrary, its Charter provides (in Chapter VII) as the ostensible means the actual waging of war "by land, sea and air" – as if by waging war one could maintain world peace. Because that same Charter, in Article 2,1, asserts that the U.N. is founded on the principle of sovereign independence of its members, states cannot be compelled, except by the threat or exercise of military action, to observe the Security Council's resolutions, and many of them to this day continue to ignore or defy them.

International Law is hamstrung by the same limitation. It is respected only when it does not conflict with what the nations perceive as their national interests, and is disregarded and violated whenever it is deemed to conflict with what a government sees as the "vital interests" of the nation. It contradicts itself by declaring that its sole subjects are sovereign states while defining sovereignty as the authority which is subject to no superior legislation. Consequently, International Law is frequently violated or just ignored by recalcitrant governments and "the tragic and futile idiocy of international anarchy" described by Curry still prevails.

Global warming, largely produced by human activity (vast emissions of green-house gases, unconscionable destruction of rain forests, unsustainable use of fossil fuels, etc.) is advancing apace, melting the polar ice-caps, producing climate change and more violent meteorological activity, which will destroy the habitat of thousands of living species, including much of our own (as sea levels rise and swamp major populated areas). Summit meetings, such as those at Rio, Kyoto, and Johannesburg seeking conventions to counteract this danger, have (with great difficulty) reached only non-binding agreement on measures inadequate to ameliorate these tendencies – measures which for the most part are not being carried out, which have been rejected by the most powerful states (USA and, until recently, Russia) and resisted by undeveloped countries, which resent the sacrifices and restraints enjoined to remedy conditions created by richer communities. The persistent reason is that sovereign governments inevitably give priority to their own national interests over environmental conservation and other global requirements.

Nor is this all. The demonizing effects of global capitalism on world trade, the vested interests of transnational corporations reduces the economies of poor countries to yet greater poverty, and the deleterious pressures of the profit motive promote unsustainable economic practises that increase the menace of environmental deterioration (see Harris, J.M., 2000, Introduction).

None of these perils overshadowing contemporary humanity can be overcome by the United Nations, as long as its members remain sovereign. The decisions of its Assembly are at best advisory to the Security Council and the resolutions of that Council, subject to the veto of the permanent members, even when agreed, are frequently ignored or flouted (e.g. by Israel, by the former apartheid regime in South Africa, and prior to 2000, by Iraq, as also by the United States and Britain in their attack on Saddam Hussein when France threatened a veto).

The U.N. cannot enforce its resolutions upon sovereign nations except by sanctions involving the threat or the actual waging of war. Economic sanctions, to be effective, need to be backed by military measures to prevent violations and are painfully slow in their effects, generally causing more distress to the innocent population than submission by the delinquent government. And the fundamental cause of all these evils is the sovereign independence of the states concerned.

That this is so is amply illustrated by the arbitrary decision of George W. Bush to attack Iraq and Tony Blair's failure, when he persuaded the American President to seek a United Nations Security Council resolution to authorize hostilities, consequent upon the threatened French veto. Aggression was then committed in defiance of International Law and led to the predicament in which the coalition has become immersed, after what looked at first like an expeditious victory, of sporadic guerilla attacks from Iraqi partisans (previously at loggerheads among themselves), and the ignominy incurred by maltreatment of Iraqi prisoners in the attempt to extract intelligence from them.

Is the human race really so stupid and unteachable? Even apart from the persistent possibility that a third and finally annihilating war might result from the prevailing climate of crisis for the reasons above outlined, the deleterious effects of climate change are terrifyingly menacing. These are global problems that can be tackled only with global remedies, if any. But no global remedies can be secured as long as national governments give priority, as they are bound to do, to their perceived national ("vital") interests in self-defense and (unsustainable) economic growth. With the best will in the world, whatever one nation does is liable to be counteracted by what others do or what they omit; and as each prefers its own national interests to those of mankind as a whole, the necessary concerted action is never achieved.

In the eighteenth century, when the British American colonies had fought a successful war to gain their independence, they found themselves in a situation not unlike that in which the nations of the world are today. They pursued rival foreign policies; they imposed import duties on one another's products; they set up different currencies, the value of which they could not maintain; they were unable to command the respect of foreign nations, and they generated rivalries that brought them to the brink of mutual war.

Led by Madison and Hamilton, however, they had the wisdom to reconcile their differences by merging their sovereignties in a federal union. In those days, when there were no examples to follow, there were many who were prejudiced against the concept of federation, but the arguments put forward by Hamilton and Madison in *The Federalist* finally overcame opposition. Can our political leaders not be persuaded, in this the eleventh hour, that they are taking us down the slippery slope to destruction? Are they incapable of appreciating the late eighteenth century example of the founders of the United States?

The abolition of the claim to sovereign independence is now the precondition of any effective measures against the ominous threats of catastrophe that we face today, because the root-source of the reluctance of governments to take effective measures to remove the perils now facing the peoples of the world, or to agree to concerted action where (as to remedy global warming) it is indispensable, is their exercise of national sovereignty. If the prevailing international anarchy is to be brought to an end with the maintenance worldwide of the Rule of Law, the one feasible means is the establishment of a federal world government constituted on sound democratic principles. Many will object that nationalities are so diverse and frequently so contrary that they could never agree to such a world union. Yet doubts on such grounds are far outweighed by the perils of the alternative.

Others object on principle to what they call a super-state. But their objections for the most part arise out of misconceptions of the nature of world government that are widely entertained among the public. The fear is common that world government would be centralized, autocratic and authoritarian; but this is the precise opposite of the truth. It might be true if global governance were imposed on the nations by force or the hegemony of a superpower, but not if it was willingly accepted by the peoples who would be subject to it. A properly constituted democratic federation would be the diametrical opposite of centralized power; it is, in fact the paradigm case of devolved government, because the federal authority would be constitutionally restricted to those departments of government dealing with matters of common concern (such as world peace and global warming) that the member states, with their limited jurisdiction, cannot severally regulate, while the rights of national administrations to control local matters would be constitutionally protected. At the same time, a suitable constitution would set up an Ombudsmus to guard against corruption and the abuse of power throughout the union.

Another prevalent misconception is that world government would be excessively bureaucratic and cumbersome, for which there are no grounds. It would be no more so than the United Nations is at present, while it would be competent to deal with world problems, as the U.N. by recognizing the sovereignty of its members is not. Nor would federation eliminate national feelings of patriotism, as is often feared, although that feeling would differ from the chauvinism that is presently common; nationalism would go, but not nationality and national tradition.

The public ought to be disabused of these misconceptions without delay. Political theorists, philosophers, and sociologists should be correcting erroneous ideas in the minds of their students and those most likely to become politicians. Publicists and commentators on current affairs should be discussing the pros and cons of federal world government and doing all they can to dissipate the prevailing misunderstandings. Why is this not happening?

It is not as though we have any excuse for ignorance of the dangers that confront us. Scientists have reported the facts of atmospheric pollution and climate change quite unambiguously. There is no significant difference of scientific opinion that human activity (industrial, transportational and other, the burning of fossil fuels and the wasteful use of energy) is increasing global warming, whatever natural causes may be operative as well. We need no special instruction to make us aware that wars are continuing without means of prevention or control, that many of the poorer nations are suffering or are threatened with acute famine, as well as the ravages of AIDS and malaria.

Our rulers leave us in no doubt that there is a serious threat of terrorism everywhere in the world. But the bedevilment of international relations by national sovereignty is recognized scarcely at all, although this is the root cause of our ills. Again, there is no excuse for this ignorance, because for decades it has been repeatedly pointed out by distinguished international theorists (e.g., George Keeton and Georg Schwartzenberger) and by writers like W.B. Curry.*

Much of the resistance to and neglect of the need for world government is due to our early upbringing and subsequent education in childhood, which is habitually nationalistic in the wrong zenophobic sense. This habit would by now have been combatted and reversed, had the lessons taught us by the writers mentioned above along with the experience of two catastrophic world wars and their aftermath been learned.

Among the several World Federalist Associations at present active, the majority concentrate on "reform" of the United Nations (as a presumed first step towards their ultimate aim); but the recommended changes are highly unlikely ever to occur. The advocated establishment of a democratically elected Assembly to advise the General Assembly, even if approved, could make no difference to the incompetence of the organization, because the General Assembly is already no more than an advisory body and could never be other as long as the nations remain sovereign; the addition of a second advisory body (democratically elected or not) could for the same reason have no legislative authority.

---

* The relevant bibliography contains over forty titles by distinguished authors including George Keeton, K.C.Wheare, Georg Schwartzenberger, B. Ferencz, and R.M. Hutchins. I myself have written four books on the subject: *The Survival of Political Man* (1950), *Annihilation and Utopia* 1966), *One World or None* (1993) (revised as *Earth Federation Now*, 2005), *Apocalypse and Paradigm* (2000), and have co-edited another: *Toward Genuine Global Governance* (1999).

Other so-called reforms are to increase the membership of the Security Council which would make little, if any, difference, and to abolish the veto, which would never be approved by the Permanent Members. Furthermore, even were such "reforms" implemented, the subsequent progress towards federal union would be far too slow, for time is fast running out – scientists have told us that global warming will soon be, if it is not already, irreversible, and the other interrelated world problems cry out to be urgently addressed and combatted.

Federalists who advocate these changes ought instead to be insisting on the abolition of sovereign rights and the effective imposition of the Rule of Law in international relations, which can be achieved only if the Charter of the United Nations is replaced by a workable *Constitution for the Federation of Earth*, empowering a world government to enact laws that can be enforced on individuals by police action (instead of on states, impossible except by war).

One federalist body, however, has taken practical steps to implement this course: the World Constitution and Parliament Association. At several conventions, with the help of eminent international lawyers, it as drafted a comprehensive and well thought out world constitution, repeatedly revised, amended and improved. This constitution is now being offered for ratification by individuals, NGOs, and state governments. There are some who object to the *Constitution* because the body that drafted it was not democratically elected, but what makes a constitution democratic is not how, or by whom, it was drafted but whether it is freely accepted by those who are to become subject to its provisions.

Others object to details of the draft, but that need not prevent them from ratifying it because it provides for its own amendment, immediately on becoming operative and at prescribed intervals thereafter, as may be required by popular petition or a sufficient majority of the World Parliament. It has so far been ratified by over a hundred individuals and several thousand nongovernmental organizations, but not by any national government. What is lacking at the present time is the necessary public pressure, and the will and insight among politicians.

The establishment of a world federation so constituted is the only legitimate method of overcoming the obstacle presented by national sovereignty to world peace and the universal rule of law; and unless the nations of the world take this vital step without delay, there can be little hope that Curry's prediction will not be realized that "the human experiment" will come to a dismal end before recourse can be taken to any adequate remedial measures. As matters now stand, this may well occur sooner than the mass of the people and their political leaders expect.

World Legal Revolution

Eugenia Almand
Secretary, Provisional World Parliament

...To secure [unalienable Rights], Governments are instituted among Men,
deriving their just powers from the consent of the governed...Whenever any
Form of Government becomes destructive of [unalienable Rights], it is the
Right of the People to alter or to abolish it, and to institute new Government,
laying its foundation on such principles and organizing its powers in such
form, as to them shall seem most likely to effect their Safety and Happiness...When a long train of abuses and usurpations, pursuing invariably the
same Object evinces a design to reduce them under absolute Despotism, it
is their right, it is their duty, to throw off such Government, and to provide
new Guards for their future security.

From the United States Declaration of Independence

Because of the constitutional foundation set by the *Constitution for
the Federation of Earth*, together with the encompassing world legislation of the Provisional World Parliament, there is currently a worldwide
underlying legal revolution in progress. This legal revolution is bound to
affect the development of further world law. Likewise, it is bound to affect
any other process that might be labeled revolutionary during the years to
come.

The Provisional World Parliament, between 2003 and 2004, began
the overhaul of world legislation from convention law format to parliamentary law format. This new development has true legal revolutionary
significance that has not yet been fully recognized by either the mass media, or even by the majority of civil society organizations purporting to
advocate for the World Parliament.

The international conventions and statutes before 2003 have typi-
cally included characteristic convention flaws:

1) Nations are recognized to have some "right" to deny jurisdiction;

2) Nations are recognized to have some "right" to withdraw from
the international convention; and

3) The United Nations Security Council is given veto power over
the implementation of the convention, or may override the convention by
unanimous consent.

These characteristic flaws weaken convention law to the degree that critics often call it not true law at all. Its ultimate enforcement is the resort to war. Hence, an anarchic state was enshrined by convention within each international statute or convention.

The way out of this trap is not by convention, but by the direct utilization of binding world parliamentary process. The Provisional World Parliament has been addressing this problem during recent sessions (since 2003), to strike the conventional provisions from the body of generally accepted international law, and to thereby begin the process of true binding statutes at the world jurisdictional level.

With binding parliamentary statutes, each national government is empowered to address world statutes through parliamentary process. If the national government has representation at the World Parliament, then the national delegate or delegates may move or vote for amendment of the statutes directly. There is no longer a national level process for the disregard of world legislation, or for the disempowerment of world jurisdictional affairs.

Many thinkers have argued for the creation of a world parliament as an advisory body, with the power only to recommend to the United Nations General Assembly under Article 22 of the United Nations Charter. Such a deliberative body might yet be established, but by definition it won't initiate the necessary binding action within global legislation. Therefore, world law asserts that the nature of the world legislation referred to here is not advisory in nature, but rather that the world legislation is enacted with the intent of binding, enforceable character, with provisions for true legal enforcement at a world jurisdictional level.

Therefore, the following listed statutes are world law, not mere proposals for possible consideration or accession.

30 world statutes enacted and amended to date by the Provisional World Parliament:

World Legislative Act (Number & Short Title)	Date	PWP Session adopted
WLA 01 Weapons of Mass Destruction prohibition	1982	1
WLA 02 World Economic Development Organization	1982	1
WLA 03 World Oceans and Seabeds Authority	1982	1
WLA 04 Graduate School of World Problems	1982	1
WLA 05 Provisional District World Courts	1982	1
WLA 06 Emergency Earth Rescue Administration	1985	2
WLA 07 Earth Financial Funding Corporation	1985	2
WLA 08 World Commission on Terrorism	1985	2
WLA 09 Global Ministry on Environment	1987	3
WLA 10 World Hydrogen Energy Authority	1987	3
WLA 11 Earth Financial Credit Corporation	1987	3
WLA 12 Omnibus Act(First Manifesto)	2000	5

WLA_13 World Peace Act	2003	6
WLA_14 World Security Act	2003	6
WLA_15 Statute for the World Court on Human Rights	2003	6
WLA_16 Hydrocarbon Resource Act	2003	6
WLA_17 Commission for Legislative Review	2003	6
WLA_18 Provisional Office for World Revenue	2003	6
WLA_19 Penalty Code	2003	7
WLA_20 World Bench for Criminal Cases	2003	7
WLA_21 World Patents Act	2003	7
WLA_22 Equity Act	2004	8
WLA_23 Global Accounting & Auditing Standards Act	2003	7
WLA_24 Rules for Procedure & Evidence	2003	7
WLA_25 Preservation of World Government Records	2003	7
WLA_26 Education Act	2004	8
WLA_27 Child Rights	2004	8
WLA_28 World Bench for Juvenile Cases	2004	8
WLA_29 Elections Act	2004	8
WLA_30 Water Act	2004	8

Each of the World Legislative Acts is vitally important for the smooth functioning of the overall system. However, some of these Acts may be seen to be of more import regarding the enforcement and security aspects of the program. Also, recent legislative amendments to the fiscal structure of the program make the overall system more viable. Here are abstracts of some significant portions:

WLA#1 – Prohibits Weapons of Mass Destruction and outlines a world disarmament agency to address the enforcement of prohibiting WMDs. Different aspects of activity related to weapons of mass destruction are addressed:

1.1. design, engage in research thereon, or

test (class 6 felony)

1.2. produce, manufacture, fabricate (class 1 felony)

1.3. transport, deploy, install (class 1 felony)

1.4. maintain, store, stockpile (class 1 felony)

1.5. sell (class 5 felony)

1.6. buy (class 6 felony)

1.7. detonate (class 7 felony) or

1.8. direct violation of world legislation by request or command (one classification level higher than violation, except if class 7 felony, then class 7 felony)

WLA#7 – Establishes a means by which individuals, organizations, corporations, and nations can support the transition to Earth Federation without fiscal sacrifice and without mere voluntarism.

WLA#8 – World Commission on Terrorism. This legislation is from 1985, predating nearly all other steps toward international security against terrorism.

WLA#11 – Establishes an Earth Financial Credit Corporation, including quantification of the value of the Earth credit and Earth currency, independent of dollarization. The concept (introduced by Nobel Laureate Robert Mundell and others), for a world credit and currency system is recognized. The Earth credit and currency has a basket of commodities linked to the value of time in labor as its basis. The basket? [(1 kilogram wheat + 1 kilogram rice + 1 kilogram corn + 1 kilogram potato + 1 kilogram manioc + 1 kilogram soya + 1 kilogram peanut + 1 kilogram lentil+ 1 kilogram pea + 1 kilogram garbanzo + 1 kilogram nyam) / 11] + 10 litres of pure, potable water + 1 litre crude oil + [(100 grams iron + 100 grams aluminum + 100 grams copper) / 3] = 1 unit of Earth credit or Earth currency = 4 hours labor at minimum wage (@ ɵ0.25 units per hour minimum) = 1 day's wage.

This basis for the value of the currency establishes a value that is independent of mere relative values between national currencies. Under WLA#22 – The Equity Act, the global credit and currency is conceived within a greater program for fiscal evaluation of the global system, including a measurable Gross Economic Product of the Earth Federation (GEP), and a worldwide Federal Wage and Price Standard, provisions for minimum and maximum wages, including wages of the Members of World Parliament and all offices of the Earth Federation. This legislation emerges in the context of the widely-accepted Global Accounting and Auditing System.

WLA#13 – The Peace Act prohibits a variety of activities, including both war activities and activities leading to war, many of which were not addressed in the original Elements of Crime (Assembly of States Parties), and which were not addressed in World Legislative Act #1.

WLA#14 – The World Security Act provides legal guidelines for the implementation of the adequately strong world police force, empowering the World Disarmament Agency, without further need for any international military force. National military forces are now able to begin to phase themselves out securely without risk to the people.

WLA#19 – A Criminal Code Penalty Classification creates the framework for just sentencing based upon parliamentary statutes, as is the custom among all the parliamentary democracies. Therefore, there are sentencing parameters defined to the World Court system. Any sentencing by the World Court has to conform to the sentencing parameters.

WLA#20 – World Bench for Criminal Cases is the upgraded form of the International Criminal Court. The World Bench is currently in effect under the *Earth Constitution*. In the upgraded World Court, nations may not decline jurisdiction, may not withdraw, the United Nations Security Council may neither veto nor circumvent the compulsory jurisdiction of the World Court.

The World Court has the power of mandamus, which is the Court Order, and is no longer subjected to groveling to national governments with so-called "Requests." The upgrade of the World Court does not require accession by national level ratification of the world legislation. No amendment to the original Rome Statute is required. However, national governments may ratify the *Earth Constitution*, and the member representatives of national governments may thereafter motion and vote in deliberative actions of the World Parliament to amend the World Court statute or any other world legislation.

Knowing the emerging world law (while also being fully apprised of the risks) individual world citizens may now take stronger, more forceful legal positions. These more forceful legal positions may include threat of legal suit, citizen arrest (as developed from the common law), and participation in world police action as world law enforcement officers, as well as other appropriate legal revolutionary measures.

Of course, there are still risks involved in any legal action or inaction. When world criminals or other sociopaths intend harm, they may yet do harm while the world police force is yet gathering strength. Individuals who decide to enforce or help enforce the world law might be physically stopped, injured or killed, in spite of world legislation in place to prohibit resistance to world law enforcement. Some world citizens may even be illegally arrested, imprisoned or sentenced by rogue forces at international, national or sub-national levels.

The new system addresses this potential for misuse of sub-jurisdictional police powers, in which world police actions may be mislabeled, for instance as "kidnapping," "abduction," "hostage-taking," or "terrorism." The law draws clear distinctions between that of terrorist acts and the acts of citizens and officials who enforce the world law.

Interference in the actions of persons who are enforcing the world law carries stiff penalties. It would be wise for everyone to be aware of these developments and either steer clear of enforcement actions in progress, or to otherwise assist in World Law enforcement actions, if this is possible or requested by persons engaged in world law enforcement.

Distinction between terrorists acts and the just, proper arrest of violators of World Legislation:

Terrorist Acts. Not founded on law, but on unresolved cases of vengeance. Targets the public. Requires maiming or killing. Based upon a controversy of sides where someone must lose. Victims and perpetrators have no mutually recognized rights or powers. Weapons of mass destruction might be used. No legal warrant is involved.

Civil Arrest of World Lawbreakers. Founded on law: the common law, customary law, the *Earth Constitution*, and on subsequent legislation based on that *Earth Constitution*. Targets individual suspected lawbreakers. Any maiming or killing of suspect is incidental, unintentional, and accountable. Based on direct observed evidence of unlawful acts. There are not necessarily any losers. Both victims and alleged violators have rights and may have powers. Only weapons suitable for law enforcement may be used. Police officials are required to obtain a legal warrant identifying the person to be arrested, and the alleged violation(s), prior to arrest. In the case of citizen's arrest, without signed warrant, the citizen must have factual knowledge or direct observation that the accused has committed a felony.

The above contrast between civil world law enforcement and terrorist acts is dramatic and discerning. It is therefore no longer necessary for the public to sit around on their hands for fear of being labeled a terrorist for enforcement while atrocities are being committed. The remaining question is only whether we have the power to affect the arrest of the world lawbreakers. The power to enforce is addressed in this next section.

Do we yet have the power to bell the proverbial cat? With a clear comprehension of world law, I think this power is emerging.

For many years, there has been intelligent and legitimate resistance to the United Nations system, in part because the United Nations system is loathe to recognize the right of the people to self-protection. Although self-defense is ostensibly recognized in Chapter 7, Article 51 of the United Nations Charter ("Nothing in the present Charter shall impair the inherent right of individual or collective self-defense"), any cursory legal analysis of this provision will show that Article 51 refers to a presumed individual member-state right of defense, rather than to a citizen's right to defense. Years of effort by United Nations conferences, aimed at putting down so-called "illicit" trade in weapons (citizen purchase) has thoroughly discredited the United Nations in terms of its propensity to guarantee anyone's civil or human rights to self-protection in the sense originally developed by various rights declarations during the course of centuries.

When we speak of world legal revolution and the creation of enforceable world law, we necessarily are speaking in terms of legal force more powerful than any criminal force. This implies appropriate instruments of defense with which to enforce the law against world criminals using lethal force.

For this to be just and effective, the world citizenry must have a recognized and guaranteed right to self-protection. Both a world police and a world private citizenry must have the physical means for self-protection.

This implies a strengthened form of what has historically been called the right to keep and bear arms.

There was a dilemma in that originally, in many declarations of rights, there was never any clarification of what constituted arms. It was not enough to say just anything one desired, because there was a conflict with legitimate law enforcement through the use of weapons of mass destruction and through blind weapons (weapons that upon activation are not necessarily guided directly by intelligence, or for which the target hit is not always clear, such as land mines or grenades. These are against the widely recognized gun safety principle of clear targets.)

World Legislative Act #13, the World Peace Act, was able to justly and effectively address this dilemma by clarifying the right to keep and bear arms into the right to self-protection by the following wording (of which variations might be derived):

> WLA#13.6.3. The individual right to uphold the Earth Federation, bearing only arms suitable for law enforcement purposes and civil order, may not be infringed. The Earth Federation agents, representatives and officials shall only develop, keep and bear arms that are legal also, without requirement of citizen permit, registration or display, to the citizens of the Earth Federation. Article XII of the *Earth Constitution* does not protect incitement to armed insurrection to interfere with the operation of the Earth Federation. The Earth Federation does not recognize any right of agencies, corporations, organizations or governments at any level to possess weapons of any kind.

This effectively turns the gun control argument on its head, because under these global provisions, the world citizens have greater freedom to bear arms than does the world government itself. This is, in fact, as it should be. Individuals have rights. Organizations, corporations, and governments have powers. Rights take legal precedence.

Because the provisions of the world law clarify the right to self-protection far beyond any earlier documents or rights declarations, the pathway clears for just legal enforcement of world law on a global basis, without true and legally defensible resistance.

This is not a guarantee of peace, but it is a guarantee that the means employed by the Earth Federation for the enforcement of world law shall be just and also in true recognition of customary rights declarations of societies around the world.

This brings us to a transition point. Is the transition under the direction of the Blue Helmets? That is, does the world police emerge from the empowerment of a United Nations rapid deployment military force?

The envisioned United Nations rapid deployment force concept has been flawed because it has not recognized the right of the people to self-protection. Its concept of human rights has not evolved beyond that of the Universal Declaration of Human Rights, which is inadequate in that the UDHR still places national sovereignty above the rights of the world citizen. Under UDHR alone, the citizen has no recourse to universal jurisdiction in the event of rights abuse, only recourse at the national level, which is often the source of the abuse.

Also problematic with the rapid deployment force concept is the fact that there has not been proper differentiation between civil police action and military action. This is partly why, historically, the United Nations forces have been repeatedly accused of human rights abuses. From Korea, to the Congo, from Somalia to Nepal and beyond, the Blue Helmets have gained an ugly reputation. Until the system for legal enforcement of world law under the *Earth Constitution* is recognized, there is likelihood that the abuses will continue with impunity. Consequently, there will be continued resistance on the part of the people, until a just order is established and firmly in place.

True and just police action is not possible under the jurisdiction of the United Nations Security Council, because the Security Council is constituted on a strictly military basis, and not on the basis of civil enforcement using civilian police, a warrant system, and due process. Any rapid deployment force that is military or para-military in structure is bound to fail the test for justice.

In other words, World Police action implies the requirement of a system of warrants and due process of law, with each arrest followed up by recognition of the right to trial by jury. This is lacking in virtually all military actions and actions of the United Nations forces.

When a minimum number of national governments, perhaps two dozen, come together with an agreement to accede to the *Earth Constitution*, the political and economic foundation for a secure and just civil world parliamentary system will be in place. There will be no effective resistance, even by the more powerful nations. Attempts to discredit the new system will be overwhelmed by serious study of the new paradigm. The *Manifesto for the Earth Federation* (Chapter Three in this volume) clearly shows how the system will operate with greater efficiency and greater justice than the antiquated system of supposedly sovereign nation-states.

The Philosophy of Nonviolence
and World Revolution Through World Law

Glen T. Martin

The philosophy of nonviolence that has been developed through much of the twentieth century has made an indispensable contribution to all theories of legitimate revolutionary social change. Yet the implications of the philosophy of nonviolence are often not well understood. Nonviolence is integral to the realization of authentic democracy on our planet, just as it is integral to creating a global economics of universal prosperity rather than today's agonizing scarcity for sixty percent of the Earth's people. It is also, of course, integral to the process of world demilitarization and the activation of a civilized world order for the first time in history.

Neither Mahatma Gandhi nor most of the subsequent philosophers of nonviolent revolutionary social change repudiated all use of force. Gandhi himself said that if one lacked the courage to fight injustice through nonviolent means, one should pick up a gun. Worse than using a gun to fight injustice is cowardice: doing nothing, refusing to act: "I have been repeating over and over again that he who cannot protect himself or his nearest and dearest or their honor by nonviolently facing death may and ought to do so by violently dealing with the oppressor" (1987, p. 144).

What Gandhi advocates in this and similar passages is not violence "as a last resort" or a "slippery slope" that opens the door to militarized violence. Rather, he is pointing out that nonviolence means an activation of the universal spirit of humanity that is within us all. He affirms that nonviolence is the activation in us of true courage, honor, faithfulness, integrity, and loyalty to truth and justice. It is not that the use of force is always prohibited, but rather that our selves and our institutions must be premised on clinging to gigantic Truth (on *Satyagraha*). If we do this, then the use of force will nearly always be the minimum necessary to protect everyone involved. It can be the actions of a civilian police force or individual self-defense, but it can never be militarized violence, which always intentionally seeks to harm a perceived "enemy."

The philosophy of nonviolence is not a utopian ideal of starry-eyed "pacifists" placing their bodies for slaughter before implacable military machines. It is a pragmatic and common sense understanding directed toward breaking the infamous "cycle of violence" that has characterized most human history to date. It understands, as Gandhi did, that the use of force is sometimes necessary, despite the fact that every human being has inalienable rights and an inviolable dignity. We live in a concrete world filled with dangerous institutions, dangerous forces, and dangerous people. The task is to deal practically with all these dangers without ourselves sinking into the cycle of violence and the corruption it entails. The task placed upon all of us is to deal with these dangers pragmatically while moving human civilization forward beyond the present nightmare of violence and corruption.

Legitimate social change within truly democratic societies, of course, is always necessarily nonviolent. Truly democratic societies institutionalize provisions (through numerous channels) for citizen participation: discussion, public debate, freedom of information, public demonstrations, referendums, election of officials, and both individual and collective forms of action. Societies that are not truly democratic (all national governments today as is explained in detail elsewhere in this volume) institutionalize empty forms of citizen participation as a propaganda mechanism for legitimating their power while in reality relegating decision-making to special power groups like corporations, the rich, dominant elites, those with "security clearances," etc.

The rule of universally applicable and fairly enforced laws is the foundation for a largely nonviolent society. Gandhi identified the institutional violence of Indian society with those features that did not conform to this pattern: the vast disparity between rich and poor, colonial privilege for a certain group, untouchability, etc. But in an interdependent world possessing horrendous high speed weapons, as well as vast inequalities, there can be no democratically run, nonviolent society anywhere unless there is the rule of democratic world law that ends most institutional violence everywhere on Earth. Only democratically legislated world law can eliminate the primary causes of imperialism, militarism, subversive violence, state terrorism, and private terrorism.

For Gandhi, and for the philosophy of nonviolence, genuine democracy very definitely requires a tremendous reduction in the gap between rich and poor. In this, he agrees with American philosopher John Dewey who argued that progress in democracy necessarily required a democratization of the sphere of economic decision-making as well as the sphere of politics (see Martin, 2004). The *Earth Constitution* is premised on both these aspects of genuine democracy, one that institutionalizes real provisions for citizen participation and nonviolent change and the other that creates a global economics of prosperity and removes the possibility of exploitation of the poor by the rich.

We have seen that the *Earth Constitution* is premised on the moral foundations of the sovereignty of the people of Earth, universal human rights, the principle of unity-in-diversity, human equality, and the right of all to a freedom compatible with the equal freedom of everyone else. For this reason, establishing a genuine world democracy requires removing the institutional violence of economic scarcity, manipulation, and exploitation: "That economics is untrue," Gandhi writes, which ignores or disregards moral values" (1972, p. 118).

Nonviolence is the activation of universal moral values in every sphere of life, since it is premised on the foundation of all moral values that is the inviolable dignity of the human person. Those moral values that claim to respect this yet try to legitimize war, economic relations that allow mass poverty and misery, or "security" arrangements that protect dominant elites from social change are false and hypocritical. Nonviolence does not abjure all use of force, but insists that social arrangements be transformed so that the use of force becomes the absolute minimum of what is necessary for the protection of everyone equally.

"The extension of the law of nonviolence in the domain of economics," Gandhi writes, "means nothing less than the introduction of moral values as a factor to be considered when regulating international commerce" (1972, p. 118). This must be true on a global scale. "Immediately as the spirit of exploitation is gone," he asserts, "armaments will be felt as a positive unbearable burden. Real disarmament cannot come unless the nations of the world cease to exploit one another" (1972, p. 112).

All militarism under the world system, like all terrorism, derives from the same undemocratic root as was explained in the above article "The Roots of Terrorism in the Sovereign Nation-state and a Path to a Secure World Order." Violence permeates nearly all the institutions of today's world as I also argued at length in Chapter Three of *Millennium Dawn* (2005). Most individual violence and private terrorist violence are consequences of, and reactions to, the pervasive institutionalized violence of modern nation-states. They are what is known as "blowback," a term made famous by both Chalmers Johnson (2001) and the CIA.

For when genuine democracy does not exist (and it cannot exist without democratic world government), then the only alternative is to institutionalize violence: to use the police and the law to repress the poor, to protect the privileged, to institutionalize lying and deceit to the public, to militarize society with the bogus threat of implacable enemies everywhere, to imperialistically control the wealth-producing process in the world to the advantage of the already wealthy and powerful in the imperial centers of capital (Smith, 2005a).

World revolution through world law means founding genuine world democracy for the first time in history. This necessarily entails not only activating citizen participation in governing but modifying global economics to one of truly universal prosperity. "If the recognized leaders of mankind," Gandhi writes, "who have control over the engines of destruction were wholly to renounce their use, with full knowledge of the implications, permanent peace can be obtained. This is clearly impossible without the Great Powers of the Earth renouncing their imperialistic design. This again seems impossible without great nations ceasing to believe in soul-destroying competition and to desire to multiply wants and, therefore, increase their material possessions" (1972, p. 111).

The "Great Powers" can only achieve this if they are federated within democratic world government and subject to demilitarization and an economic system that maintains their prosperity while also creating prosperity for everyone else on the planet. They can only achieve this if their mutual security is assured by effective enforceable world law that demilitarizes all nations and organizations equally. They can only achieve this if it is demanded by the people of Earth.

Gandhi introduced a resolution to a national committee in India on 5 August 1942 that read in part:

> "The Committee is of the opinion that the future peace, security, and ordered progress of the world demand a world federation of free nations, and on no other basis can the problems of the modern world be solved. Such a world federation would ensure the freedom of its constituent nations, the prevention of aggression and exploitation by one nation over another, the protection of national ministries, the advancement of all backward areas and peoples, and the pooling of the world's resources for the common good of all" (Hudgens, 1986, p. 14)

This is a very close description of what the *Constitution for the Federation of Earth* offers. Gandhi understood that a nonviolent world order is not only a spiritual commitment on the part of persons everywhere but must be institutionalized both politically and economically in the form of democratic world government and federated democratic government at all levels of governing.

"The entire social order has got to be reconstructed," he says, "a society based on nonviolence cannot nurture any other ideal" (1972, p. 120). "Democracy and violence can ill go together," he writes, "it is a blasphemy to say that nonviolence can only be practiced by individuals and never by nations which are a compound of individuals" (1972, p. 134). Given the cycle of violence today that also protects massive institutionalized violence, founding a demilitarized democratic world government is the most practical and common sense course of action for humanity.

A reconstructed social order would necessarily be a genuine democracy, since it would have to be founded on truth, freedom of speech, inquiry, and press, rather than on manipulation of the public by dominant elites through deception and propaganda. Its democratic framework and its ways of dealing with law-breaking: with police practices, with due process procedures, with court practices, with sentencing, forms of punishment, and imprisonment would all cultivate the spirit of nonviolence in the population. People would see for themselves that their rights were respected and that equality, freedom, and justice were promoted. Such government would by no means eliminate conflict. Rather, it would institutionalize nonviolent ways of dealing with conflict on all levels. Nonviolence does not eliminate conflict, Gandhi asserts. It eliminates the intention to harm ones opponent:

> To say or write a distasteful word is surely not violent especially when the speaker or writer believes it to be true. The essence of violence is that there must be a violent intention behind a thought, word, or act, i.e., an intention to do harm to the opponent so-called. False notions of propriety or fear of wounding susceptibilities often deter people from saying what they mean and ultimately land them on the shores of hypocrisy. But if nonviolence of thought is to be evolved in individuals or societies or nations, truth has to be told, however harsh or unpopular it may appear to be at the moment. (1972, p. 91)

Can police be trained to arrest lawbreakers with the intention of using the minimum force necessary to secure the safety of themselves, the suspect, and any innocent bystanders? Certainly. In some European nations, police are already being trained in such methods of apprehension and arrest. Conflict can be democratically institutionalized in a way that minimizes both violence and the tendency to violence in dissidents and lawbreakers. American philosopher Robert Holmes advocates a similar practical understanding of the philosophy of nonviolence:

> This doesn't require changing human nature or transforming the world into a community of saints. It does require recognizing that if we don't cherish the human person, there is no point to the many other activities and strivings that consume our time; no point to saving the environment unless we value the beings that inhabit it; no virtue in self-sacrifice when at the expense of the lives and happiness of others. It does require a massive commitment of time, energy, and moral and financial resources to exploring nonviolent ways of getting along in the world. The aim should not be to end conflict. That would be utopian and might not even be desirable. The aim should be to develop nondestructive ways of dealing with conflict. Violence by its very nature cannot do that. Nonviolence can. As Gandhi dem-

onstrated, rather than approaching conflict with a view to trying to prevail at any cost, it's possible to approach it with a view to trying to see that the truth prevail – trying to see that the best solution emerge, whether or not it be one to which you were predisposed at the outset. People can learn this. They can be trained in techniques to implement it. They can incorporate it in their institutions. (1990, p. 139)

Given the truth that nonviolence can be institutionalized to minimize the use of force in human relations, what will the nonviolent democratic world government look like? How will its police behave? How will it deal with terrorism, killers, or violent dissidents? The *Constitution for the Federation of Earth* provides the framework for a nonviolent world order. We have seen that this framework requires both genuine democracy and general economic prosperity with an end to economic exploitation. Article 10, "The Enforcement System," makes the following declaration concerning enforcement by the World Police force:

(1) The enforcement of world law and world legislation shall apply directly to individuals, and individuals shall be held responsible for compliance with world law and world legislation regardless of whether the individuals are acting in their own capacity or as agents or officials of governments at any level or of the institutions of governments, or as agents or officials of corporations, organizations, associations or groups of any kind. (2) When world law or world legislation or decisions of the world courts are violated, the Enforcement System shall operate to identify and apprehend the individuals responsible for violations. (3) Any enforcement action shall not violate the civil and human rights guaranteed under this World Constitution. (4) The enforcement of world law and world legislation shall be carried out in the context of a non-military world federation wherein all member nations shall disarm as a condition for joining and benefitting from the world federation, subject to Article X VII, Sec. C-8 and D-6. The Federation of Earth and World Government under this World Constitution shall neither keep nor use weapons of mass destruction. (5) Those agents of the enforcement system whose function shall be to apprehend and bring to court violators of world law and world legislation shall be equipped only with such weapons as are appropriate for the apprehension of the individuals responsible for violations. (6) The enforcement of world law and world legislation under this World Constitution shall be conceived and developed primarily as the processes of effective design and administration of world law and world legislation to serve the welfare of all people on Earth, with equity and justice for all, in which the resources of Earth and the funds and the credits of the World Government are used only to serve peaceful human needs, and none used for weapons of mass destruction or for war making capabilities.

This set of six principles defines the framework for the operation of the World Police and the possession of weapons. No legitimate government or democracy requires a military apparatus, since all democratic legislation applies to individuals, not governments, institutions, or corporations. Militaries are organized for mass destruction of some perceived "enemy" and that enemy's life-support systems.

But once the international anarchy and chaos of the system of "sovereign" nation-states is replaced with real world law and a federation of nations, militaries will no longer be necessary. "Nations will no longer lift up their sword against nations." At this point, enforcement will only need to apply to individuals. Therefore, the agents of democratic world government "shall be equipped only with such weapons as are appropriate for the apprehension of the individuals responsible for violations."

Since a constitution is a framework, not a body of specific laws, the question of what weapons allowed the World Police is left to the World Parliament to decide. However, they must be only those necessary to apprehend individuals. All tanks, warships, warplanes, bombs, missiles, etc., are necessarily excluded since they are military weapons, not those necessary to apprehend individuals using a minimum of force while protecting the rights and safety of all concerned. The philosophy of nonviolence implies exactly this social transformation to the point where the use of force is minimized in human relations.

It is very important here to distinguish between the role of civilian police and the role of military force, including a militarized police force. Military force is inherently undemocratic, since it is only necessary to secure an illusory protection or to enforce a system of imperial exploitation in a profoundly undemocratic world order. Its very existence destroys democracy and freedom both within and without individual nation-states (as we have seen elsewhere in this volume).

This is why the world government cannot be militarized, not because of some utopian idea that human beings will be without conflict or without requiring the occasional use of force. No democracy can be militarized and remain a democracy. That is why no nation claiming to be a democracy today is legitimate. Democracy within nations can only be realized when democratic world government has dealt with the global problems such as militarism and external threats that are beyond the scope of all nation-states (see Almand and Martin, 2005).

Civilian police, on the other hand (the only kind of police allowed under the *Constitution*) are accountable to the citizens for their behavior, their obedience to the law, their use of force, and their job security. We already have a measure of this in many cities that require a civilian review board to monitor police behavior. Civilian police are normally mandated to use (and can be trained to use) the minimum force necessary to apprehend individuals suspected of crimes.

They are required to respect the rights of all citizens and, as the slogan says, to "protect and serve." A nonviolent set of governmental institutions would insist that police are highly trained and educated in the proper function of a civilian police force, which is the antithesis of all military force. A civilian police force within a genuine democracy is mandated to use the minimum necessary force, and to make every effort to use nonlethal force.

The *Constitution* leaves it open for the World Parliament, after democratic dialogue and debate, to legislate what weapons are acceptable for the World Police. But it makes sense that these weapons would be more and more *nonlethal* as technology in nonlethal weaponry advances. Stun guns, propelled body nets, non-lethal darts, and other technology of nonlethal weaponry yet to be developed will likely become the stock and trade of the World Police.

A civilian police force within a framework of real democratic justice, respect for individual rights, and freedom will be mandated to continually examine how it can accomplish its mission of effectively apprehending criminals while at the same time continually maximizing the safety of themselves, those apprehended, and innocent bystanders. Very high quality training and education will necessarily supplement whatever weapons are authorized by the World Parliament.

The *Constitution* also leaves it open for the World Parliament to legislate what weapons are acceptable for private individuals. A constitution is not a blueprint. Many decisions must be made through the democratic processes set up by the *Constitution*. However, the Provisional World Parliament has already passed provisional world laws in this regard specifying that individuals may posses only those weapons also permitted to the World Police.

Provisional world laws are not binding on the established World Parliament once it has been activated. They will serve as guidelines, suggestions, and a preliminary groundwork. This particular provisional world law of the Provisional Parliament was controversial and by no means unanimous, yet it appears consistent with the *Constitution's* founding premise of the dignity and inviolable rights of every individual on Earth, including the right to self-defense. We saw above that Gandhi affirmed even the use of force in defense of ones self and loved-ones if a person lacked the courage to do this nonviolently.

The Provisional World Parliament has followed the *Constitution* closely by outlawing the design, development, sale, transportation, or possession of all weapons of war for individuals, groups, corporations, governments, and even the world government. So we may be assured that weapons of war will continue to be illegal everywhere on Earth (as they are now under provisional world law) once the established World Parliament is activated. If the established World Parliament sees fit to follow the Provisional World Parliament in allowing individuals the same weapons as it allows the World Police, this may serve as an incentive for the World Police to develop ever-more and better nonlethal forms of apprehension and arrest and to progressively eliminate lethal weapons. Article 12 of the *Constitution* gives each citizen of the Earth Federation the following rights:

> Safety of person from arbitrary or unreasonable arrest, detention, exile, search or seizure; requirement of warrants for searches and arrests. Prohibition against physical or psychological duress or torture during any period of investigation, arrest, detention or imprisonment, and against cruel or unusual punishment. Right of habeas corpus; no ex-post-facto laws; no double jeopardy; right to refuse self-incrimination or the incrimination of another. Prohibition against private armies and paramilitary organizations as being threats to the common peace and safety. Safety of property from arbitrary seizure; protection against exercise of the power of eminent domain without reasonable compensation. Right of privacy of person, family and association; prohibition against surveillance as a means of political control.

The security, safety, and freedom of citizens is clearly a primary focus of the *Constitution*. And, given what we have seen in this essay, it should be clear that the Earth Federation will be nonviolent regardless of whatever stun-guns, handguns, pepper spray canisters, or rifles citizens are allowed to possess. If people feel they need to possess these items, they will do so. But given the framework of a deeply nonviolent society that is built by the *Constitution* (in which true democracy is realized and institutionalized violence and exploitation are eliminated), it is unlikely that many will feel this need. The law could easily maximize their freedoms in this regard without the fear that there would be many people using such weapons to break the law or do violence.

As Gandhi made clear, if we create real democracy on Earth, and real economic justice and prosperity on Earth, we will have institutionalized nonviolence. With today's system of militarized "sovereign" nation-states and vast disparities between extreme wealth and extreme poverty, we have pervasive institutionalized violence. This violence requires the military to enforce its global system of injustice and exploitation. But if we ratify the *Constitution for the Federation of Earth* and create world institutions premised on the dignity, freedom, and equality of every person on Earth, we will eliminate the need not only for the military but also for most personal or terrorist violence. And what is even more fundamental, we will have laid the groundwork for a transformation of the human spirit.

Today, the human spirit is distorted by the violent institutions that pervade our lives. The process of realizing a democratic world order under the *Constitution* may be marred by having to contend with the violence of the nation-states that currently eat, sleep, and breathe violence through their every institution. As we have seen in Chapter Two above, the people of Earth (and each of us insofar as we act from what is universal in ourselves) not only have the right, but the duty to create democratic world government and exit the immoral state of *defacto* war and institutionalized violence under which they are currently forced to live.

Under Article Nineteen of the *Constitution*, the people of Earth have the mandate to elaborate the institutions of provisional world government until such time as the *Constitution* has been formally ratified according to the provisions set forth in Article Seventeen. This means we are building what is sometimes called a "parallel government" to the ones currently falsely claiming legitimacy in the world. This "parallel government" is not a competing claim to nation-statehood, of course, but includes the invitation to all national governments to reclaim their legitimacy and integrity by becoming part of the emerging Earth Federation. In this regard, it is not "parallel" at all but the entity representing the sovereignty of the people of Earth capable of restoring the legitimacy of the national governments as well as eliminating their violent and unjust characteristics.

Yet in our efforts to elaborate the infrastructure of world government, members of the emerging Earth Federation avail ourselves of many of the techniques of nonviolent action. Professor Gene Sharp in Part Two of *The Politics of Nonviolent Action* entitled *The Methods of Nonviolent Action* lists 198 techniques or methods of nonviolent struggle. Number 198 is listed as "dual sovereignty and parallel government." Sharp writes:

> This method involves the creation of a new government, or continued loyalty to an existing rival government to that of the opponent. If the parallel government receives overwhelming support from the populace, it may replace the opponent's established government....This general phenomenon has occurred in a variety of situations and is by no means a product of twentieth century revolutions. (1985, p. 423)

Sharp goes on to describe historical examples of when this method was used, often without conscious intent as a nonviolent method. He describes the Netherlands struggle against the Spanish king in 1575-77, the conflict in England between Charles and the Long Parliament during the 1640s, the struggle during U.S. revolutionary times between the Continental Congress and British rule, "Dorr's Rebellion" in Rhode Island in 1841-42, the Russian Revolution of 1905, and again of 1917, the general strike in Winnipeg, Canada in 1919, the Indian struggle against the British, especially during the 1930-31 campaign, and the contest in China between the Japanese and the "Border Government" during the 1930s.

Given this long history of revolutionary movements developing an alternative government to replace an existing government, one can say that the work of the Provisional World Parliament and the members of the emerging Earth Federation are definitely engaged with time-honored methods of nonviolent action. As the institutions of the Federation develop (assuming the *Constitution* has not yet been ratified by the people and nations of Earth) we will be elaborating the world ministries, the World Parliament, the world courts, and the world enforcement system of police and attorneys general.

The World Police may be called upon to apprehend criminals (for example, any persons engaged in weapons research, design, manufacture, transport, sale, purchase, or deployment, which are all criminal activities under existing provisional world law). From what has been said above, it should be clear that even the provisional World Police will be well trained in what it means to be a civilian police officer within a genuine democracy. That is, they will be trained to use the minimum force necessary to apprehend the suspect, protect themselves, ensure the safety of innocent bystanders, and follow due-process procedures ensuring the rights of all.

In addition, citizens as well as the World Ombudsmus will be free to monitor the behavior of the police to be sure that they fulfill their function of reducing the use of force to a minimum. Provisional World Legislative Act 14.3 reads in part as follows:

> Civil Empowerment. Behavior of World Police Officers while on duty may be freely audited by both non-interfering private Earth citizens and by the World Ombudsmus, to assure compliance to least necessary force and to appropriate behavior on the part of the Enforcement System. The World Ombudsmus and Earth Citizens may file legal complaints or legal charges, and seek rectification for damages arising from the improper use of weapons. At which time the World Police begins its formation and forever thereafter, the World Police Force may develop, use and possess only weapons legal to the citizens of the Earth Federation without requirement of permit, registration or disclosure."

The World Police under the Earth Federation will be truly servants and protectors of the people as this passage states. Nonviolence is therefore institutionalized within both the *Constitution* and Provisional World Law.

This is practical and common sense nonviolence in action. It does not demand some utopian abjuring of all reasonable use of force. It clearly forbids an "intention to do harm to the opponent" that Gandhi says is a defining characteristic of violence. It does not assume some "peaceful human nature" or conflict-free future for humanity.

It is action in the service of authentic democracy, which is necessarily nonviolent to every extent possible, and it is action in the service of the nonviolent method of developing a "parallel government" that appeals to the allegiance to the people of Earth precisely because it is democratic, just, liberating, and nonviolent. Just as "violent means" inevitably lead to violent results (as the institutionalized violence of today's world illustrates), so nonviolent means are the only legitimate revolutionary strategy to realize a truly new and revolutionary goal: a nonviolent world democracy of justice, freedom, equality, and peace.

Principles of Ecology
and the Emerging Earth Federation

Glen T. Martin

The principles of ecology and their significance are not widely understood even at this point in the early twenty-first century. They reveal not only the basic processes of the natural world but also the foundations of human societies and social interactions. The principles of natural ecology are complemented by the principles of social ecology. These principles point directly to the creation of an Earth Federation under the *Constitution for the Federation of Earth*. Once the *Constitution* is ratified, these principles are also legally implemented, enforced, and protected under the Federation of Earth. This essay attempts to both elucidate these principles and show their necessary connections to the emerging Earth Federation.

1. The Revolution in Ecological Understanding

An important event in the emergence of the environmental movement in the 1960s was the publication of Rachel Carson's book *Silent Spring* (1962). The book signaled the dawning of a new awareness among thoughtful human beings of the fragile nature of the planetary environment and the suicidal consequences of economic and social policies that ignore our inseparability from, and interdependence with, the environment.

Since that time, the environmental movement has spread worldwide and the new natural science of ecology has emerged to study living natural systems, their integration, and their interrelation throughout the Earth. Ecology is the scientific study of the interdependence between organisms and their environment. The understanding is growing worldwide that organisms and their environment form a fragile web of life in which disruption of even seemingly irrelevant aspects of an ecosystem can spell disaster for the entire system and the organisms that are interdependent with that system.

Millions of ecosystems have spread throughout the Earth during its four billion years of being home to living organisms. These range from tiny microscopic environments to the total environment of the planet. The total environment is sometimes called "Gaia" after the ancient Greek goddess of the Earth. Ecosystems form a web of interdependent systems that encompass the entire planet and constitute an integrated weave of life-forms within which the evolution of human beings took place and without which human beings could not have survived upon the Earth (Lovelock, 1991).

Human beings slowly became the dominant species on the planet over the course of their more than two million year history. Only after the discovery of agriculture, approximately 8-10,000 BCE, did they become able to form permanent settlements, build ever-larger cities, and begin engineering projects that altered the natural landscape of the planet to suit their designs. The record shows many ancient civilizations that used up or destroyed their natural resource base and either died out or emigrated elsewhere (Diamond, 2005). Nevertheless, human beings did not become capable of actually destroying the ecological foundations of the entire planet until the industrial revolutions of the 18th and 19th centuries.

With the vast power placed in human hands by engines, electricity, and specialized machines, the ecosystems of the Earth began to be destroyed at a rate far beyond the ability of nature to heal and repair damages caused by human interference. The technological revolutions of the 18th and 19th centuries continued into the electronic and digital revolutions of the 20th and 21st centuries placing such power in human hands that human activity in its present forms may well destroy the life-support systems of the entire planet and collapse the fabric of life to the point where higher forms of life can no longer survive upon the Earth.

The forests of the world, for example, provide the planetary ecosystem with much of the oxygen that supports all aerobic forms of life. They bind carbon dixoide that is exhaled by most living creatures and produced by all forms of combustion. They moderate the climate, provide habitats for most of the vast bio-diversity of the Earth, and draw fresh water from the ocean coasts into the interior of continents. Yet the forests of the Earth are disappearing at the rate of an area one half the size of California each year.

In addition to forests, agricultural soils of the Earth are rapidly disappearing. Unsustainable agricultural practices are rapidly depleting topsoils of the planet to the point where vast areas have become unsuitable for agriculture and have been converted to grazing lands. Yet overgrazing worldwide is turning even these areas on every continent into desert, places that cannot be used to support most life. Runnoff from the use of pesticides is poisoning water supplies and ecosystems. Billions of tons of topsoil are lost each year to erosion because of these unsustainable agricultural practices.

Regarding fresh water, the over-pumping of aquifers and overuse of water is dropping water tables worldwide, causing water crises and shortages in many areas of the world. The cities of the world, in addition, are becoming poisoners of the planet's fresh air supplies. Hundreds of millions of gasoline and internal combustion engines and other sources of air pollution spew pollutants into the air. Yet the air of the Earth is necessary to support all higher forms of life and is at the heart of the ecosystem of our planet.

These cities also produce immense amounts of polluted water, garbage, and trash wastes that are filling, and poisoning, the countrysides of nations worldwide. At the same time, the human polulation continues to grow at the rate of 80 million new persons per year, every one of whom requires basic resources, fresh water, clean air, and agricultural and forest resources to support them throught their life-spans, and every one of whom produces waste materials that are returned to the environment (Caldicott, 1992; Renner, 1996; Daly 1996).

The principle of Gaia, the idea of the entire Earth (as it has evolved over its 4.6 billion year existence) forming an encompassing ecosystem, is only slowly becoming understood by large numbers of people. This awareness grows as planetary phenomena signaling the alteration of the entire global ecosystem become widely known, phenomena such as global warming, melting of the polar ice caps, depletion of the ozone layer, collapsing of entire ocean fisheries, rapid exinction of species on a daily basis, increased planetary disasters and superstorms, and possible inversions of global ocean currents and weather patterns (Lovelock, 1991).

Thoughtful human beings today have understood that human life is inseparable from the web of life on Earth. They have understood that we must alter our economic, social, and political practices rapidly to bring human civilization into harmony with the planetary web of life that sustains us (Daly, 1996). They understand that all development must be sustainable, that it must support human life in the present in ways that do not diminish the life-prospects of future generations. Today, nearly all societies and all nations are living at the expense of future generations, both of humans and other species (Calidcott, 1992). Actualization of our life-prospects diminishes their life-prospects. At the current rate of destruction, it is even possible that we will reduce their life-prospects to zero.

2. Social Ecology

Ecology teaches us that human beings and all living organisms are part of the web of life, the fabric of which can be torn to the point of no return.

Social ecology, a science that has also emerged during the late 20th century, teaches us that not only are humans part of the web of life but human societies themselves are best formed around the principle of unity-in-diversity which is the basic principle of a healthy community. Human life has emerged from nature following the same principles of interdependency and interrelationship that are fundamental in the natural world.

During the famous Axial Period in human history that included the six hundred years before the beginning of the Common Era, human consciousness was transformed into its present subject-object structure. This new structure allowed people to self-consciously distance themselves from nature or other persons and objectify the world, other people, or living creatures. This capacity for objectification placed tremendous power into the hands of human beings, power that began to systematically violate the principles of social ecology, as well as those of natural ecology, in the service of the drive to domination, control, and mastery of nature and other people (Martin, 2005).

Systems of domination and disregard of human interdependency developed rapidly and continued into the early modern world until the present. The principles of social ecology only began to be understood with the elaboration of democratic theory in the 18th century through the work of such writers as Immanuel Kant, Jean-Jacques Rousseau, John Stuart Mill, and John Locke. Even though there had long been ideas of our common human dignity (humans made in the image of God) and of the fundamental role played by human reason (from Plato to Aquinas and natural law theory), the idea of the necessary integration of human communities into democratic forms based on liberty, equality, and community only developed fully during the period of the 18th century Enlightenment. This movement, focusing on universal human rights and a universal human rationality as the basis for democracy, developed the early forms of the principle of social ecology.

In that era, it dawned on many thinkers that reason was a common human trait that made all people potentially capable of excercizing responsible freedom and contributing to the well-being of their community. Today, it is becoming understood that the social ecological principle is best exemplified in political life in precisely this idea of democracy whereby liberty, equality, and community point to, as American philosopher John Dewey (1993) expresses it, democracy as a moral-spiritual form of association expressing the relationships of interdependence and cooperation that should prevail among human beings. Human beings are intensely social animals radically dependent not only upon natural processes but upon one another.

The idea of democracy was extended in the 19th and 20th centuries to include the concept of economic democracy. It became ever more clearly understood that industrial and service operations are cooperative in nature with many people working together to produce wealth. It was understood that the private appropriation of cooperatively produced wealth violated not only the integrity of people but damaged the community spirit required in productive and service projects. Twentieth century thinkers such as Gregory Batson (1972), Erich Fromm (1947), Jürgen Habermas (1984), Errol E. Harris (2000), Robert J. Liften (1993), and Pierre Teilhard de Chardin (1959) began to formulate the principles of social ecology in terms of the interdependency and interrelation of persons within communties and the ways in which society best functions as a successful community.

Just as with natural ecology, social ecology has not yet penetrated the awareness of most persons. This is in part because of the gigantic propaganda efforts of imperial governments along with the propaganda that spews forth from immense concentrations of private capital that benefit from the older, anti-ecological system of human relationships. Most economic, political, and community processes are still top-down, heirarchical systems that marginalize, exploit, and exclude the majority at the base of the social-economic pyramid.

Social ecology understands that there is a social Gaia principle for the Earth, that human life on Earth is a whole, a fabric of social, political, and economic activities in which activities on one part of the Earth impact human as well as natural life on other parts of the Earth. Human life is a web of tiny communties (families) integrated into ever-larger wholes (social and ecological systems) from the village to the province to the nation to the world. The Gaia principle for the Earth means that human beings must create nonmilitary democratic world government based on the social ecological principle of unity-in-diversity for all nations, peoples, and individuals. Such a principle would do for fragmented and destructive human societies what the natural Gaia principle does for the environment of the Earth. Both are necessary to make sustainable fourishing upon the Earth possible.

3. The Emerging Earth Federation

After the nations of the world discovered the technology for developing nuclear and other weapons of mass destruction at the close of the Second World War, many thinkers recognized the need for democratic world government. The list includes such eminant personalities as Mortimer J. Adler (1991), Sri Aurobindo (1997) Albert Einstein (1950), Errol

E. Harris (1993), Emery Reves (1946), and Pierre Teilhard de Chardin (1959). Awareness the pending collapse of the global environment did not come until later. Among the earliest to understand the implications of the impending destruction of Gaia were the founders of the World Constitution and Parliament Association in 1958, leaders and visionaries such as Philip and Margaret Isely, Dr. Terence Amerasinghe, and Dr. Reinhart Ruge. For the next 30 years they worked continuously with thousands of world citizens from many countries to hold four Constituent Assemblies that developed and approved the *Constitution for the Federation of Earth*.

The *Constitution*, once ratified, will become the actualization of the social ecological Gaia principle for the Earth. The Preamble to the *Constitution* describes the realization of this principle as "a new age when war shall be outlawed and peace shall prevail," and "when the Earth's total resources shall be equitably used for human welfare." The *World Constitution* does for humanity what natural evolution has done for nature. It creates a world order based on the principle of the whole – Gaia. There can be no effective political, social, and economic respect for the whole of nature unless there are polical, social, and economic institutions based on the whole of humanity.

These two dimensions of ecology are inseparable. The basic principle of ecology must apply to both our human relationship to nature and the relationship of human beings to one another. Wholeness, as philosopher of science Errol E. Harris has pointed out (2000), is fundamental to the entire human and natural world order. Natural processes have created Gaia, the principle of the whole of the global ecosystem based upon the integration and interdependency of overlapping systems as parts. Both human society and the natural world require this principle. This "synergy" is explicitly understood by Peter Russell in his book *The Global Brain Awakens* (1995). Its continued violation will ultimately spell planetary suicide.

Our present world order is in violation of the social principle of ecology in at least three fundamental ways. The first way involves a world order divided into approximately 191 so-called "sovereign" nation-states. The very existence of the perverse concept of a "sovereign" nation-state (supposedly independent in its external relations and autonomous over its internal affairs) destroys the wholeness and integrity of human life on this planet. Because it violates the principle of social ecology so deeply, it makes impossible respect for the principle of natural ecology, the whole of the planetary natural environment. The "sovereign" nation-state breeds violence and fragmentation through its political structure that institutionalizes a fragmented and destructive world view. This impacts the thought patterns of most of the world's population.

The second way the present world order violates the principle of social ecology is through the promotion of aggressive and competitive individualism. This egoistic self-assertion cultivated by economic, social, and political processes in the modern world order finds its consequences in masses of people who do not care about the common good, the whole, or the planetary community. Such people act solely out of naked self-interest and are therefore directly destructive of both the natural and social principles of ecology. The social production of this sort of destructive individualism is clearly connected with the existence of sovereign nation-states on the one hand and the global economic system of unbridled greed and self-interest on the other.

The third way that the present world order is in violation of ecology is through the legal institution of corporate personhood and the system of *"exclusive-titles-to-nature's-wealth"* (Smith 2005a). Corporations doing business for the private accumulation of wealth are legally protected as if they were private persons not responsible to the common good or the communities within which they operate. They are top-down, totalitarian institutions, with decisions made in secret by tiny groups of executives and owners, whose sole mission it to accumulate private profit.

If monopolization of these exclusive titles is eliminated, thereby giving full and equal rights to each person, then those exclusive rights will be properly restructured to *conditional rights*. With that simple change, mass accumulations (appropriations) of wealth produced by others is impossible. The system of corporate personhood involves the denial of full and equal rights to real persons and is at the base of global monopoly capitalism.

This entire system is protected by law in most countries with the result that horror-story after horror-story emerges concerning corporate destruction and disregard of nature, persons, and communities in the pursuit of unlimited private accumulations of wealth (Chossudovsky, 1999; Korten, 2001; Siva 2002). This global system of corporate irresponsibility destroys both the natural and social principles of ecology and portends the ultimate destruction of life itself. It will mean the end of Earth's ability to support higher forms of life by the close of the 21st century.

The *Constitution for the Federation of Earth* was written with all three of these failures of the present world order in mind. First, it abolishes the dangerous and fragmented system of so-called "sovereign" nation-states and federates the nations into a whole based on the principle of unity-in-diversity which is at the heart of social ecology. Second, through a number of specific requirements given throughout the document, it promotes human cooperation, a sense of responsiblity to the community, to the whole, and to authentic democracy in which liberty is inseparable from equality and community.

Finally, the *Constitution* explicitly gives the World Parliament the legal mandate and authority to regulate corporations for the common good of humanity and the environment. It recognizes businesses and corporations as important for the global economy but insists that a sustainable economy requires regulation of corporations for the protection of both the environment and future generations. This necessarily means conversion of exclusive titles to nature's wealth into conditional titles. The principle of social ecology embodied in the *Constitution for the Federation of Earth* is the key to transforming the anti-ecological attitudes and institutions now threatening the very existence of higher life-forms on Earth.

The *Constitution* also explicitly requires the government of the Earth Federation to protect the ecological fabric of life on Earth, that is, to respect the Gaia principle with all its ramifications. The very first article gives six "broad functions" of the Federation of Earth. Number five states that the Earth Federation must function "To protect the environment and the ecological fabric of life from all sources of damage, and to control technological innovations whose effects transcend national boundries, for the purpose of keeping Earth a safe, healthy and happy home for humanity."

Not only does the *Constitution* make this a primary mandate of the Earth Federation, but in its second bill of rights (Article 13, which covers social, environmental, and economic rights) the *Constitution* makes respect for the Gaia principle a right of the people of Earth themselves and a "directive principle for the world government" to actualize this right. Numbers 9, 10, and 11 read as follows. People have a right to "(9) Protection of the natural environment which is the common heritage of humanity against pollution, ecological disruption or damage which could imperil life or lower the quality of life. (10) Conservation of those natural resources of Earth which are limited so that present and future generations may continue to enjoy life on planet Earth. (11) Assurance for everyone of adequate housing, of adequate and nutritious food supplies, of safe and adequate water supplies, of pure air with protection of oxygen supplies and the ozone layer, and in general for the continuance of an environment which can sustain healthy living for all."

Clearly here again the *Constitution* explicitly recognizes the need for human economic, political, and social institutions to conform to the Gaia principle (which is the principle of sustainability) protecting the whole of the planetary environment for future generations. The key to a sustainable civilization is not only to promote education concerning the principles of natural ecology. For this effort alone is insufficient and will ultimately fail unless the anti-ecological institutions of the modern world described above are also transformed on the principles social ecology.

The entire human community must be joined together through the dynamic of genuine unity-in-diversity. Only through realizing the principle of social ecology in human life and uniting all people under nonmilitary democratic world government can the Gaia principle become a guiding principle for all human political, economic, and social processes. The principles of social ecology are inseparable from the principles of natural ecology. It is necessary to do for humanity what the natural Gaia principle does for nature. The *Constitution for the Federation of the Earth* joins the two together to create a truly ecological and sustainable world order.

Chapter Seven: Conclusion

Pledge,

Resolution,

and

Revolution

Pledge of Allegiance
to the Earth Constitution

I pledge allegiance to the Constitution for the
Federation of Earth,
and to the Republic of free world citizens
for which it stands,

One Earth Federation, protecting by law
the rich diversity of the Earth's citizens,
One Earth Federation, protecting
the precious ecology of our planet.

I pledge allegiance to the World Parliament
representing all nations and peoples, and to
the democratic processes by which it proceeds,

One law for the Earth,
with freedom and equality for all,
One standard of justice,
with a bill of rights protecting each.

I pledge allegiance to the future generations
protected by the Earth Constitution,
And to the unity, integrity, and beauty
of humankind, living in harmony on the Earth,

One Earth Federation, conceived in love, truth, and hope,
with peace and prosperity for all.

Commentary on the Pledge of Allegiance

Glen T. Martin

The Pledge of Allegiance expresses the highest allegiance a person can give to the human community. Unlike the vague and generalized pledges to the Earth or to future generations that some organizations have promoted in the 20th and 21st centuries, the Pledge of Allegiance is not a commitment to a vague hope that may be realized in the future but to a real *Constitution* embodying real values that is the ultimate global legal document in the here and now. This means taking this pledge does not simply express some ideal. Rather, in real measure, every person, organization, community, or nation taking the Pledge increases the power and scope of the transformed world order embodied in the *Earth Constitution*.

This pledge was unanimously approved at the Seventh Session of the Provisional World Parliament in Chennai, India in December 2003. Since that time it has been widely distributed among members and chapters of the World Constitution and Parliament Association. People sign the pledge and send it to world headquarters as a way of becoming personal ratifiers of the *Earth Constitution*. The pledge is also signed by all delegates to the Provisional World Parliament. (Observers at these Parliaments need not sign the pledge.)

The Pledge is not made to a flag or a symbol but that legal document organizing the world order on the principles of justice, freedom, peace, and prosperity. The *Constitution* "stands" for all these things because it concretely embodies them. It stands for the republic of "free and equal" world citizens that represents the end of the tragic and ugly prehistory of humanity and the beginning of a higher human civilization based upon the realization of our true potential. There can only be one "Republic of free world citizens" for there is only one Earth.

The Earth Federation is one. It is a unity. But precisely because it is a unity, it has the ability to protect the genuinely "rich diversity of the Earth's citizens." Without the unity of world law founded on the principle of unity-in-diversity, there can be no protection of diversity. The stronger culture, economy, military, or propaganda system will always overwhelm the weaker. Ultimately small cultures, nations, languages, ethnic groups, or religions will become absorbed by the larger. True diversity can only be protected by the unity of world law.

"One Earth Federation" is also necessary to protect the ecology of our planet. The planet is a single ecosystem and the global environmental crisis is insoluble without the Earth Emergency Rescue Administration and the other departments of world government working on restoring the fisheries, farmlands, grazing lands, clean sources of water, clean air, and forests to the Earth. One Earth Federation is necessary for this task since it requires global monitoring, planning, and coordination. There is no other way it can be accomplished.

The Pledge of Allegiance is also a pledge to the World Parliament and its democratic processes. The *Constitution* sets up a parliamentary system in which the combined three houses of Parliament are the supreme legal authority. The other organs of government are subordinate. This protects the people of Earth from the danger inherent in any system that has an independent executive branch, or independent enforcement branch.

History is full of examples where these branches have taken over governing and ignored the legislative branch. The *Constitution* provides a true safety system where authority is in the hands of about 1500 representatives in the combined houses. This does not mean that the World Executive will not be able to respond to natural or other disasters effectively. It does mean that Parliament will almost certainly operate by "democratic processes" and this is what deserves the loyalty of the people of Earth.

"One law for the Earth," and only this, can give true freedom and equality anywhere on Earth. There cannot be democracy if people in rich countries have immense privileges denied to people from poor countries. "One standard of justice," will mean for the first time in history human beings will have a consistent universal standard by which to measure their rapid progress toward a peaceful and prosperous world order.

Yet "one standard" cannot be effective unless it protects each individual. The *Constitution* has two bills of rights, one for political rights (Article 12) and one for economic, social, and environmental rights (Article 13). One standard of justice is embodied in the entire *Constitution*, but this means in practice that each person on Earth must be protected politically, economically, and ecologically. This deserves our allegiance.

Finally, the pledge includes "future generations." There is literally no possible decent future for our children, humanity, or the environment unless world government under this *Constitution* is realized rapidly. But the future generations and our pledge to them is a fundamental reason why we act in the present to have the people and nations of Earth ratify the *Constitution*. The "unity, integrity, and beauty of humankind" is concretely embodied in a ratified *Earth Constitution*. Otherwise, it is a merely utopian ideal. However, with this embodiment, this beauty and integrity becomes ever more fully actualized under provisions such as

Article 13. The *Constitution* that enables this richly deserves our loyalty.

The *Constitution* was indeed conceived in "love, truth, and hope." The love of humanity, the truth of our basic sameness as human beings, and the practical hope that a truly just world order can be realized if this vision is embodied in a concrete document that can serve as a foundation for a truly new era in human history. That is why the Pledge ends with the words "peace and prosperity for all." There can be no peace without a decent livelihood for all, just as there can be no peace as long as military organizations are equipped and maintained. War, militarism, and violence go together with poverty, misery, and injustice.

Peace and prosperity also truly go together. Today's immense waste of life, resources, and the environment will only come to an end when we have demilitarized the world and instituted the enforceable rule of law above all the nations. The Pledge of Allegiance, hanging on the wall of every classroom of every school on Earth, would itself point to a transformed existence for humanity, true unity-in-diversity with peace, justice, and prosperity for all.

Campaign for a Transformed World Order

The sample draft for a "Resolution for the Creation of a Democratic World Parliament" that appears on the following page is one of the many initiatives by the World Constitution and Parliament Association to move the world closer to democratic world government under the *Constitution for the Federation of Earth*. All people everywhere concerned about the future of our planet, the survival of life on Earth, freedom, and dignity for all human beings should join together to quickly transform the world order to one of genuine democratic law under a world parliament.

We should form chapters of the Earth Federation Movement in every country and every city, dedicated to bringing pressure on local and national governments to ratify the *Constitution for the Federation of Earth*. One way to do this is to contact members of city, state, and national parliaments to introduce a version of this resolution into their parliaments. It does not matter at first if the resolution has a chance of passing. It is important that the issue be debated and get out into the open in as many parliaments around the world as possible.

We should conduct signature campaigns to get people to personally ratify the *Constitution* by signing the Pledge of Allegiance. Copies of the Pledge can be reproduced cheaply and distributed widely. Signed copies of the Pledge can then be collected and sent for recording and deposit to the world headquarters offices of the World Constitution and Parliament Association.

We should form study groups of the documents in this book and become knowledgeable about the coming new world order and the impossibility of continuing the old, rotten world order. We should reproduce and widely distribute these documents. We should raise funds to support the World Constitution and Parliament Association and the Institute On World Problems who coordinate and spearhead this work worldwide.

Resolution for the Creation of a Democratic World Parliament

This house, being of the opinion that,

— in the present state of world political anarchy, where international agreements and conventions are flouted, and judgments of the World Court are treated as matters of no concern,

— in the present state of world militarism, where national governments feel forced to spend vast sums of money on weapons and military defense, while global insecurity continues to increase,

— in the present state of world environmental destruction, where vital resources necessary for life are diminishing, and where ice caps and glaciers are melting, the oceans are rising, and global weather patterns are becoming destructive,

— in the present state of world economic inequality, where the wealthy of the world continue to accumulate unimaginable wealth while each year many billions of US dollars are transferred from the poorest regions of the world to the wealthiest regions of the world,

This house calls upon the government of _____, in collaboration with other national governments, to make earnest efforts to convene a World Constituent Assembly, as the first step towards the establishment of a Democratic World Government, with a World Parliament representing all nations and peoples equally, under an enforceable, nonmilitary democratic *Constitution for the Federation of Earth*.

The Urgency of World Revolution Through World Law

Glen T. Martin

(Address to the closing session of the World Peace
Congress 2005, Kolkata, India, January 9, 2005)

Today, we stand at the dawn of the 21st century, at the dawn of the third millennium. We see all around us the possibilities for fulfillment and the achievement of a decent and just world order. Medicine is capable of healing most diseases and creating a healthy world population. Yet everywhere we see unnecessary disease, suffering, and death.

We know how to create clean water and sanitation systems for the people of Earth, yet everywhere we find filth and pollution, leading to massive epidemics of preventable diseases, while fresh water is rapidly disappearing from the Earth.

We know how to create sustainable agricultural production to feed the people of Earth. We know that enough food is grown right now to feed every person on Earth. Yet more than one billion of our fellow citizens are malnourished and starving, while the agricultural lands of the Earth are turning to desert before our very eyes from erosion and unsustainable agricultural practices.

Today, we understand the principles of ecology, and the role of forests, plants, animals, water, and air systems that keep our planetary ecosystem in health and balance. Yet we know that the Earth loses 17 million hectares of forest each year and that the oceans of Earth are becoming polluted as the dumping ground for toxic pollutants for our unsustainable civilization. These are the lungs of the Earth! We are destroying the lungs of the Earth and impairing the future survival of all the creatures that live upon the Earth.

We have the scientific knowledge today to build housing systems, sanitation and water systems, sustainable farming systems, to make the Earth a safe and happy place for all the people who live upon it. Yet our scientific research is on weapons of war and destruction, and our industrial production is devoted to warplanes, warships, bombs, and other diabolical weapons for the purpose of destroying people and their life-support systems. Every year we spend nearly one trillion U.S. dollars on militarism while the poor of the Earth rot in their living hell and the ecosystem of our planet turns to dust before our eyes.

Some place their naive hopes in the U.N. Organization that has presided over 150 wars since its founding with some 25 million deaths, 90 percent of which were civilians. Some place their naive hopes in the ideology of a global economic system that has presided over the accumulation of wealth in the hands of 243 individual persons that is equivalent to the combined wealth of the entire bottom 50 percent of humanity. 243 people have a wealth equivalent to 3.5 billion of their fellow humans!

Why don't we revolt? How much do we have to endure before we are willing to create a revolution upon the Earth? Do we have to wait until the last tree is cut down? Do we have to wait until the ice caps are melted and much of the continents are swallowed by the oceans? Do we have to wait until the Superpower has placed its weapons of mass destruction in space and created a totalitarian dictatorship over the entire world? Do we have to wait for the Superpower to use its tactical nuclear weapons against poor people and poor countries wherever in the world they rebel against the present unjust world order?

We say over and over that all human beings are one family and children of God. Then why do we not revolt when God's children are being bombed, maimed, starved, and brutalized in Iraq, Palestine, Afghanistan, Columbia, the Sudan, and elsewhere?

What is a revolutionary situation? How much does a people have to endure before they become galvanized to create a revolution? If the people of Iraq are our brothers and sisters, why do we say that their destruction is no concern of ours? If the starving masses of Africa, South America, and South Asia are our brothers and sisters, why do we allow them to starve to death? Are we so blinded by the outmoded ideology of so-called "sovereign" nation-states that we do not see that we are first and foremost human beings and citizens of the Earth?

My country is the world! And your country is the world! Why do we then cling to the absurdity of this ideology of ill-defined "sovereignty," while our fellow countrymen in Africa, South America, Asia, and the Middle East writhe in agony? Why do we let those who rule the world order financially and militarily use the system of sovereign nation-states to divide and conquer the vast majority of human beings in their global system of domination and exploitation? They invade Iraq, defying the entire world and crushing that hapless people, and the people of this country do nothing, saying "It is not my country." But if they are our brothers and sisters, then our country is the world, and we are in a situation calling for revolutionary action.

What form can revolutionary action take when the oppressor is *systems of institutionalized violence and domination*, not an identifiable group of persons and their minions? Removing George W. Bush from office will not change the economic and political systems of the world created by the European and North American colonial powers and enforced today as a system of neocolonial exploitation. Removing Tony Blair from office will change nothing.

Mahatma Gandhi spoke of the need for a new world order, a new economic and political order for the world based upon nonviolence and respect for each human being as a uniquely valuable expression of God. He said that the struggle in India was just the beginning and must become worldwide if human beings are to survive on this planet.

What does nonviolent revolutionary action look like directed toward creating a decent and just order for our country, the world? What could it possibly look like except action to ratify the *Constitution for the Federation of Earth?*

The most revolutionary word in the lexicon of political terms is the word "all" (Adler, 1991, p. 90). It is this word that sends shivers through the spines of oppressors everywhere. Gandhi embraced the Untouchables of India in the name of the word "all." Nelson Mandela struggled against Apartheid in South Africa in the name of the word "all." The Bolsheviks in Russia overthrew the Czar and his Aristocracy in the name of *all*.

At the dawn of the 21st century we now know that those "alls" were only partial and insufficient. There is a larger *all – all* human beings who live upon this planet. It is the only valid "all" and the only valid form of sovereignty – the sovereignty of all the people who live upon the Earth!

How long will we wait until we are moved to revolutionary action? Will we wait until the chains of totalitarianism under the Superpower have hardened around the neck of every person on Earth? Will we wait until the forests and clean water and agricultural lands of the Earth are totally destroyed? What does a revolutionary situation look like if not the nightmare of the world today presided over by institutions of fragmentation and division – a global economic system that creates poverty for the majority and a system of so-called "sovereign" nation-states that makes militarism, terrorism, and war inevitable?

My country is the world, and all human beings are my brothers and sisters. Revolutionary action today means that we must embody these truths in planetary institutions that protect and unify every person on Earth.

The most revolutionary and most noble document on our planet is the *Constitution for the Federation of Earth*. It guarantees a world economic system directed toward the prosperity of all, not the tiny elite of super-wealthy who now exploit the poor of the world. It federates the nations, and eliminates all weapons of war from the Earth so that powerful nations can no longer dominate weaker nations and all nations are equal for the first time.

It guarantees political freedom to all peoples, not just to those who happen to be born in democracies. And it guarantees health-care, housing, clean water, sanitation systems, free education, social security, and decent wages to every person living on Earth. The Earth is very rich and the wasted wealth now spent on militarism alone can easily create a decent world order. This *Constitution* is the only immediately available hope for eliminating global poverty and environmental destruction.

We are facing the final revolution – the final nonviolent struggle in the name of all. No other revolution has included all human beings, and that is why all other revolutions have failed. Gandhi's revolution in the name of "all" in India has failed, as did Nelson Mandela's revolution and the Communist revolution. Just look at the tens of thousands of people sleeping on the streets of Kolkata or Dhaka City! Just look at the poverty of people in the lands of the former Soviet Union today!

We are facing the final hope for planet Earth. Either we go down into total destruction of the Earth and its creatures under the fragmented systems of our global economic order and so called "sovereign" nation-states, or we institutionalize the principle of *all* upon the Earth.

The principle of *all* is both the most revolutionary principle and the most dynamic principle in the philosophy of nonviolence. But nonviolence must be institutionalized in a nonmilitary, democratic, planetary world order. For the first time in history, we can create a truly nonviolent world order by ratifying the *Constitution for the Federation of Earth*. The principle of *all* is embodied in the sovereignty of all the people of Earth and institutionalized by the *Constitution*. It is affirmed, honored, and embraced by the Pledge of Allegiance.

The Pledge of Allegiance is the supreme act of civil obedience for every citizen on Earth. We should memorize it and repeat it daily. We should act on it by deligitimizing the claims to "sovereignty" of the merely local (national) governments. They are not legitimate as "sovereign" entities, but only as states within the Earth Federation.

We restore their legitimacy by affirming *the principle of all* as this is embodied in the sovereignty of the people of Earth. The only legitimate sovereignty is the dignity, equality, and freedom of every person on Earth as this is expressed in the *Earth Constitution*. World revolution through world law means acting in the here and now on this gigantic truth. We must recognize that the only legitimate law is law that protects everyone on Earth equally. Local laws derive their legitimacy from planetary law, not the reverse.

We do not need the permission of the illegitimate so-called "sovereign" nations to perform *the act of civil obedience* and begin a new world order free of the fragmentation and perversions of the past. The laws passed by the Provisional World Parliament and the ratification process of the *Constitution for the Federation of Earth* proceed as legitimate representations of the people of Earth. The nation-state system with its economic system of exploitation and domination and its self-contractory claims to being the "ultimate" political unit is dead.

We must disobey and deligitimize this system in the name of the sovereignty of the people of Earth and the rule of just, democratic law for everyone on Earth equally. We must obey the most revolutionary and the most moral principle in the lexicon of political terms: this principle of *all: equality to all people, human rights to all people, a decent environment for all people, freedom, peace, and prosperity to all people.*

There is no way in Heaven or Earth to achieve a decent, legitimate world order without ratification of the *Constitution for the Federation of Earth*. But this possibility can only be realized if we act today. For tomorrow, it will be too late. The time for a genuine act of civil obedience is now. The time for world revolution through world law is now.

Appendix

The Development of a World Parliament
A Brief History

1958. Agreement to Call a World Constitutional Convention initiated by four persons, circulated worldwide for signatures, requesting both national governments and people of each country to send delegates.

1959-1960. World Committee for a World Constitutional Convention formed. Thousands sign the Agreement, including many prominent leaders. Organizers of this action travel around the world to enlist support.

1961-1962. Definitive Call to the World Constitutional Convention adopted. Many persons sign, including Heads of five national governments.

1963-1964. First Preparatory Congress held Denver, Colorado, USA, with delegates from five continents. Call to the World Constitutional Convention is publicly issued, then circulated for more signers and response.

1965-1966. Second Preparatory Congress held at Milan, Italy. Outline for Debate and Drafting of a World Constitution is formulated, on basis on alternative choices. Plan agreed for a Peoples' World Parliament to meet concurrently.

1967. Decision made at Third Preparatory Congress to begin Convention in 1968, even if no government sends delegates. 300 Peoples Delegates pledged.

1968. First working sessions of World Constitutional Convention and Peoples' World Convention held at Interlaken, Switzerland, and Wolfach, W. Germany with 200 Peoples Delegates from 27 countries, of five continents. Work begun on drafting the World Constitution.

1969-1971. Strategy for Reclaiming Earth for Humanity is circulated. Emergency Council of World Trustees meets, Santa Barbara, Calif., and issues First Decree for Protection of Life, outlawing nuclear weapons. Directions given to drafting commission.

1972. World Constitution drafting commission of four persons works for two months, almost completes first draft of *Constitution for the Federation of Earth.*

1973-1975. First draft finished, printed in 1974, then circulated worldwide for comment, together with Call to the second session in 1977, now defined as the World Constituent Assembly. Comments on first draft complied.

1976. Drafting Commission meets again. Second draft completed, circulated, 1977. Second Session of World Constituent Assembly held in June, Innsbruck, Austria. *Earth Constitution* debated paragraph by paragraph, amended, then adopted with 138 original signers from 25 countries of 6 continents. Call for ratification by the nations and peoples of Earth is issued. *Constitution* is sent to U.N. General Assembly and to all national governments.

1978-1980. *Earth Constitution* is circulated worldwide for debate and ratification. Third session of World Constituent Assembly held January, 1979, Colombo, Sri Lanka; adopts Rationale For a World Constituent Assembly, defining right of people to convene Assembly, draft constitution, and obtain ratification. Appeal issued for national parliaments to ratify.

1981. World Constitution & Parliament Assn. meets at New Delhi, India. Call issued for Provisional World Parliament to convene 1982 under terms of Article 19 of the *Earth Constitution.* Honorary Sponsor list of 150 prominent persons enrolled.

1982. First Session of Provisional World Parliament meets at Brighton, England. Delegates form 25 countries of 6 continents. Five world Legislative Acts are adopted: for World Disarmament Agency, World Economic Development, Ownership of Oceans & Seabeds, Graduate School of World Problems, and World Courts.

1983-1984. First Provisional District World Court organized in Los Angeles; takes up case of outlawing nuclear weapons. Plans for Provisional World Parliament in Sudan and Nigeria thwarted by military coups.

1985. Second Session of Provisional World Parliament held New Delhi, India. Opened by President of India, presided by speaker of Lok Sabha. Three more World Legislative Acts adopted: for Emergency Earth Rescue Administration, World Government Funding, and Commission on Terrorism.

1986. Campaign continued for "provisional" ratification of the *Constitution for the Federation of Earth*, pending review at next World Constituent Assembly.

1987. Third session of Provisional World Parliament held Miami Beach, Florida. Three more World Legislative Acts are adopted: for Global Finance System, Environment Protection, and Hydrogen Energy. Provisional World Cabinet begun.

1988-1989. Plan launched for collaboration by many organizations to prepare next session of World Constituent Assembly. 150 organizations join in Preparatory Committee. Two meetings held in New York with U. N. Ambassadors, to explain and solicit help. List of Honorary Sponsors reconfirmed and expanded.

1990. Government of Egypt agrees to host Assembly. Three preparatory meetings held. Call circulated for Governments and People to send delegates.

1991. Location of 4th session World Constituent Assembly abruptly changed due to the 1991 Gulf War. Held at Troia, Portugal, in May. Delegates adopt 59 minor amendments to the *Earth Constitution*. New ratification campaign begun, appealing to both people and governments. Most Honorary Sponsors personally ratify.

1992.   Global Ratification & Elections Network organized, including several hundred organizations, to promote ratification of the *Constitution for the Federation of Earth*, then election of delegates to World Parliament. Government heads should also ratify.

1996. The Fourth Session of the Provisional World Parliament held at Barcelona, Spain in September. A number of resolutions passed as well as a "Manifesto" declaring the oceans the property of the people of Earth under the authority of the *Earth Constitution*.

2000. The Fifth Session of the Provisional World Parliament is held on the Island of Malta, November 22nd to 27th. One Omnibus legislative act and a number of resolutions passed.

2003. The Sixth Session of the Provisional World Parliament held in Bangkok, Thailand, March 23rd to 28th. Several important legislative acts passed: a World Peace Act, a World Security Act, a Provisional Office of World Revenue Act, a Hydrocarbon Resource Act, and a Statute for the World Court on Human Rights. The Commission for Legislative Review is formed. Parliamentary law format commenses with the Sixth Session.

2003. The Seventh Session of the Provisional World Parliament is held at Chennai, India, December 23-29. Several important legislative acts passed: a Criminal Penalty Code, Rules for Procedure and Evidence, a World Bench for Criminal Cases Act, a World Patents Act, a Global Accounting and Auditing Standards Act, and a Preservation of World Government Records Act. *The Manifesto of the Earth Federation* (Chapter Three above) and the "Pledge of Allegiance to the *Earth Constitution*" (part of Chapter Seven above) are unamimously ratified by the Parliament.

2004. The Eighth Session of the Provisional World Parliament held at Lucknow, India in August. Several important legislative acts passed, including creation of a World Bench for Juvenile Cases, a Child Rights Act, an Elections Act, and a Water Act. The International Criminal Court in the Hague is empowered by world legislation. A global Education Act is passed as well as a World Economic Equity Act establishing the Earth Currency on an independent and fully democratic basis. A Global People's Assembly is created to activate grass roots participation in the House of Peoples. The "Declaration on the Rights of Peoples" (part of Chapter Two above) is unanimously ratified.

2005-2006. Action begins for transforming the Global Ratification and Elections Network into the *Earth Federation Movement*. Planning continues for the Ninth Session of the Provisional World Parliament to be held in Libya, Africa, February-March, 2006.

Note: Most of the above legislative acts can be found on the websites of WCPA (www.wcpa.biz) and IOWP (www.worldproblems.net). The full texts of all, along with summaries and analyses, can be found in the forthcoming volume: *Emerging World Law,* Eugenia Almand and Glen T. Martin, eds., Sun City, AZ: Institute for Economic Democracy Press, 2006.

Select Bibliography and Works Cited

Adler, Mortimer J. (1991). *Haves Without Have Nots. Essays for the 21st Century on Democracy and Socialism.* New York: Macmillan.

Ahmed, Nafeez Mosaddeq (2002). *The War On Freedom: How and Why America was Attacked, September 11, 2001.* Joshua Tree, California: Tree of Life Publications.

Albert, Michael (2003). *Parecon: Participatory Economics.* New York: Verso.

Allott, Philip (1990). *Eunomia: New Order for a New World.* Oxford: Oxford University Press.

Almand, Eugenia and Martin, Glen T. (2006). *Emerging World Law. Key Documents and Decisions of the Global People's Assemblies and Provisional World Parliament.* Forthcoming: Sun City, Arizona: Institute for Economic Democracy Press.

Amin, Samir (2004). *The Liberal Virus: Permanent War and the Americanization of the World.* New York: Monthly Review Press.

Amin, Samir (1997). *Capitalism in the Age of Globalization.* New York & London: Zed Books.

Aurobindo, Sri (1997). *The Human Cycle, The Ideal of Human Unity, War and Self-determination.* Pondicherry, India: Sri Aurobindo Ashram.

Bateson, Gregory (1972). *Steps to an Ecology of Mind.* New York: Ballantine Books.

Bidmead, Harold S. (1992). *A Parliament of Man: The Federation of the World.* Swimbridge, England: Patton Publications.

Biersteker, Thomas J. and Weber, Cynthia, eds. (1996). *State Sovereignty as Social Construct.* Cambridge, UK: Cambridge University Press.

Blain, Bob (2004a). *The Most Wealth for the Least Work Through Cooperation.* Bloomington, IN: Author House Publishers.

Blain, Bob (2004b). *Weaving Golden Threads of Sociological Theory.* Bloomington, IN: Author House Publishers.

Blum, William (2000). *Rogue State. A Guide to the World's Only Superpower.* Monroe, Maine: Common Courage Press.

Blum, William (1995). *Killing Hope: U.S. Military and CIA Interventions Since World War II.* Monroe, Maine: Common Courage Press.

Boswell and Chase-Dunn (2000). *The Spiral of Capitalism and Socialism: Toward Global Democracy.* Boulder, CO: Lynne Rienner Publishers.

Boucher, Douglas H. (1999). *The Paradox of Plenty: Hunger in a Bountiful World.* Oakland, CA: Food First Books.

Brecher, Jeremy and Costello, Tim (1994). *Global Village or Global Pillage: Economic Reconstruction from the Bottom Up.* Boston: South End Press.

Brown, Lester R. (2001). *Eco-Economy: Building an Economy for the Earth.* New York: W. W. Norton & Co.

Burbach, Roger and Clarke, Ben, eds. (2002). *September 11 and the U.S. War: Beyond the Curtain of Smoke.* San Francisco: City Light Books.

Caldicott, Helen (1994). *Nuclear Madness.* Revised Edition. New York: W. W. Norton & Co.

Caldicott, Helen (1992). *If You Love This Planet.* New York: W.W. Norton & Co.

Carson, Rachel (1962). *Silent Spring.* New York: Fawcet Publishers

Caufield, Catherine (1996). *Masters of Illusion. The World Bank and the Poverty of Nations.* New York: Henry Holt and Company.

Chase-Dunn, Christopher (1998). *Global Formation: Structures of World Economy.* Updated Edition. New York: Rowman & Littlefield.

Chomsky, Noam (2003). *Hegemony or Survival: America's Quest for Global Dominance.* New York: Henry Holt & Company.

Chomsky, Noam (1996). *What Uncle Sam Really Wants.* Berkeley: Odonian Press.

Chomsky, Noam (1993). *Year 501: The Conquest Continues. Boston:* South End Press.

Chomsky, Noam (1989). *Necessary Illusions: Thought Control in Democratic Societies.* Boston: South End Press.

Chomsky, Noam, and Herman, Edward S. (1979). *The Washington Connection and Third World Fascism.* Boston: South End Press.

Chossudovsky, Michel (1999). *The Globalization of Poverty: Impacts of IMF and World Bank Reforms.* London: Zed Books LTD.

Coicaud, Jean-Marc (2002). *Legitimacy and Politics: A Contribution to the Study of Political Right and Political Responsibility.* David Ames Curtis, trans. Cambridge, U.K.: Cambridge University Press.

Commission on Global Governance. (1995). *Our Global Neighborhood: Report of the Commission on Global Governance.* Oxford: Oxford University Press.

Daly, Herman E. (1996). *Beyond Growth: The Economics of Sustainable Development.* Boston: Beacon Press.

Daly, Herman E. and Cobb, John B. (1994). *For the Common Good: Redirecting the economy toward community, the environment, and a sustainable future.* Boston: Beacon Press.

Davis, Garry (2004). *Letters to World Citizens.* Burlington, Vermont: World Government House.

Davis, Garry (2003). *World Government, ready or not!* Burlington, Vermont: World Government House.

Davis, Gary, with Guma, Greg (1992). *Passport to Freedom: A Guide for World Citizens.* Cabin John, Maryland: Seven Locks Press.

Dewey, John (1993). *The Political Writings.* Debra Morris and Ian Shapiro, eds. Indianapolis: Hackett Publishing Co.

Diamond, Jared (2005). *Collapse: How Societies Choose to Fail or Succeed.* New York: Viking Books.

Einstein, Albert (1950). *Out of My Later Years.* New York: Philosophical Library.

Falk, Richard (1992). *Explorations at the Edge of Time. Prospects for World Order.* Philadelphia: Temple University Press.

Flavin, Christopher, et al. (2002). *State of the World 2002.* New York: W. W. Norton & Co.

Foster, John Bellamy and McChesney, Robert, editors (2004). *Pox Americana: Exposing the American Empire.* New York: Monthly Review Press.

Fromm, Erich (1947). *Man for Himself – An Inquiry into the Psychology of Ethics.* New York: Holt, Rhinehart, and Winston.

Galeano, Edwardo (1973). *The Open Veins of Latin America – Five Centuries of the Pillage of a Continent.* Cedric Belfrage, trans. New York: Monthly Review Press.

Gandhi, M. K. (1987). *The Mind of Mahatma Gandhi.* R.K. Prabhu and U.R. Rao, eds. Ahmedabad: Navajivan Publishing House.

Gandhi, M. K. (1972). *All Men Are Brothers. Life and Thoughts of Mahatma Gandhi.* Krishna Kripalani, ed. New York: World Without War Publications.

Gandhi, M. K. (1929). *An Autobiography or My Experiments With Truth.* Mahadev Desai, trans. Ahmedabad: Navajivan Publishing House.

George, Henry (1935). *Progress and Poverty: An Inquiry into the Cause of Industrial Depressions and of Increase of Want with Increase of Wealth.* New York: Robert Schalkenbach Foundation.

Glossop, Ronald J. (1993). *World Federation? A Critical Analysis of Federal World Government.* Jefferson, NC and London: McFarland & Company.

Goff, Stan (2004). *Full Spectrum Disorder: The Military in the New American Century.* Brooklyn, N.Y.: Soft Skull Press.

Griffin, David Ray (2004). *The New Pearl Harbor: Disturbing Questions about the Bush Administration and 9/11.* Northampton, Massachusetts: Olive Branch Press.

Habermas, Jürgen (2001). *The Postnational Constellation: Political Essays.* Cambridge, MA: The MIT Press.

Habermas, Jürgen (1984). *The Theory of Communicative Action, Volume One: Reason and the Rationalization of Society.* Thomas McCarthy, trans. Boston: Beacon Press.

Habermas, Jürgen (1975). *Legitimation Crisis.* Boston: Beacon Press.

Harris, Errol E. (2005). *Earth Federation Now: Tomorrow is Too Late.* Sun City, Arizona, Institute for Economic Democracy Press.

Harris, Errol E. (2000). *Apocalypse and Paradigm: Science and Everyday Thinking.* Westport, CT: Praeger.

Harris, Errol E. (1993). *One World or None: Prescription for Survival.* Atlantic Highlands, NJ.

Harris, Errol E. and Yunker, James A., eds. (1999). *Towards Genuine Global Governance: Critical Reactions to "Our Global Neighborhood."* Westport, CT: Praeger

Harris, J.M. (2000). *Rethinking Sustainability: Power, Knowledge, and Institutions.* Ann Arbor: University of Michigan Press.

Harris, William H. and Levy, Judith S. (1975). *The New Columbia Encyclopedia.* New York: Columbia University Press.

Herman, Edward S. (1982). *The Real Terror Network: Terrorism in Fact and Propaganda.* Boston: South End Press.

Hodge, James and Cooper, Linda (2004). *Disturbing the Peace: The Story of Father Roy Bourgeois and the Movement to Close the School of the Americas.* Maryknoll, New York: Orbis Books.

Holmes, Robert L., ed. *Nonviolence in Theory and Practice.* Belmont, California: Wadsworth Publishing Company.

Hudgens, Tom A. (1986). *Let's Abolish War.* Denver: BILR Corporation.

Hudson, Michael (2003). *Super Imperialism: The Origins and Fundamentals of U.S. World Dominance.* London: Pluto Press.

Hudson, Michael, editor (1996). *Merchants of Misery: How Corporate America Profits from Poverty.* Monroe, Maine: Common Courage Press.

Isely, Philip (2000). *Immediate Economic Benefits of World Government.* Lakewood, Colorado: Emergency Earth Rescue Administration of the World Constitution and Parliament Assoc.

Jesudasan, Ignatius, S. J. (1984). *A Gandhian Theology of Liberation.* Maryknoll, New York: Orbis Books.

Johnson, Chalmers (2001). *Blowback: The Costs and Consequences of American Empire.* New York: Henry Holt and Company.

Johnson, Chalmers (2004). *The Sorrows of Empire: Militarism, Secrecy, and the End of the Republic.* New York: Henry Holt & Company.

Kant, Immanuel (1957). *Perpetual Peace.* Louis White Beck, trans. New York: Macmillan.

Keeton, G. W. (1939). *National Sovereignty and International Order.* London: Peace Book Co.

Kiang, John (1984). *One World: The Approach to Permanent Peace on Earth and the General Happiness of Mankind.* Notre Dame, IN: One World Publishing Company.

Korten, David C. (2001) *When Corporations Rule the World.* Second Edition. Bloomfield, CT: Kumarian Press.

Korten, David C. (1999). *The Post-Corporate World. Life After Capitalism.* West Hartford, CT: Kumarian Press, Inc.

Lifton, Robert Jay (1993). *The Protean Self: Human Resilience in an Age of Fragmentation.* New York: Basic Books.

Lovelock, James (1991). *Healing Gaia: Practical Medicine for the Planet.* New York: Harmony Books.

Mander, Jerry and Goldsmith, Edward (1996). *The Case Against the Global Economy: And for a Turn Toward the Local.* San Francisco: Sierra Club Books.

Mahajan, Rahul (2003). *Full Spectrum Dominance: U.S. Power in Iraq and Beyond.* New York: Seven Stories Press.

Martin, Glen T. (2005). *Millennium Dawn. The Philosophy of Planetary Crisis and Human Liberation.* Sun City, Arizona: Institute for Economic Democracy Press.

Martin, Glen T. (2003). "Revolutionary Democracy and the Problem of The Other - John Dewey, the Philosophy Of Liberation, and Human Spirituality." Under "Three Philosophical Papers" on the web site: www.radford.edu/~gmartin/

Martin, Glen T. (2002). "Unity in Diversity as the Foundation for World Peace." *Community, Diversity, and Difference: Implications for Peace.* Alison Bailey and Paula J. Smithka, eds. Amsterdam: Rodopi Press, pp. 309-325.

Martin, Glen T. (1999a). "A Planetary Paradigm for Global Government." *Toward Genuine Global Governance: Critical Reactions to "Our Global Neighborhood,"* Errol E. Harris and James A. Yunker, eds. London: Praeger, pp. 1-18.

Martin, Glen T. (1999b). "Three Stages in the Dialectical Realization of Democracy and the Constitution for the Federation of Earth," Part One. *Across Frontiers - A WCPA/GREN Publication for Humanity,* March-April, 1999, pp. 19-20. Part Two, *Across Frontiers,* May-June, 1999, pp. 20-22.

Marx, Karl and Engels, Friedrich (1978). *The Marx-Engels Reader.* Second Edition. Robert C. Tucker, ed. New York: W. W. Norton & Co.

Mayne, Richard and Pinder, John (1990). *Federal Union: The Pioneers. A History of Federal Union.* New York: St. Martin's Press.

Mayur, Rashmi (2002). *Beyond Johannesburg: Where Do We Go From Here?* Mumbai: International Institute for Sustainable Future.

Mcgehee, Ralph W. (1999). *Deadly Deceits: My 25 Years in the CIA.* Melbourne, New York: Ocean Press.

Monthly Review Magazine. "The Failure of Empire." Harry Magdoff, et. al. New York: Vol. 56, No. 8, January 2005.

Palast, Greg (2003). *The Best Democracy Money Can Buy.* New York: Plume Books of Penguin Publishers.

Perkins, John (2004). *Confessions of an Economic Hit Man.* San Francisco: Berrett Koehler Publishers.

Philpott, Daniel (2001). *Revolutions in Sovereignty: How Ideas Shaped Modern International Relations.* Princeton: Princeton University Press.

Pines, Christopher L. (1993). *Ideology and False Consciousness. Marx and His Historical Progenitors.* Albany: SUNY Press.

Renner, Michael. (1996). *Fighting for Survival: Environmental Decline, Social Conflict, and the New Age of Insecurity.* New York: W. W. Norton & Co.

Reves, Emery (1946). *The Anatomy of Peace.* New York: Harper & Brothers.

Rich, Bruce (1994). *Mortgaging the Earth. The World Bank, Environmental Impoverishment, and the Crisis of Development.* Boston: Beacon Press.

Russell, Peter, (1995). *The Global Brain Awakens: Our Next Evolutionary Leap.* Palo Alto, CA: Global Brain, Inc.

Sáenz, Mario. ed. (2002). *Latin American Perspectives on Globalization: Ethics, Politics, and Alternative Visions.* Lanham, MD: Rowman & Littlefield Publishers.

Seligson, Mitchell A. and Passe-Smith, John T. (1993). *Development and Underdevelopment: The Political Economy of Inequality.* Boulder, CO: Lynne Rienner Publishers.

Sharp, Gene (1973). *The Methods of Nonviolent Action, Part Two of The Politics of Nonviolent Action*. Boston: Extending Horizons Books.

Shiva, Vandana (2002). *Water Wars: Privatization, Pollution, and Profit*. Boston: South End Press.

Shiva, Vandana (2000). *Stolen Harvest: The Hijacking of the Global Food Supply*. Boston: South End Press.

Shiva, Vandana (1997). *Biopiracy: The Plunder of Nature and Knowledge*. Boston: South End Press.

Singer, Peter (2002). *One World: the Ethics of Globalization*. New Haven: Yale University Press.

Sivard, Ruth (1996). *World Military and Social Expenditures*. 16th Edition. Washington, DC: World Priorities, Inc.

Smith, J. W. (1994). *The World's Wasted Wealth 2*. Sun City, Arizona: Institute for Economic Democracy Press.

Smith, J. W. (2005a). *Economic Democracy – The Political Struggle of the Twenty-first Century*. Sun City, Arizona: Institute for Economic Democracy Press.

Smith, J. W. (2005b). *Why? The Deeper History Behind the September 11, 2001, Terrorist Attack on America*. Sun City, Arizona: Institute for Economic Democracy Press.

Smith, J. W. (2005c). *Cooperative Capitalism: A Blueprint for Global Peace and Prosperity*. Sun City, Arizona: Institute for Economic Democracy & Institute for Cooperative Capitalism.

Solomon, Robert C. (1995). *A Passion for Justice: Emotions and the Origins of the Social Contract*. Lanham, MD: Rowman & Littlefield Publishers.

Stiglitz, Joseph E. (2002). *Globalization and its Discontents*. New York: W. W. Norton & Co.

Stockwell, John (1991). *The Praetorian Guard: The U.S. Role in the New World Order*. Cambridge: South End Press.

Teilhard de Chardin, Pierre (1959). *The Phenomenon of Man*. Bernard Wall, trans. New York: Harper & Brothers.

Tetalman, Jerry and Belitsos, Byron (2005). *One World Democracy: A Progressive Vision for Enforceable Global Law*. San Rafael, California: Origin Press.

Tokar, Brian (1997). *Earth for Sale: Reclaiming Ecology in the Age of Corporate Greenwash*. Boston: South End Press.

Vidal, Gore (2002). *Perpetual War for Perpetual Peace: How We Got to Be So Hated*. New York: Thunder's Mouth Press.

Weston, Burns H., Falk, Richard A., and D'Amato, Anthony (1990). *International Law and World Order. A Problem-Oriented Coursebook*. Second Edition. St. Paul, Minnesota.: West Publishing Co.

Zarlinga, Stephen (2002). *The Lost Science of Money. The Mythology of Money – The Story of Power*. Valatie, NY: American Monetary Institute.

Zinn, Howard (1990). *Declerations of Independence: Cross-examining American Ideology*. New York: Harper-Collins Publishers.

Index

9 780975 355534